MW01275456

SEP

LIBRARY
Red River Community College

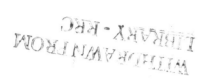

WITHDRAWN FROM
LIBRARY - RRC

LITTLE FREE LIBRARY.org.
TAKE A BOOK · RETURN A BOOK

Take a Book – Return a Book
Always a Gift – Never for Sale

Library Steward - G3 Books
"Books are your friends"

CANADIAN MEDICAL LIVES

R.M. BUCKE
Journey to
Cosmic Consciousness

Peter A. Rechnitzer

Series Editor: T.P. Morley

Associated Medical Services, Inc.
&
Fitzhenry & Whiteside
1994

RED RIVER COMMUNITY COLLEGE

Copyright © Associated Medical Services Incorporated/The Hannah Institute
for the History of Medicine, 1994

Fitzhenry & Whiteside
195 Allstate Parkway
Markham, Ontario L3R 4T8

All rights reserved. No part of this publication may be reproduced, stored in
a retrieval system, or transmitted in any form or by any means, electronic,
mechanical, photocopying, recording, or otherwise, except brief passages for
purposes of review, without the prior permission of Fitzhenry & Whiteside.

Jacket design: Arne Roosman
Copy Editor: Frank English
Typesetting: Jay Tee Graphics Ltd.
Printing and Binding: Best/Gagné Book Manufacturers Inc.

Fitzhenry & Whiteside wishes to acknowledge the generous assistance and ongo-
ing support of **The Book Publishing Industry Development Programme** of the
Department of Communications, The Canada Council, and **The Ontario Arts
Council.**

Care has been taken to trace the ownership of copyright material used in the
text, including the illustrations. The author and publisher welcome any information enabling them to rectify any reference or credit in subsequent editions.

Canadian Cataloguing in Publication Data

Rechnitzer, Peter
   R.M. Bucke

(Canadian medical lives : no. 12)
Co-published by the Hannah Institute.
Includes bibliographical references and index.
ISBN 1-55041-155-1

1. Bucke, Richard Maurice, 1837–1902.
2. Psychiatrists – Canada – Biography. I. Hannah
Institute for the History of Medicine. II. Title.
III. Series.

RC438.6.B8R4 1994   616.89′0092   C94-930503-0

CANADIAN MEDICAL LIVES SERIES

The story of the Hannah Institute for the History of Medicine has been told by John B. Neilson and G.R. Paterson in *Associated Medical Services Incorporated: A History* (1987). Dr. Donald R. Wilson, President of AMS, and the Board of Directors decided that the Institute should produce this series of biographies as one of its undertakings.

The first ten biographies have now been published and can be obtained through the retail book trade or from Dundurn Press Ltd., 2181 Queen Street East, Suite 301, Toronto, Canada, M4E 1E5, and Dundurn Distribution, 73 Lime Walk, Headington, Oxford, England, OX3 7AD. The second group, of which this is the first volume, can also be obtained through retail book stores or from the publisher, Fitzhenry & Whiteside.

Richard Maurice Bucke (1837-1902) grew up and practised psychiatric medicine in London, Ontario, where he became Superintendent of the London Asylum. As a young man he spent four years wandering the United States picking up whatever work he could find. In the course of his mining adventures he came within an inch of death crossing the Sierra Nevada but survived with frost-bitten feet (which had to be amputated).

Bucke came to international prominence through his unusual friendship with Walt Whitman. Whitman served as an inspiration for Bucke's *Cosmic Consciousness*. In this work Bucke wrote his prescription for the human millennium, an apocalyptic vision with *Leaves of Grass* as the Bible of Democracy.

Peter Rechnitzer unravels the complex threads of Bucke's life: his adventures, his denial of his father and his adoration of Whitman who became his Messiah. Bucke was convinced that only mankind itself can shape its future into perfection, and that guilt, penitence and absolution are regressive steps reversing the march to happiness.

Future volumes include *William Henry Drummond* (J.B. Lyons) and *William Beaumont* (Julian Smith).

There is no shortage of meritorious subjects. Willing and capable authors are harder to acquire. The Institute is therefore deeply grateful to authors who have committed their time and skill to the series.

T.P. Morley
Series Editor
1994

CANADIAN MEDICAL LIVES SERIES

CONTENTS

To Lili

Acknowledgements

I received invaluable assistance and encouragement from the staff of the Special Collections Department of the D.B. Weldon Library at the University of Western Ontario. I was introduced to the Bucke papers by the late Beth Miller. John Lutman, Molly Farmer, Lucy Kowalchuk and John Martin responded to my endless requests with enviable good humour. A special thanks to my secretary, Edna Marek, who typed the first draft in my clinical office amidst welcoming patients and answering the telephone. Subsequent versions were typed by Patricia Andrew, Maureen Morris and Nancy Patrick. Adrienne O'Hanley offered much needed expertise in preparing the bibliography. Dr. Paul Potter very kindly helped me with the initial revision. I am indebted to the Hannah Institute for the History of Medicine/Associated Medical Services Inc. for making the publication of this book possible. The project also enabled me to meet Dr. R.M. Bucke's grandson William Bucke and his wife Ann to discuss one of the most fascinating physicians this country has produced.

Preface

At Bon Echo Provincial Park, one hundred kilometres north of Belleville, Ontario, a gigantic Gibraltar of old Laurentian granite rises perpendicularly 300 feet into the air at the junction of upper and lower Lake Mazinaw.

As a young camp counsellor, I canoed regularly beneath the dark, overwhelming presence of that rock, feeling both excitement and dread. At the base of the rock is carved in bold letters,

> My foothold is tenon'd and mortis'd in granite
> I laugh at what you call dissolution
> And I know the amplitude of time.
>
> Horace Traubel

I responded to the affirmation of those lines which expressed my own youthful struggle to become master of my own fate. I learned that the rock had the sobriquet "Old Walt" and that the lines were those of Walt Whitman. But the name Horace Traubel remained a mystery, and no one seemed to know why Whitman's words were inscribed on that awesome granite.

I carried those words with me over a good number of decades before I finally understood them, realizing the deep truth in Eliot's lines:

And the end of all our exploring
Will be to arrive where we started
And know the place for the first time.

My trail of discovery led off a few years back with the impulse to write a book about medicine in southwestern Ontario a hundred years ago. I planned to model my work on Lytton Strachey's *Eminent Victorians*, in which several short biographies of that era coalesce to tell the story of the time.

I chose to start with Dr. Richard Maurice Bucke (1837-1902), whom I knew to have been a notable physician in London, Ontario, where I have lived most of my life. The grand plan was never realized: I stayed with Bucke.

Bucke's journey included a new theory of consciousness, an obsession that Bacon wrote Shakespeare and a most unusual friendship with Walt Whitman. My journey was an unravelling of the mystery of the words on that huge rock.

— Chapter 1 —
Childhood Prelude to Adventure

In 1838 Horatio Walpole Bucke left his curacy in the town of Methwold, Norfolk with his pregnant wife Clarissa and seven children. The family settled on one hundred acres of Crown land, three miles east of the village of London in Upper Canada. Their youngest child, aged one at the time, was Richard Maurice, whose early life unfolded on that farm, and whose later life as psychiatrist and visionary was spent less than a mile away.

Horatio Walpole Bucke was born on 26 December 1802, in Worlington, Suffolk, son of Thomas George Bucke of Methwold in Norfolk and Georgina Walpole, illegitimate daughter of George Walpole, 3rd Earl of Orford and grandson of Sir Robert Walpole, once Prime Minister of Great Britain.[1]* The wedding of Thomas and Georgina was attended by the most prominent families of Norfolk, Suffolk and the City, including Horatio Lord Nelson and his wife. Horatio Walpole Bucke was thus named after both the Walpoles and the Nelsons.

In 1819, at age 17, H.W. Bucke entered Trinity College, Cambridge, obtaining his BA in 1825 and MA in 1828. Bucke partially financed his education at Cambridge by becoming a "sizar" (a "sizar" received a

---

* For all numbers or letter references please see Notes section at back of book.

reduction in fees in return for some part-time valet duties to other students). As sizar, Bucke met and was greatly influenced by his contemporaries in the Apostles' Club, including Tennyson and Arthur Henry Hallam, the gifted young writer whose tragic death at age 22 was immortalized seventeen years later in Tennyson's "In Memoriam".[2]

After leaving Cambridge the Rev. H.W. Bucke received the appointment of curate of the parish of Methwold, situated in the village of Methwold in the fen country, just fifteen miles from Mildenhall where he had grown up. Three years later, in 1828, he married Clarissa Andrews, also from Mildenhall. During the next decade several children were born to them: George Walpole, Edward Horatio, Philip Eustace, Augustus Henry, Anne Mary Georgina, Helen Augustus and Richard Maurice, who was born on 18 March 1837.

Rev. Bucke's reasons for emigrating to Canada, though unknown, were likely financial. The family was no longer well off, the curacy paid little and education, especially higher education, was expensive, with Cambridge fees up to three hundred pounds a year. Bucke was likely influenced in his choice by Captain Frederick Marryat, a neighbour and well-known author and explorer, who had visited Canada; Marryat had described Upper Canada as having a population of forty thousand in an area capable of supporting many millions, and thought it "the most favoured spot in North America".

On 21 June 1838, the Rev. Bucke purchased a 100-acre farm, later called Creek Farm after the river which bisected the land from north to south, three miles east of the then village of London. It must have been a hectic menagerie when Clarissa Bucke, after one day in her new surroundings with seven children under age 11, gave birth to her eighth child, Alice Clarissa. Two years later, twin boys, Julius Poussett and Julian Rivers, completed the family.

Six years before the Bucke family's arrival, London had experienced a cholera epidemic from which it was beginning to recover. In 1838 London's growth was given an impetus by becoming the Military Headquarters for Western Canada. At that time the town contained some two hundred frame or brick houses, three or four small schools and the jail which was full of convicted rebels from the Mackenzie uprising:

> Besides the seven taverns, there is a number of little grocery
> stores, which are, in fact, drinking houses. And though a law

exists which forbids the sale of spirituous liquor in small quantities by any but licensed publicans, they easily contrive to evade
the law.[3]

Very little is known of Rev. Bucke's life in Canada. He brought with
him a library of several thousand volumes including books in Hebrew,
Greek, Latin, French, Italian and Spanish. There is no record of his having had a parish, although he performed a marriage ceremony in St.
Paul's Cathedral and delivered a non-ecclesiastic address on "Commerce
of Antiquity" in the Anglican Church at the nearby village of Adelaide.[4]
He was also elected an honorary member of the London Mechanics Institute on 13 January 1845.

Rev. Bucke's library on Creek Farm served as the children's school
and Richard Maurice grew up in a familiar nineteenth century pattern,
doing his share of duties on the farm and spending much time reading
in solitude. His father's influence is obvious in his early passion for books
and he remained a bibliophile until the end of his life.

Life changed suddenly on 25 January 1845, when Clarissa died.
Bucke's later accounts of the time between his mother's death when he
was seven and his departure from the family at sixteen, are evasive if
not actually misleading,[5] (CC, 8):

When only a few years old I lost my mother and shortly afterwards my father. Affairs at home went badly for me. I was ill-
treated and early in '53 being then sixteen years old, I made up
my mind that I would live elsewhere.[6]

In fact, Bucke's father did not die shortly after his mother, but re-married
eight months later.[7] Rev. Bucke's emotional life after his first wife's death
can be charted to some extent by the poems he wrote. A poem written
in December 1846, three months after his second marriage is addressed
to his new wife Elizabeth, née O'Reilly:

To Exxxx
What gives my troubled soul its rest?
What — but my gentle xx's breast.
What drives away the heavy sigh?
What — but my xx's sparkling eye.

Should all the world from me depart,
Yet leave my xx's warm, warm heart.
I'd rather have it far, than all
Men riches, grandeur, pleasures, call.
For there the depth of honour dwells,
And there, are love's romantic spells.
And thine — affections' holy ties —
For me it lives — for me, it dies![8]

That joy, however, proved short-lived as Elizabeth died two months later.[4]

Nor was this the end of the elder Bucke's amatory life, at least on a literary level, as a long series of poems addressed to female subjects shows. An undated, unfinished poem begins:

Behold the cruel moment near,
Thou goest my love from me:
How can I live in torment here,
So far, dear girl from thee?
. . .
How often shall my thoughts return
To those sweet plains, where we
Did once with mutual ardour burn
Where once I roved with thee![9]

Another poem dated 15 May 1848:

What will be the words they'll say
Of thee and me from day to day?
. . .
Of thee, my Lady they will say
The kindness that thou shewest to me
Is but the just reward I pray
    For all the love I feel for thee:
    That firm and constant thou will prove
    The dear effects of woman's love .... what or
Of me, the speech will always hold
That all for thee I could forsake

Or justly dread the wrath of God
Would soon my guilty head o'ertake
Oh dearest girl! how envy tries
In vain, to break our sacred ties!
   Of thee how loved would be the praise,
   Did they but know thy gentle heart
   Tho' some may boast a fairer face
   And some the syren's witching art
   Thy sweetest charms in life will be
   The kindness that thou shewest to me
Of me the rumour well may go
How high I dared my hopes to strain
How proud in me, a thought to win
The dear reward I trust to gain
But he that will not lift his eyes
From off the ground will never rise!

What will be the words they'll say
Of thee and me from day to day.[10]

This is succeeded on the following day by a poem entitled *"Les Yeux Bleus et les Yeux Noirs"*, in which the poet depicts his dilemma of choosing between a blond with blue eyes who "shall be gifted with the balm that soothes to rest"[11] and a brunette with black eyes who has "the pointed dart which burns the feverish breast."[11] In Rev. Bucke's handwriting at the bottom of this poem is the message that it was sent to a Miss Lowell Alison in April 1853, i.e., five years after it had been written and at the time of R.M. Bucke's departure.

   There are three more poems. The first is addressed to a young lady who asked for a sermon on the text "Thou shalt not steal" and which describes the young lady's stealing the tortured poet's heart. It concludes with the quatrain,

Lay thy dear hand upon thy heart
And make confession, sweet, sincere:
Act, act no more the traitor's part
And let one still be happy here! [12]

The second poem, written on 5 October 1849, is entitled "Ill, Melancholy and Alone''; it depicts the poet ill and dying without the comfort of his mother and sister or his beloved.

The last poem, written on 17 November 1853, and entitled "L.C.A.", is addressed presumably to the Miss Alison to whom the Rev. Bucke had sent his 16 May 1848 poem *"Les Yeux Bleus et les Yeux Noirs"* seven months earlier:

Sweet Syren! sing that song no more,
    or do not sing for me:
My youth, my love, they both are o'er
    You only torture me.

Yet stay — yet stay — those heavenly notes
    recall my happiest days;
As when the lightening rends the clouds,
    A bright, a deadly blaze.

Fond memory's bitter sense recalls
    The shade of joyous hours,
And round the wreck of hope it falls,
    And dark and cheerless lours.

Yet stay — the fleeting moment throws
    A light, tho' sad and dim;
A brightness all my spirit knows,
    The beacon in the waste of time.[13]

A month before this poem was written, Rev. Bucke's oldest son, George Walpole, then twenty-five, had sold "Creek Farm", of which he had assumed control two years earlier, and with his share of some money left him by his mother bought a farm sixty miles away in Moore Township near Sarnia. With him in his move went his father and all the younger siblings except Richard Maurice, whose unhappiness had become so intense just prior to this that he left home; in June 1853, he walked twenty-five miles to Port Stanley and crossed Lake Erie into Ohio.

Bucke's oft repeated account of his youth and the beginning of his adolescent adventures always included the mis-dating of his father's death to before his leaving home. Bucke was fully aware of his father's tormented emotions, because on the page of his father's last poem, "L.C.A.", follows, in Bucke's handwriting, a poem of his own written in 1859, and describing the beauty of the Sierra Nevadas. There may well have been general family disapprobation, or at least personal disapproval on young Bucke's part of his father's doomed liaison. Perhaps for the young Bucke his father symbolically *had* died by 1853. In fact, the Rev. H.W. Bucke died only on 31 March 1856.[14] By this time, Bucke had been gone three years, and was about to join a wagon train leaving Leavenworth, Kansas for the West. Those three years had been filled with adventures, but even more exciting ones were yet to come.

—— Chapter 2 ——

Near Fatality in
the Sierra Nevadas

BUCKE WORKED initially as a gardener near Columbus, Ohio but soon moved to the southwest and worked near Cincinnati on the railroad and on several farms. In the fall of 1854, with thirty-five dollars he had saved, he boarded a boat on the Ohio River which took two weeks to reach Cairo, Missouri where it ran aground. Bucke transferred to the *Arabia*, a steamer going down the Mississippi. On board he met a man who was going to Louisiana to make staves and Bucke was hired on at twenty dollars a month.

They disembarked at Plaquemine, Louisiana and the next day they started down the Bayou Plaquemine which had sugar cane farms along each side. They entered the Grand River and the following day they began to build their winter quarters.

There were thirteen men in the party: the head man and three assistants who had been given the contract to make 300,000 molasses staves; six men, including Bucke, were hired to help make the staves; and three other men were to make flat roads to the different piles of staves, and flat boats on which the staves could be loaded in the spring when the floods came.

After only eleven days Bucke developed diarrhoea and was not strong enough to work all winter. For a month he could do nothing, but thereafter he was given the job of cook and a reduction in pay from twenty dollars a month to fifteen. In the spring he joined the others in taking the staves in small boats to larger boats in the Bayou and on to Franklin on Bayou Task where they were sold.¹ For his winter's work, Bucke had earned sixty dollars.

He worked during 1855 on several steamboats on the Mississippi, Ohio, Missouri and Cumberland rivers. The era of steamboats for passenger and commercial travel was approaching its zenith. In 1850, the number of steamboats afloat was approximately 850 and by 1859 it had increased to 2000. Travel was treacherous and in the later years there were many fires, explosions and groundings, which took their toll and led to the eventual demise of steamboat traffic.²

By the spring of 1856, Bucke had tired of steamboating. He decided to go west, and while travelling up the Missouri from St. Louis, he was hired for twenty-five dollars a month on a wagon train leaving Leavenworth, Kansas on April 2nd. The train consisted of twenty-six wagons with six yoke of oxen to each wagon. The wagons were loaded with supplies for the garrison at Fort Laramie which they reached in early June. The train returned, and at the Big Blue River in northern Kansas in mid-July they met another wagon train going west to Salt Lake City with dry goods, groceries and hardware for the Mormon market. Bucke changed trains and hired on to the westbound wagon train at thirty dollars a month. Although they met Pawnees at Fort Carney, and a large party of Sioux at Fort Laramie, they were not attacked and completed the twelve-hundred-mile trek to Salt Lake City in mid-September.

Bucke and his travelling companions soon became restless there and decided within a few days to go to California. They divided themselves into parties of five to ten men and each group bought a wagon, two horses and the necessary provisions. They departed sequentially over several days with each man taking his turn at driving the wagon, the others walking along beside it. They covered about thirty miles a day.

Bucke was one of ten men in the second wagon to leave Salt Lake City. Their first contact with other white men would be at Sam Black's trading post, 450 miles of wilderness away at the Sink of the Humboldt River in what was then Utah. One day, at a point about two hundred miles from their destination, having stopped for a mid-day meal, they saw a group of men approaching from the west. They were six men from the first party, which had left Salt Lake City two days before Bucke's wagon. They told of being beaten and robbed by the Shoshone Indians, but had escaped with their lives by leaving all their possessions behind.

What to do? Bucke's group would now have six additional men to feed. No one wanted to return to Salt Lake City. Safety in numbers seemed an attractive strategy, so they camped where they were, waiting for parties three and four to catch up. After three days, the other parties had not appeared, and food provisions shared by sixteen rather than ten, began to get low. They, therefore, decided to go on. They planned to proceed to within a few miles of where the Shoshones had attacked, wait for darkness and pass through the enemy territory at night. It seemed a naïve plan to Bucke in retrospect. Indeed, after a night march of twenty-five miles, they camped on the Humboldt, only to see smoke rising beyond some willow trees further down the river. In traditional style, a second and third column of smoke appeared up and down the river, followed by the war whooping of a hundred or more Indians.

They decided to fight on the march. The Indians attacked with two or three guns and a shower of arrows, one of which struck Bucke's friend, Stewart, between the shoulders. The Indians immediately retreated as the white men fired at them, and did not charge again, but changed their strategy. Two or three of them, each with a gun, would run past the wagon out of gunshot and then crouch by the trail and wait. When the wagon approached, they would suddenly stand up and fire. The counterstrategy of Bucke's company was to appoint two men to watch the Indians as they ran by, and to mark where they squatted in the sage brush. The armed white men would then know where to fix their gaze and their barrel and would fire as soon as the Indian stood up. By afternoon they were out of danger, but a more terrible threat became apparent.

That morning, with the breakfast interrupted by the Indians, the wagon party had moved on without replenishing their water supply. By early afternoon there was no water for throats scorched by the tension and activity of the morning, as well as by the desert sun. Bucke said later that the parched feeling that day was harder to endure than the four days without food or warmth he would face a year later.

At nine that night they reached the river. Bucke wrote years later,

> We rushed into the water knee deep, some of us waist deep and drank from tins, from our hands, from the river itself. A man would drink all he could, perhaps from one to two quarts, and

in less than three minutes he would be just as thirsty; he would again fill his stomach with the same result. A man had a vessel in which to take water to a wounded man, who he knew was almost at the point of death for want of it. This man drank at least four quarts of water at the river then filled the can and started for the wagon, perhaps fifty yards away, to take the water to Butler. Before he reached the wagon, although he fully realized Butler's condition, he became so thirsty that he actually stopped, drank the water from the can and returned to the river for more for the wounded man. He again drank freely at the river and then succeeded in getting water to Butler.[3]

The party pushed on for six more days with nothing but flour and water, which they made into a kind of porridge. They arrived at Sam Black's trading post at the Sink of the Humboldt, and had no trouble disposing of meat, game, vegetables, hot biscuits and coffee. Bucke wrote later that for many days their appetites were insatiable, and that they ate raw meat with as much satisfaction as cooked meat, and unbaked dough as eagerly as bread. For several weeks they regarded bread and meat as sacred and divine.

The next day they bought a two-year-old heifer, flour, salt and other culinary basics, and settled down briefly near the trading post. After a three-day rest they crossed the desert from the Sink of the Humboldt to the Carson River and arrived at Gold Canyon. It was now November and too late in the season to cross the cold Sierra Nevadas into California. Bucke and the others sold their wagon and horses, took up claims, bought the necessary tools and began to look for gold in Gold Canyon. The Sierra Nevadas would have to wait until the next year when Bucke would cross them several times.

Bucke's fate in 1857 became entwined with that of two young miners, Allen and Hosea Grosh, who had come to California via Mexico in 1849. The Grosh brothers were sons of a Universalist clergyman, the Rev. A.B. Grosh of Marietta, Pennsylvania, and had set out from Philadelphia to join a party of some forty men who had paid a J.R. West to take them to California.

They sailed to the east coast of Mexico, landing at Tampico, and after buying mules, horses and provisions set out for the west coast. The Grosh brothers' start was unlucky, and the first in an eight-year catalogue of misfortunes occurred when West abandoned the party some eighty miles from the west coast. They took possession of the horses, mules and wagons and reached San Blas, completing a seventy-four day trek punctuated with dysentery, lack of water and malaria.

The Grosh brothers had enough money for about half the steerage fare and, after giving the captain of the sailing vessel *Olga* of Boston, their mules, wagons and harness, they were taken on and reached San Francisco forty-nine days later on August 12th. They worked at odd jobs until June 1850, when they went to the mines in the neighbourhood of Colma, Eldorado County. In their first year, which was probably their best, they made two thousand dollars. However, they subsequently lost it in building a dam to divert a river out of its bed which could then be washed for gold — no gold was found.

During the next two years they continued to mine unsuccessfully and became ill. They started a ranch which they soon gave up, and in July 1853, crossed the Sierra Nevadas for the first time. After crossing the western summit they prospected for gold in the valley south of Lake Tahoe. They then walked over the eastern summit into Utah (Nevada after 1864) and settled down for the winter to mine in Gold Canyon, where a little gold had been discovered three years earlier.[4]

After mining without success through the spring and summer of 1854, they returned to California and prospected for quartz veins in Eldorado County. Their bad luck continued through 1855 and into 1856. On March 31st, the first mention of silver in Gold Canyon was made in a letter to their father. They returned to Utah in September 1856 and stayed for two months. It was during this period that they discovered "two veins of silver at the forks of the Gold Canyon and one of the veins is a perfect monster".[5] They returned once more to Eldorado County to mine for gold but were again unsuccessful. In the spring of 1857 they returned to Gold Canyon trying to follow the vein they had discovered several months earlier. Theirs was the first discovery of silver in Nevada and although the vein that they found did not turn out to be a rich one, within two years the silver rush had gathered momentum and the fabulous Comstock Lode was beginning to yield its treasures. Neither Allen nor Hosea Grosh realized any profit from it. By the end of 1857 both were dead.

In the spring of 1857 the Grosh brothers had interested a cattle rancher named George Brown in nearby Carson Valley in financing the development of the vein they had discovered. But one day that summer George

Brown was murdered at his trading post by some Arkansas men staying nearby, who accused him without evidence of having let Indians steal their horses.

Bucke spent the winter of 1856-57 mining at Gold Canyon, but had earned barely enough to live on. In the spring, he wanted to try his luck on the other side of the mountains in California. Together with three other men he crossed the Sierra Nevadas and found work in Marysville where he stayed for approximately six weeks. Still unsettled, he crossed back again to Nevada and stayed for only a week in Flower Lake Valley, about 140 miles north of Carson Valley. Dissatisfied with Flower Lake Valley, he returned to Gold Canyon where he began mining again.

Bucke had begun to tire of this life, and while in Marysville he had written home, presumably to his older brother, George, asking for three hundred dollars to get him home. No reply had come while he remained there, and a letter to Marysville requesting his mail be forwarded brought no answer. Bucke, therefore, decided to go back once more and collect his letters. He crossed through the Sierra Nevadas again, and at Marysville picked up some letters but no money. His family, apparently fearful that some imposter might have made the request, was reluctant to send money. Bucke returned to Gold Canyon, a distance of 175 miles, after an absence of three weeks. He later described the incident, wryly, as "a long walk that, to the Post Office".

While Bucke was mining in Gold Canyon, Allen Grosh had showed Bucke a button of silver extracted by his brother Hosea and himself in the neighbourhood of Gold Canyon, and told him of other finds, though he did not indicate their exact locations. While making plans to develop their silver discovery, the Grosh brothers continued to try to make a living mining for gold. On August 19th, Hosea struck his left ankle with a pick. The injury was not considered serious at first, but within a few days he became ill and died of septicaemia on September 2nd.

On September 11th, Allen wrote to his father,

By Hosea's death you fall heir to his share of the silver claims. We have so far four veins — three of them promise much.

Bucke assisted at the burial service and became closer to the bereaved Allen, who continued to work to pay off a debt of $60 accumulated through Hosea's illness and death. Allen's plan to find financial backing for his silver discovery persisted, and by November he wanted to cross to California. The two men arranged to go together. Allen had a donkey which they packed with their clothes, some cooking utensils and a few days' provisions.

The distance to be travelled to the western side of the Sierra Nevadas was about a hundred miles along the Washoe trail, used by Indians or occasional foot travellers and, as related, already traversed by Bucke twice each way. From Washoe Valley (Plate I, please see page 26) the trail ascends the eastern summit to the shore of Lake Tahoe. It skirts the north east shore of Lake Tahoe for about ten miles until it reaches the junction of the Truckee River and Lake Tahoe. The trail then runs north along the east bank of the Truckee River for eight miles, crosses the stream into Squaw Valley for a few miles which lies close under the western summit of the Sierra Nevadas, at an elevation of about eleven thousand feet. The distance from Squaw Valley down the western slope to the first settlement is about fifty miles.

On November 15th, they set off from Gold Canyon and camped in Eagle Valley (Plate I). In the morning the donkey was missing. They looked for him all day and found his tracks at sunset, eight miles away. Grosh returned to their camp and Bucke followed the tracks and found the donkey. Next morning, November 17th, Bucke and the donkey returned to Grosh. They crossed the ten-mile Washoe Valley and camped in an old house at the foot of the eastern summit of the Sierra Nevadas.

Awakening on November 18th, they found the donkey had strayed again and looked unsuccessfully for him all day long. On November 19th, they continued along the path leading into the mountains but having more than they could carry, they detoured to a lone house a mile away where a man lived whom they knew. While there, they met another man who said he had seen a donkey the day before back in Eagle Valley. Grosh took their belongings back to where they had camped the night before and Bucke returned to Eagle Valley for the donkey. Reaching Eagle Valley, Bucke encountered a man who told him that the donkey had been taken back to Gold Canyon by someone, thinking Grosh was there. So Bucke plodded back to the starting point at Gold Canyon, found the donkey and immediately set off again.

On November 20th, Bucke and the unreliable beast of burden reached Grosh and started over the eastern summit where they camped that night. By noon on November 22nd, they had reached the Truckee River and

PLATE I — *Bucke and Grosh's 23-day trek across the Sierra Nevadas, 1857.*

Day 1 — November 15 — began trek from Gold Canyon

Day 2 — November 16 — donkey escaped, found 8 miles away

Day 3 — November 17 — reached Washoe Lake

Day 4 — November 18 — donkey escaped again

Day 5 — November 19 — Bucke returned to Eagle Valley in search of the donkey

Day 6 — November 20 — returned to the starting point at Gold Canyon found the donkey, and went west again

Day 7 — November 21 — reached Lake Tahoe

Day 8 — November 22 — reached Squaw Valley

Day 9 — November 23 — snow — no progress

Day 10 — November 24 — donkey killed

Day 11 — November 25 — snow — remained in Squaw Valley

Day 12 — November 26 — snow — remained in Squaw Valley

Day 13 — November 27 — snow — remained in Squaw Valley

Day 14 — November 28 — unable to reach summit, returned to Squaw Valley

Day 15 — November 29 — passed summit and took shelter in a cabin

Day 16 — November 30 — snow — remained in cabin

Day 17 — December 1 — snow — remained in cabin

Day 18 — December 2 — missed the trail, walked in a circle

Day 19 — December 3 — resumed walking with no sense of direction

Day 20 — December 4 — struggled on, no food, slept under snow

Day 21 — December 5 — very weak, no food, but continued to walk

Day 22 — December 6 — Bucke proposed they lie down and die

Day 23 — December 7 — staggered on, reached Little Duncan, eight miles from Last Chance where they were taken on December 15.

followed it into Squaw Valley. The several-days delay because of the wandering donkey proved crucial. It had now begun to snow, and before they had gone halfway to the western summit, the trail was no longer visible. It began to grow dark and they had no alternative but to return to Squaw Valley again and camp there.

On November 23rd, they tried again but the snow was too deep for the donkey to travel and it was bitterly cold so once again they returned to the valley. They decided the next day it would be impossible to get over the pass with the donkey, so they killed and skinned him, and with very little food left, ate only donkey meat from then on. The following three days were cloudy and snowy. They remained in the valley and tried to make snowshoes, and to keep warm by the fire, while they considered various plans of action.

Four possibilities presented themselves. The first was to push on, and either reach their destination or die. The second was to return to Gold Canyon, which was now as far back as their intended destination was ahead, the third was to follow the Truckee River and hope to find some houses, and the fourth, was to stay in Squaw Valley until spring. Bucke weighed the choices carefully, and he and Grosh agreed that their best chance was to try to make it over the summit to the other side.

November 28th was clear and fine. They packed as much donkey meat as they could carry and set out to find the trail, but were unsuccessful. Finally they decided to guess its location, and spent most of the day climbing toward the summit. Once they reached it, they saw that they were separated from the trail down the western side by a one-thousand-foot ravine, and though they could from their vantage point now see the proper trail, they had no choice but to return again to Squaw Valley, which they reached, exhausted, at about 10 p.m., only to find their matches wet. They used their guns to start a fire, rested, and started out again the next morning.

That day they passed the summit and in the evening reached a cabin Bucke knew: on his crossing back in the summer he had stayed briefly with some men who lived in this cabin. Bucke hoped that some flour and bacon which the men had left hidden in the cabin would still be there, but Indians had discovered the supplies and taken them.

By December 2nd it had stopped snowing, and Grosh and Bucke set off on their home-made snowshoes, which they soon discovered were of no help. Only half a pound of donkey meat was left. They had difficulty staying on the trail: as long as there were trees, blazes marked the way, but towards evening they came to a ridge devoid of trees, and could only guess at the direction of the trail. About sundown they discovered fresh tracks, which for a moment or two they misinterpreted as evidence of other human beings in the vicinity: the numbing realization soon followed that the tracks were their own, and that they had simply walked in a circle. It was now snowing, and becoming colder. The next shock was to discover, when they set out to build a fire, that their gun was damp and would not fire.

Bucke and Grosh realized that their only chance of survival was to find some form of shelter from the cold. They abandoned their possessions, including Allen's papers, keeping only their blankets, a butcher's knife and a tin cup containing the last few scraps of the donkey meat. Unencumbered, they made their way down from the ridge, and before dark reached a valley well wooded with evergreens.

How were they to survive the night? They decided to sleep under the snow. After clearing a bed space, they covered the ground with three or four inches of evergreen boughs, placed their blankets on these and layered a foot of snow on top. They ate half the remaining meat, crawled in under the blankets, and waited for morning.

On December 3rd, they resumed walking, but without a definite sense of direction. They reasoned that the ravine would eventually lead to a river, which they hoped to find muddy, an indication that miners were not far away. They did not reach a river that day, but bedded down that night as before, after eating the last of their meat.

About noon the following day they reached a river; Bucke estimated they had walked about ten miles. They stayed close to the river, and slept for the third time under the snow. December 5th provided no respite.

On December 6th they plodded on following a small stream which fed into the river, and looking in vain for the muddy colour. Bucke recalled that Grosh was weaker than he was, but more resolute. That afternoon, exhausted and overwhelmed with despair, Bucke began to weep and wanted to give up. He proposed to Grosh that they just lie down and die. Grosh insisted that they keep on as long as they could move, and persuaded Bucke to make a last effort. That night Bucke recalled his words to Grosh.

Let us make up our bed for the last time, for we shall never leave this place.[6]

Grosh again insisted that if they were still alive in the morning, they would walk or crawl on. They slept little but were too weak to talk to each other; in the morning they were still able to stand. They staggered on, and about 11 o'clock Grosh said he heard a dog bark. Bucke thought Grosh was hallucinating, but the stream became muddy, and soon they sighted a few houses. Thus, on December 7th, they reached Little Duncan, after three days of walking without food, and four nights survival under the snow.[7]

By the next day neither could walk, and it was apparent that their feet were frozen. Bucke recalled twenty-five years later that they became delirious, but Grosh was able to write a letter, his last, to his father on December 12th. He referred to Bucke as a young Englishman and

> though not yet 21 years of age, has shown the high Norman blood in encountering our difficulties and trials, which has enabled that race to keep its position as the governors of England, even to the present day.

Grosh apparently had no intimation he would not survive and wrote:

> I think that in three or four days I will start for the Sugar Loaf. . . . Neither of us can walk. Our friends will try and have us packed out to Michigan Bluff through the snow. We are 6 or 7 miles above Last Chance and 18 or 20 above the Bluff.

The plans to move Bucke and Grosh were completed, and a number of men came up from Last Chance with two sleighs and hauled them away on December 15th. Word was sent to Michigan Bluff for a doctor. Four days later a physician arrived, but Grosh became weaker and more delirious and died that evening. Nine days later, Bucke's feet were amputated; the right one four inches above the ankle joint, and the left halfway down the foot. He eventually wore a prosthesis on the right leg and although the stumps did not thoroughly heal for more than forty years, he very seldom complained of the discomfort.[8]

When Bucke was well enough to get up, it was suggested to him

by the Spaniard who owned the shanty that he should go around among
the mining camps and try to solicit enough money to get back to Ontario.
Bucke replied that he would rather starve than beg, whereupon the
miners called a meeting, and Bucke was placed on a table in the middle
of the room while one of the men made a speech. He told them that
Bucke was a miner like themselves and that his case might have been
theirs — it was a situation which called for subscriptions and he hoped
that they would be liberal.

The miners, who had come prepared, filed past the table where they
deposited gold dust and nuggets. Bucke's physician gave him a letter
to an influential businessman, a Mr. Alpheus Bull of San Francisco, setting forth Bucke's plight and asking for assistance. Mr. Bull secured a
ticket to pay Bucke's way from San Francisco to New York through the
Panama Railway.

On his way home Bucke stopped in Washington where he visited
the Rev. A.B. Grosh, now a government clerk. He also visited Grosh
in Marietta, Pennsylvania the following year, and they became warm
friends. Rev. Grosh wrote Bucke on 5 November 1858, referring to the
latter's visit,

> and it seemed to me, more than ever, that you stood in his place
> [i.e., his son's] for us to regard and love.[9]

In all his later accounts of the Sierra Nevada adventure Bucke seldom referred to his feelings about it. In 1896 he wrote:

> pain, of course, is unpleasant especially when it gives me bad
> nights but I am not at all sure that it is well to be entirely with-
> out it — it seems to me that it is as important (for character)
> to learn to bear and to face pain (as in operations) as to learn
> French or mathematics.[10]

In 1858, Bucke wrote a poem about the Sierra Nevadas. This is the
first entry he made in the Poetry record book, immediately following Rev.
Bucke's last entry:

> I once did stand upon Nevada's peak
> The loftiest height for many miles around

The eastern side my wondering gaze did seek
It almost seemed that prospect had no bound
So far on every side it stretched; no sound
Of living thing above, around, below
Was there to mar that solitude profound
Naught but the rugged rocks whose peaks did glow
With dazzling height reflected from the purest snow.

And far as eye could reach in distance dim
Peak above peak, mount above mount arose;
And Humboldt's mountains in the east did seem
Like many piles of everlasting snows;
Their lofty peaks the horizon did close
Three hundred miles lay 'tween their base and I;
Down from their side the roaring Humboldt flows
Their summits mingle with and kiss the sky
Scarce might the haughty eagle soar so wondrous high.

The snow clad peaks at Carson River's head
Were in the distance seen and o'er their tops
The vast Nevadas rose; upon them fed
The hardy mountain sheep who joyfull crops
The grass upon their fertile base or lops
The mountain twig where herbage is not seen
And if he hears a sound full soon he stops
And looks around where late his mate has been
Then seeing all is still turns once more to the green.

And turning to the west before me lay
All California's land in vast extent.
The coast-range mountains, and Francisco's bay
Seen through them where the Sacramento rent
The massy hills in twain; the sky seemed blent
Inseparably with the watery sheet
So great a mist the enormous distance lent
The Sacramento valley 'neath my feet
Smiled like a second Eden lovely, fair and sweet.

Great gift it is to those who thus may stand
On ancient mounts whose peaks untrod by men
Look o'er that wild and solitary land
That prospect vast of varied hill and glen
Well might he wish to stand there once again
He who that glorious vision once doth see
Forgets it not again; or if so then
Together sinks his life with memory
Of what while life did last could ne'er forgotten be.[11]

—— Chapter 3 ——

Postgraduate Studies Abroad

IN OCTOBER 1858, Bucke, accompanied by Mr. Pousett, an old family friend from Sarnia, travelled to Montreal where he entered medical school. There is virtually no record of his life during the four years he was there. He carried on a correspondence with the Rev. A.B. Grosh but only Grosh's letters have survived. They deal mainly with family matters and the possible legitimacy of claim to the silver discoveries rapidly unfolding in Nevada. This was the first intimation Bucke had of the fabulous Comstock Lode and the eventual litigation which would take him back to California in 1864.

By 1859, he had met his future wife, Jessie Gurd, and on November 19th, in Hamilton en route back to Montreal, wrote her a letter asking if he might correspond. He anticipated resistance.

> though *why* you should be so prejudiced against writing I am sure I cannot see.... you cannot surely dear Jessie refuse to write just this once if it is even to say that you will not write to me again nor allow me to write to you.[1]

However, his plea was successful and on 19 August 1860 Bucke wrote Jessie from Montreal lamenting his lonely life and wishing he was with her.

How I should like to have a ride with you along the river and
see all the old places again — but it is idle to wish, that time
is past — perhaps never to return.[2]

Bucke seems to jump from his own unhappiness and longing to the theme
of human suffering and the purpose of existence which was to occupy
much of his energy and imagination, and then back to one of the rare
instances of self-pity.

Can you wonder dearest Jessie that I should get very sad sometimes, here all alone, when I sit in my room all by myself and
think of *what has been — what is — and what might have been —*
much misery upon this earth, what was its beginning and why
it was ever called into existence we cannot tell — the *fact* of its
existence we know and the *reason* of that we hope one day to
be cleared up — you must forgive me dear Jessie for getting so
dull over my letter but I will not offend again, the fact is it is
rather hard to keep from complaining sometimes although we
all know it never does any good.[3]

Of other suitors little is known, except for a Theo Brookes from
Chicago who spent the summer of 1862 near Sarnia and who wrote Jessie after his departure, asking if they might correspond and requesting
a lock of hair. In fact, he wrote four letters[4] and Jessie finally replied declining the invitation.[5]

Bucke was also in Sarnia briefly at the beginning of that summer,
following his graduation from medical school. On June 30th, he entered
in his diary that he had written some verses in Jessie's album, prior to
his departure for England.

. . . they are some of the worst I ever wrote, and they are so
from the simple fact that they were not written in accordance
with my feelings (i.e., are not soft enough); were it not for the
admonitions of Aunt and Julius I believe I should have left
Canada engaged to that girl ... and, if it was not that I want to
go to England so bad I might be induced easily to give up the
scheme and marry her for I do not imagine there would be the
least difficulty in obtaining her consent *now*.[6]

But the diary entry in July includes not only the sanctioned verses which went into Jessie's album, but the intended version, preferred by Bucke. The sanctioned verses are polite and express fondness, the intended lines express the anguish of a lover's rejection.

'Tis thou hath set our lives apart,
'Tis thou hath cast a shade on mine,
And given half my life to pine,
The rest to science and to art.

And left me only half a man
To gather hints of law; and grope
In desert places, seeking hope
Of knowledge, and the boundless plan

Of nature; while the nobler part
That makes us not as thinking things
Is withered by disuse its wings
Are clipped; and darkness hides my heart.[7]

Thus there must have been a rapprochement during the days between the composition of the verses and the diary entry with its confident assertion that Bucke could obtain Jessie's consent "*now*".

June 1862 had been a busy month for Bucke, ending with the intense, emotional fluctuations of his relationship with Jessie and the excitement of his approaching departure for England. At the beginning of the month he had been awarded the Governor's prize for his thesis for the degree of MD CM, "The Correlation of Physical and Vital Forces". It was defended before the Medical Faculty of McGill on May 2nd and subsequently published in the *British American Journal*.[8]

Bucke's hypothesis was that the distinction between inorganic and organic form (mineral vs. animal/vegetable) is simply a difference in the way forces acting on those forms are transformed. Physical forces such as heat and light become altered into vital life forces (forces peculiar to a living organism) in the cell by virtue of a chemical change. The type of vital force depends on the nature of the cell: a nerve cell converts a non-biological stimulus such as heat or light into a nervous force carried to its destination by the nerve.

The energy to carry out the functions of the body results from the change of organic compounds in food of complex chemical construction into simpler, more stable compounds with a resultant release of energy, a vital force whose nature depends upon the type of cell acting as mediator: a muscle cell transforms the force into a contraction, a neuron into a propagated electrical impulse along the nerve.

Bucke introduced both a personal and a metaphysical note in explaining this transformation of forces with the release of vital energy:

I was once for five days and four nights exposed to a temperature of from zero to below that point to a few degrees above the freezing point: during this time I was supplied with no food, no artificial heat, and travelled every day on foot through deep snow from morning till night. Now, I ask, could the muscular force employed, the heat evolved, and the vis nervosa put forth (without speaking of other forms of force liberated in less amount), have been derived from the decomposition of the tissues lost during that time? I make no doubt that the reply must be in the affirmative.[9]

In attempting to explain this, Bucke gives examples of energy transformation where a resultant force appears to have increased. For example, the small amount of oil burned in a lamp would yield vast quantities of light. But he also invokes the Creator's help.

That the animal body should be far superior to any machine of mere human contrivance as an economist of force, is nothing more than we should expect, and may fairly infer from its origin, being planned and formed by a Mind and Hand so infinitely superior in wisdom and power to those that work among us. And it must be regarded as a result of this economizing that so great a proportion of the force given off takes the form of motion, which as we have seen is a much cheaper form of force — so as to speak — than any of the rest.[10]

Bucke sailed for England on July 16th. His uncle, Joseph Andrews, provided the financial assistance which enabled him to pursue his postgraduate studies.

The main source of information on Bucke's life abroad over the next eighteen months is his diary, though the entries from 16 July 1862 to 12 March 1863 have been destroyed. March 12th found him based at University College Hospital recording details of hospital rounds and the operations he observed; his reading at this time was extensive and eclectic. He goes on:

> Have been in a curious psychical condition all day — felt as if something awful had just happened to me or was just about to happen, tried to analyse the feeling but could not do it satisfactorily — but think that sitting up the other night half falling in love, the near prospect of a move, and some other little things have together brought on an irritable condition of the brain. Must try and see Miss B before I leave town, the girl has half made a fool of me that's a fact — I dare say I shall get better of it in a few days.[11]

Then with a quiet self-reprimand he adds,

> I ought to attend the old Scotchman's great rule and "ay keep the bowels open". Perhaps if I should see her once more the charm might be broken.

But Bucke did not see her again, nor did he succeed in meeting a girl whom he saw passing in a chaise on Good Friday, three weeks later in Suffolk.

> About 7, as it was beginning to get a little dusk a chaise passed the window to which my uncle called my attention, there were a couple of girls in it, one had a lovely head of hair — dark brown curls — I did not see her face.[12]

His uncle prophesied correctly that she was going to the Post Office and Bucke suddenly decided he needed stamps.

> Faced her at the office door and had a good look at her face; lost all recollection of the stamps, and walked on. Got round the corner and turned back again — saw her again. She looked

full at me each time — she did not seem to have any narrow prejudices against being looked at. The loveliest girl I think I ever saw — such eyes! Mein Gott — complexion, hair, nose, mouth, as far as I could see, all perfect; I was half in love.[13]

The next day his uncle drove him to where she lived. Bucke saw her mother and grandmother as they drove past, but not the girl. The only other mention of a female encounter of any kind was on October 1st in London: coming up St. Martin's Lane he was approached by a prostitute whom he shunned.

His reading at the time included for the second time Charles Kingsley's *Westward Ho!* He returned to this romantic novel repeatedly. It is an adventure story set in Elizabethan times, and immensely popular with Victorians following its publication in 1855. The hero Amyas Leigh is a fearless sailor, devoted son and faithful brother, who leads an expedition to America to discover gold and to rout the bellicose Spaniards. In so doing, he is away for three years and returns with an untamed Indian maiden, named Ayacanora, who loves Amyas but who is kept kindly, but at arm's length, with him and his old mother forever after.

Bucke's nostalgia and loneliness are expressed vividly in his diary entry of May 5th.

It is the very God of novels, I was wholly carried away from the dim east and north once more westward to that most divine land of America, fairly wallowing in the glorious sunshine & rich vegetation of the south and west, the wild grandeur of the western wilderness that I know so well! but must, never more see except in such visions — ye mighty scenes of mountain river, forest, and lovely valley, how ye passed before me, almost turning my brain with indescribable longings, regret, exultation & despair — to think to have seen such & never more to see, a cripple, a wreck — and that scene in the valley with the two Seamen and their Indian wives, and Amyas and Ayacanora, it is like a glimpse into the Elysium of the Gods of highest heaven — the beauty of the book is perfectly awfull.[14]

In this scene, Amyas and Ayacanora, whom Amyas won't let himself love, come upon two of Amyas Leigh's renegade seamen with two

Indian maidens they have taken unto themselves in a paradisiacal setting. One of the seamen taunts Amyas that he, Amyas, is wasting his
life chasing fame and fortune. Amyas is spellbound and although he
chastizes the men for their sloth and heathen ways, he has ambivalent
feelings for the only time in the book, dreaming of life with Ayacanora
in this Garden of Eden. She looks to him for a decision but it is made
for him by the sudden and fatal attack on one of the Indian maidens
by a jaguar. Amyas then kills the jaguar as it was attacking one of the
seamen.

> "Oh Lord Jesus", said Amyas to himself, "thou hast answered
> the devil for me! And this is the selfish rest for which I would
> have bartered the rest which comes where thou has put me!"[15]

This scene represents for Bucke the conflict between the self-
indulgence of sybaritic pleasure and the resolute adherence to a life
governed by duty and responsibility.

In the spring of 1863, Bucke was also reading Auguste Comte's
Catechisme positiviste. He had been led to Comte through Lewes's two
volume *Biographical History of Philosophy*, which ends with an exposition
of Comte's philosophy. Between April and December 1863, he also
worked his way through Comte's *Politique positive* twice, Littré's *Paroles
de philosophie positive* and Comte's magnum opus *Cours de philosophie
positiviste*.

Bucke's great admiration for Comte is particularly interesting in the
light of his later transcendental philosophy which culminated in *Cosmic
Consciousness*. The fundamental theme of Comte's positivism is to consider all phenomena as subject to invariable natural laws. The discovery
of these laws using the scientific method and their reduction to the least
possible number was the object of the system. Comte postulated an
intellectual progression through history from theological and metaphysical
reasoning to his scientific approach. He regarded the search after what
are called first or final causes as futile.

Comte's philosophy had an important influence on Bucke at this time.
In his McGill thesis he had hypothesized that physical and chemical forces
in the body became transformed into organic vital forces, the exact nature
of which depended upon the nature of the type of cell in which the transformation occurred. This was entirely consonant with Comte's view that

the laws of science are applicable to all phenomena and would enable the new science of biology to elucidate them. That is, biology would provide the methodology to confirm his materialistic concept of life.

There were several reasons why this philosophical system appealed to Bucke. The first was an extension of the theme of his McGill essay, namely, that the genesis of vital forces, including our moral or emotional nature, had a somatic origin. He came to believe that it lay in the sympathetic nervous system.

Comte also believed that man's mind was evolving from an earlier theological stage of superstition, through a period of metaphysical philosophies to the modern era of scientific truth.[16] This evolutionary upward travel would become a central theme in two of Bucke's books. In *Man's Moral Nature*, Bucke affirmed that man's moral development, seated anatomically in the sympathetic nervous system, would continue inexorably along its upward path. His theory that the alleged site of man's moral nature was in the sympathetic nervous system was not widely held even at that time and is now known to be incorrect. In his later, more celebrated book, *Cosmic Consciousness*, he would depict how acquisition of the elevated cosmic sense was occurring in ever increasing numbers of individuals. Comte's anticlerical approach also appealed to him as it suited Bucke's philosophical atheism at that time.

However, two aspects of Comte's system were at variance with Bucke's later convictions. Although Comte included the belief that the collective consciousness of all individuals was incorporated into a "Great Being", he did not believe an apocalyptic experience in each person to be the prerequisite for a personal transcendental union, with the subsequent acquisition of anything corresponding to Bucke's cosmic sense. Comte's view of immortality was also different from Bucke's. He viewed man's immortality rather abstractly as the effect which memory of the deceased had on the survivors. Bucke later became certain of personal immortality, a conviction that proved invaluable in sustaining him through the loss of two people who had by then become very important to him.

Bucke also read Herbert Spencer's essay on the "Genesis of Science" in which Spencer attempts to refute one aspect of Comte's philosophy. Comte viewed the sciences as following one another, both logically and historically in order of their decreasing generality. Thus, for example, mathematics becomes the instrument of astronomy and physics. Spencer believed that not infrequently the more abstract sciences were advanced

only at the instigation of a more concrete science. Bucke noted his disagreement with the essay in his diary of September 26th:

I find it rather too much for my knowledge and faculties to effect
a reconciliation between him and Comte. I thought some of trying to write a paper to attempt to do this but am afraid I have
neither the requisite time or ability.[17]

Bucke could not have foreseen that the gap between Spencer's criticism and Comte's general philosophic system was a mere crack compared to the chasm that would later exist between Comte's rationalism
and Bucke's mysticism sparked by his illumination in 1872. Most interesting is the absence of any subsequent acknowledgement of this.

During these months in 1863 in England and France, in addition to
reading Comte, Bucke became familiar with Wordsworth, Coleridge,
Browning, Keats and Shelley, the latter being his favourite poet, until
his initial exposure to Whitman six years later. His novel reading included
Anne Bronte's *The Tenant of Wildfell Hall*, Scott's *Waverly*, Goethe's *Wil-
helm Meister*, George Eliot's *Mill on the Floss, Adam Bede* and *Silas Marner*
and Cooper's *The Last of the Mohicans*. He also read Irving's *Life of Gold-
smith*, Mill's *On Liberty*, De Quincey's *Confessions of an English Opium Eater*,
Prescott's *Conquest of Peru* and Ernest Renan's *Vie de Jésus*.

Bucke spent the early part of 1863 in London, doing rounds in the
morning with the consultants such as Sydney Ringer, at University College Hospital. On March 23rd, he received a letter from Palmer Howard,
one of his former professors at McGill, encouraging him to do a few
months of study on the continent rather than taking a higher degree in
England. This suited Bucke perfectly, and he began at once to form his
plans for going to Paris.

On April 15th he left Folkstone by boat. In Paris by 9:30 a.m. the
next morning, he took a cab to the Mazarin Hotel, washed up and went
straightaway to the Ecole de Médecine where he heard a lecture on frac-
tures of the femur, not a word of which he understood. He found lodg-
ings the next day, and settled in for four months. His routine included
doing hospital rounds in the morning and attending lectures by Armand
Trousseau, whose two-volume *Clinique Médicale* he read.

Bucke was lonely in Paris, made few friends, and was very happy
on May 15th to welcome a Dr. Van Buskirk, another postgraduate stu-

dent whom he had met in London. His stay was also marred by illness: on June 12th he developed an acute febrile illness which kept him confined to his room for a month. His own diagnosis was typhoid fever, but he had no medical supervision except for Dr. Van Buskirk who prescribed quinine. Bucke wanted to continue on to Berlin, but decided that would be beyond his means.

Before coming to Paris, Bucke had begun what turned out to be a lifelong friendship with two brothers, Alfred and Harry Forman, both in the publishing business. Alfred arrived in Paris on July 25th to visit Bucke, and they spent two weeks together visiting the Louvre and the Tuileries. Bucke returned with Alfred to London on August 8th, only to find that there would be very little medical teaching until October. He then spent a month with his relatives in Suffolk.

He returned to London on September 23rd and found a room in Bloomsbury. Until early December, Bucke spent most days at the Ophthalmic Hospital, University College Hospital, or Kings College Hospital. In the first week of December, he received two important letters. On December 4th, a letter from a Mr. Bull in San Francisco informed him of pending litigation about the ownership of newly discovered silver deposits in Nevada, and requesting Bucke's testimony. The second letter, received three days later, informed him of his brother's serious illness. Edward Horatio Bucke, the second eldest brother, had graduated from McGill Medical School in 1852 and practised in Sarnia. Bucke was unsettled by this news and within a few days had decided to return to Canada. His post-graduate days were over. It had been a year-and-a-half of disciplined reading, a new-found familiarity with his ancestral background and the ripening of important friendships with the Forman brothers.

— Chapter 4 —

Return to California

A T NOON on December 24th, Bucke sailed out of Liverpool and after an uneventful crossing docked at Portland, Maine on January 9th. He went on to Montreal by train and spent four days there seeing old friends including his former teacher Palmer Howard. He also learned that his brother Edward had died. On January 15th, Bucke arrived in Sarnia. Over the following ten days he deliberated where to set up practice. Friends of the family, the Poussetts, had a son Arthur, a physician, who had set up practice in Sarnia immediately after Edward Bucke's death. Mr. Poussett offered an inducement of $300, to be paid against the late Dr. Bucke's mortgage, if R.M. Bucke would leave Sarnia and start practice in Montreal. Bucke initially considered accepting the offer, but the next day decided it was more prudent to practise for a year in the nearby hamlet of Moore and to pay off the mortgage from his own earnings.

At this time Bucke spent some evenings with Jessie and her mother, and on January 17th recorded that it was quite possible he might marry Jessie "especially if I stay in this part of the country". By January 24th, having reconsidered the options, Bucke chose to settle in Sarnia. He secured an office above the drugstore and shared the rooms with his younger brother Julius. He saw patients both in his office and in the neighbouring communities of Wyoming and Oil Springs.

On February 14th, Bucke signed a pact with Robert Gurd, Jessie's brother, that during the month of July 1865 they would each, on the same day, be married. The defaulting party would be liable for the expenses of a wedding trip to Portland, Oregon. The pact was affixed with a seal and witnessed.

Bucke's new life in Sarnia was quickly interrupted by the receipt of a telegram on 5 March 1864 from Mr. Alpheus Bull of San Francisco.[1] He had met Mr. Bull in San Francisco in 1858 after his disastrous adventure in the Sierra Nevadas, and it was the same Mr. Bull who had purchased a ticket for him, enabling him to return home to Canada. Bull was now seeking Bucke's assistance in a lawsuit that had been filed against the Gould and Curry Mining Co., of which he was a trustee. Following the Grosh brothers' discovery of silver in 1857, other discoveries of great importance were made over the next few years, leading to considerable litigation concerning ownership. Ironically, Rev. Grosh, who had developed a warm, avuncular friendship with Bucke, found himself aligned with the plaintiff, the Grosh Consolidated Gold and Silver Mining Co.. Grosh had hoped for some financial reward from the family's mining activities ever since his son Allen had written him on 11 September 1857 after the unexpected loss of his brother:

By Hosea's death you fall heir to his share of the silver claims.

What Bull wanted from Bucke was his testimony that the land mined by the Grosh brothers, in which, in 1857, they had found "two veins of silver at the forks of Gold Canyon and one of these is a perfect monster",[2] was not the site of the Comstock Lode.

Bucke must have felt some conflict of conscience in starting out from Sarnia to give evidence that would only jeopardize the Rev. Grosh's chance of obtaining money he needed badly. Indeed, on 31 March 1864 Rev. Grosh wrote Bucke:

I was bitterly disappointed at not seeing you before you went; but doubt not that you acted in the whole affair, as to your judgement seemed necessary — and not only so, but *right* and *best* — and hence I commend *you*, however much I felt disappointed by your *action*. Just as I should expect commendation under similar circumstances of motive and judgement. And I assure you that whatever you may feel called on to do or say throughout this whole affair, I shall undoubtingly believe to be dictated *by* a good conscience and the best judgement you can form of duty under the circumstances in which you may be placed and I shall trust that you now know enough of *me*, to believe that I would not counsel you to wrong your own conviction of duty, truth and right, though you could thereby enrich yourself, and me also. Poor as I am, and poorer as I have been and may be in many things, I hope never to be *so* poor as to desire *profit* by wrong, falsehood, or unrighteousness of any kind. So "be sure you are *right*, then go *ahead!*"

The litigation was the outcome of discoveries made in 1859 by two Irishmen digging in Gold Hill at Gold Canyon. They had found some yellowish sand mixed with bits of quartz and friable black rock. The black colour was due to argentile, the sulphide of silver and with it were mingled specks of gold.

The two Irishmen set about to locate two 50-foot placer claims. As they did so, a lanky young Canadian from Trenton, Ontario, Henry Tompkins Paige Comstock came along. On fingering the gold, he impudently told the two Irishmen that this was his property and that he would let them continue only if they gave him and an accomplice, Penrod, equal shares in the claim. The two Irishmen were taken in and agreed. Subsequently, a piece of the black ore was taken to California and shown to a James Walsh who had it assayed. It contained $3000 in silver and $876 in gold. Walsh hurried to Grand Canyon and succeeded in obtaining an option on Comstock's fraudulent share for $11,000. This site, the famous Orphir, Gould and Curry mining operation, over the next four years turned out enormous amounts of bullion.[3]

When Allen Grosh died of exposure in December 1857, Comstock had laid claim to the Grosh brothers' silver discovery and had sold the claim for a small sum to the Grosh Consolidated Gold and Silver Mining Company. Rev. Grosh felt entitled to some part of the profits and agreed to transfer any claim he might have to the Company for $10,000, of which $5,000 was to be sent immediately. Grosh, who was not the least bit avaricious, and who was naïve concerning the tactics of this variety of capitalistic venture, signed the deed and returned it, without having actually received the $5,000 initial payment. It was the land being successfully mined by the Gould and Curry Company that the Grosh Consolidated claimed and was attempting to obtain by litigation. Gould and Curry wanted Bucke's testimony that the land in question was not the site at which the Grosh brothers had found silver in 1857. Comstock, by the way, who realized only $11,000 from the sale of his share which made millions in the first few years of the silver rush, committed suicide in 1863.

After Bucke received the request to leave for California he told Jessie who "seemed rather taken down".[4] One does not sense any disappointment on Bucke's part in this sudden and dramatic change in plans. On the contrary, there are intimations that he was glad to get away. On the afternoon of March 9th, he bade goodbye to Jessie.

Got that happily accomplished without any accident then round to rooms where found Gustin, Julius, Gurd and Peter Miles, we got in beer and whisky and got drunk at that....[5]

More explicitly, Bucke recorded five days later while sailing on the *Ocean Queen* from New York to Panama:

Feel on the whole pretty lively and in condition to appreciate a decent book pretty fairly. Do not feel to say, bad about leaving Canada, and "the girl of my 'art". Rather glad indeed to get away from this last character who was running things somewhat strong. Feel as if very little would make me stay in California, specially if I could get Julius to live there too. By and by might get a wife from England, — or a Washoe Queen from over the mountains according to Julius' and my idea of running a ranch.[6]

Bucke had boarded the *Ocean Queen* in New York after picking up $750 on Wall Street to cover his travelling expenses. In addition, Bull promised him a retainer fee and a monthly allowance of $250. One senses from Bucke's diary a feeling of liberation from the encroaching ties, spiced by the prospect of adventure and money.

Bucke enjoyed the trip to Panama, reading Comte, Shelley and Wordsworth on the warm deck. He reached Aspinwall on March 23rd, and the following day took the train across the isthmus to Panama. On the evening of March 25th, Bucke and a shipboard acquaintance rowed out into Panama Bay and boarded the *Golden City* which was to take him up the west coast to San Francisco, where he disembarked on April 9th. After finding a room and re-establishing his acquaintanceship with Mr. Bull, plans were made for both to visit the site where Allen and Hosea Grosh had sunk their shaft. On April 18th Bucke and Bull took a boat up the Sacramento River to Sacramento and then travelled by train and stage to Virginia City. They visited the Gould and Curry office there and three days later took a team over to Gold Canyon where they identified the site of the Grosh brothers' living quarters. There was a silver mine there but it was not a part of the Gould and Curry operation. The next day they looked for Hosea's grave. Bucke found what he thought were the two stones he had put there six-and-a-half years earlier. They were told that Hosea's body had been moved to a proper graveyard and that those were indeed the stones that Bucke and Allen Grosh had sadly laid in place in 1857. A few days later they returned to San Francisco with Bucke firmly convinced that the Gould and Curry operations were not on the site originally mined by the Grosh brothers.

Bucke returned to the Lake Tahoe district on May 13th and remained there for four months. He took some medicines along with him so that he could see a few patients. This period was one of the most leisurely in Bucke's life. He spent his days writing letters, playing billiards with friends and reading. He was still reading Comte, he enjoyed *Les Misérables* and he explored Tennyson and Browning. The evenings often included music:

> Some one sang an old song that Fanny P (Poussett) used to sing when I was in love with her, I was in my room and leaned out the window to hear it, in the meantime looking over the lake — the blending of the emotions of the three periods (when I was in California before and saw this lady — when I heard Fanny sing the song, and now) produced a most peculiar state of mind....

On July 30th Bucke "had a tolerably long winded letter from Jessie, not very affectionate of which not very sorry."

Bucke had strong inclinations to remain in California and must have written about this to Harry Buxton Forman, who then replied on August 28th,

Your enjoyment of your old scenes seems to be perfect, but you would not, of course, care to spend all your days in so uncivilized part of the new world as that where you now are. You may get your books out to "Lake House", but you cannot get the sort of society that's necessary for you, and with which you can dispense for a few months by way of change — you mention a mysterious plan for making piles of money and having piles of leisure to spend it in, but you do not tell us what it is.

On September 12th, Bucke rode on horseback over to Last Chance, the haven that had ended his terrifying ordeal six years earlier. He rode along the Truckee River to Squaw Valley and back again. Two days later he visited Squaw Valley again and saw the barrel of the rifle that he and Grosh had left there in 1857.[7]

Bucke returned to San Francisco on September 29th, met Bull at the Gould and Curry office, and learned that the court hearing had been postponed another three months. He decided to move from Lick House, the small hotel where he had stayed previously, to rooms at 759 Market Street. He also decided to spend his time learning German. To this end, he took lessons daily from a Mr. Muller at $1 each and worked at German several hours a day. On December 5th, he moved in with a German family in order to improve his conversation. It was a happy interlude in Bucke's life.

He read, over the next three months, in addition to his German, an eclectic assortment of works, such as *Tom Jones, Amelia,* Comte, *Enoch Arden, Sartor Resartus,* Shelley's letters, Chatterton's poetry, Herbert Spencer, *Vie de Jésus, The Tempest,* some Goethe and *Vanity Fair.* His evenings were spent playing whist or billiards and drinking wine with friends. He saw Kean play Shylock and Lear, and thought Mrs. Kean some fifty years too old for the role of Portia. It is not surprising to read in his diary entry for December 17th that he

spoke to Mr. Bull about making me an allowance and mentioned 2 to 300 a month as about the thing. Bull said: "we'll say $250" — If I can only have this all straightened out and get my $250 in a shape in which I can feel sure of it I shall be as jolly as a jug here, and as long as I keep hard at my German I shall have the comfort of feeling I am not losing my time.

Bucke's plans remained unsettled. On January 14th he recorded, "I have still some little notion that I shall go out there in the spring and try for a pile."

Perhaps this was the "mysterious plan" Forman had queried Bucke about in a letter of August 28th.

Bucke's ambivalence is clearly expressed in an entry on 28 February 1865:

> It seems that there is some chance of the suit coming off next week. I don't care much myself. I should like first rate to go home and see Julius — Jack — and the rest of them — but at the same time I should hardly light on anything so good East as I have here — and besides I should like to get on further with my German before I left Muller — The scales are pretty well balanced — and that is a very comfortable state of things as it saves me from anxiety.

There is no mention of Jessie in this equation. Three days later Bucke recorded having met a girl named Etta with whom he went riding.

> I begin to think Etta is a dear little girl — I suppose I shan't see her more than a couple of times more so now is the time to be falling in love when no harm can come of it!

Thus Bucke seems to have decided to return to Canada, and recorded on March 16th, the day after the case was finally called and dismissed,

> It is certainly a good thing that I am about leaving as in a few more weeks I believe I should be fairly in love with that girl — though she is not good looking — clever — or possessed of good manners there is still something very charming about her — which I suppose is the simple fact that she is 15 years old and has still many of the simple ways of a child.

But the following day he recorded that he had agreed to go with some ten men to the Goose Creek Mountains in the spring to look for gold. He even wrote:

and after making them solemnly promise there should be no backing out about it I agreed to wait here till the spring opened and then go with them.

This reversal was short-lived and ten days later he had made his reservation to sail on April 13th. His feelings that first night at sea were expressed as follows:

> Walking melancholily up and down the deck we experienced profoundly the sadness of the first night at sea of a long voyage; — a feeling dismal and peculiar — composed of the conscienciousness of complete isolation — made more complete by the crowds of strangers around — and of the solemn sense of the vague and vast that the ocean gives to everyone.

Perhaps the source of his melancholy lay elsewhere. Bucke had experienced a year of leisure, financial security, new friends and little responsibility. Though he was returning home, what awaited him was uncertain, including his own feelings.

Chapter 5

A Change in Perspective Through Cosmic Consciousness

BUCKE ARRIVED back in Sarnia on 25 May 1865 and stayed with Robert Gurd. He renewed his friendships and resumed his courtship of Jessie. On June 9th, he wrote to his old teacher, Dr. Howard, in Montreal, asking about prospects there. Dr. Howard replied, encouraging Bucke, but warning him that it would take four or five years before he could make a living. By June 23rd he had decided to stay in Sarnia and begin practice again.

On July 21st, Bucke finally made up his mind to marry Jessie and the date of the wedding was set for 7 September 1865.

August was spent largely in preparation: he bought a carriage, secured a wedding ring, and arranged tickets for his wedding trip to Quebec. The wedding took place at 9 a.m. in Moore, and after the wedding breakfast, Dr. and Mrs. Richard Bucke drove to Sarnia and caught the train to London where they spent their wedding night in the Tecumseh Hotel.

They were back in Sarnia by September 21st, and the next day Bucke recorded that several people consulted him, none of them a paying patient. His first major case was Raymond Baby, who had fractured his left leg into the ankle joint. Bucke set the fracture and visited Baby almost daily; when infection set in amputation became necessary which, together with another physician, he carried out on November 2nd.

Bucke fell into the inevitable routine of a busy practice; on 4 March 1866 he records as the penultimate entry in his diary:

Closed my log on last page but one after continuing it four years all but a part of a month, the trouble was that it was getting too mechanical, and feeling bound to write every day more or less it was a nuisance, then I wrote in such a hurry that I doubt it did more to corrupt than to improve my handwriting and style. My life also that I am fairly married and settled down to work is so monotonous that what is said of it one day answers for every other day, and there is no object in keeping a diary record of my doings.

Little information is available concerning the details of Bucke's life between March 1866 and November 1868. A daughter, born in 1866, died ten months later, and his first son Maurice Andrew, was born on 21 November 1868. It was in this setting of long working hours, which Bucke's growing medical practice demanded, that a conversation occurred which changed his life. As he recalled many years later,

The first time I ever heard pronounced the name of the author of "Leaves of Grass". It was in mid-winter 1867-8. A friend of mine, who then lived in Montreal, the Mineralogist to the Geological Survey of Canada, a first-class chemist, geologist and scientist generally, Dr. T. Sterry Hunt was visiting me in Sarnia, where I then lived and practiced. One evening we were sitting together in my office, before a cheerful wood fire in an old-fashioned fire place, talking poetry, philosophy and science, when Dr. Hunt rose from his chair, and, standing with his back to the blaze, asked: "Did you ever hear of a man named Walt Whitman?" I replied: "No: who is he?" Dr. Hunt answered: "He is an American poet who writes in a very peculiar style — something between prose and verse." And he went on to quote all he could recollect — only a line or two — from the "Leaves".[1]

Bucke managed to obtain a copy of the Rossetti edition the following summer and in 1870, while visiting Dr. Hunt in Montreal, he found in Hunt's library a copy of the 1855 edition which he borrowed and took home with him to Sarnia. The experience of reading those poems prepared the way for Bucke's illumination of 1872, and formed the first chapter in the events leading to his unusual friendship with Whitman.

The first edition of *Leaves of Grass* had gone on sale 4 July 1855. Although it was perhaps the most important appearance in the history of American letters, at the time it was a non-event. Whitman, born in 1819, had grown up in a poor family in Brooklyn where, after several jobs with short-lived Manhattan newspapers, he became editor of the *Brooklyn Daily Eagle* in 1846. He had acquired something of a reputation as a polemical journalist and had written some bad poems and negligible stories; there was no sign of budding genius. Yet in 1855 he published the most unusual book of poems ever to be written in the United States.

Whitman had persuaded two friends, James and Thomas Rome, who owned a printing shop, to print his book. Whitman spent much of his time in the spring of 1855 revising and correcting proofs. Seven hundred and ninety-five copies were printed, the book was unsigned and the collection of twelve poems was untitled. A picture of the author, facing the title page, shows the engraved three-quarters portrait of a man who does not look like a writer at all. He seems to be a working man, with an open-necked shirt, broad brimmed hat, his right hand on his hip and his facial expression cocky and defiant.

The first poem, by far the longest, was entitled "Walt Whitman" in earlier editions, and "Song of Myself" from the edition of 1881 on. It is a non-narrative mystical poem celebrating the union of mind and body in the person of the idealized figure of a representative American working man. It is a powerful, long-winded, unashamed, sensual, fearless, bold and honest affirmation of man. He believes that the Self is of the same essence as the universal spirit and that true knowledge is not acquired through the senses or the intellect, but through union with the Self. This belief was echoed by Bucke after his 1872 illumination.

Like Whitman, Bucke also believed, after his 1872 illumination, that when man becomes self-actualized, he is awakened and "the gum is washed from [his] eyes." He responds to Blake's assertion that when man expresses his divinity through his imagination he is able

To see a world in a grain of sand,
And a heaven in a wild flower;
Hold infinity in the palm of your hand,
And eternity in an hour.[2]

Whitman claimed that discovering a mouse "is miracle enough to stagger sextillions of infidels." Like Blake, and unlike traditional mystics, Whitman celebrated man's sexuality. Indeed, Whitman uses sexual imagery in "Song of Myself" to describe the mystical union of mind and body, in which both are equal partners.

Leaves of Grass was saved from oblivion by Ralph Waldo Emerson, America's most famous man of letters at the time, who wrote the following letter to the *New York Times*:

> Concord 21 July
> Masstts 1855

Dear Sir,

I am not blind to the worth of the wonderful gift of Leaves of Grass. I find it the most extraordinary piece of wit and wisdom that America has yet contributed. I am very happy in reading it, as great power makes us happy. It meets the demand I am always making of what seemed the sterile and stingy Nature, as if too much handiwork or too much lymph in the temperament were making our western wits fat and mean.

I give you joy of your free and brave thought, I have great joy in it. I find incomparable things said incomparably well, as they must be. I find the courage of treatment, which so delights us, and which large perception can only inspire.

I greet you at the beginning of a great career, which yet must have had a long foreground somewhere, for such a start. I rubbed my eyes a little, to see if this sunbeam were no illusion; but the solid sense of the book is a sober certainty. It has the best merits, namely of fortifying and encouraging.

I did not know until I last night saw the book advertized in a newspaper, that I could trust the name as real and available for a post-office. I wish to see my benefactor, and have felt much like striking my tasks, and visiting New York to pay you my respects.

R.W. Emerson.

From 1854 to 1857 Whitman's suddenly erupted creative powers produced a large number of poems of the first order. In the second edition of 1856 there were 32 poems, and by 1867 the fourth edition contained 154 poems from the 1860 edition, 53 poems called "Drum Taps" and the magnificent "President Lincoln's Burial Hymn".

From the time of his departure from England in December 1863 until the end of his life, Bucke maintained an avid correspondence with his two friends the Forman brothers, particularly Harry Buxton Forman. Harry Forman was a literary editor and, like Bucke, an addicted bibliophile. He served, not only as a friend with whom Bucke could exchange views of poems, novels, essays, etc, but also as an agent, sending him books and articles impossible to obtain in Canada West. Bucke's first mention of Whitman occurred in a letter to Forman on 19 February 1869.

> You will have seen the collection of Walt Whitman's poems that have been edited by Rossetti and published by John Camden Hutton Son, 1868. You will probably have got a copy and taken it home and looked into it, but have you *soaked* through the crust into the heart of it? Have you seen that here is the modern poet? Especially the American poet, the only one so far, the founder of American literature as Goethe was of German literature .... For this is a *man* and he reveals *himself.*

Forman replied on March 18:

> Your mention of Walt Whitman opens up a subject of steadily-growing enthusiasm with me; I have read him a little from a friend's copy*, some time ago, and a good deal from my own copy of Rossetti's edition. Almost all you say of him I seem to agree with. The "crust" does not repel me though it is not attractive like the crust of Swinburne's work; the *man* is obviously as noble as the other is ignoble.
> (* the friend's copy was the 1860 edition)

Bucke, warming to the subject, wrote Forman on April 11th:

> But here is a man who receives images of spiritual and material things from without and transmits them again without the least

thought of what will the world say of this idea and how will the world like this form of expression .... There is nothing in modern literature like it. This, according to me, is his claim to praise, a claim that must not be distorted. Praise that will live while the English language is read ....

William Michael Rossetti's selection of Whitman's poems contained less than half Whitman's output. Rossetti had decided "to omit entirely every poem which could with any tolerable fairness be deemed offensive to the feeling of morals or propriety in this peculiarly nervous age."[3] The omission included "Song of Myself"! The poem Bucke singled out in his letter for special praise from the Rossetti edition was "President Lincoln's Funeral Hymn", with its now celebrated first stanza

When lilacs last in the dooryard bloom'd,
And the great star early droop'd in the western sky in the night,
I mourned, and yet shall mourn with ever-returning spring.

Ever-returning spring, trinity sure to me you bring,
Lilac blooming perennial and drooping star in the west,
And thought of him I love.[4]

The influence of Whitman's poems on Bucke was immeasurable. Gone was Comte's empiricism and diminished in importance were the Romantic poets including his favourite, Shelley. By 1870, when he first read "Song of Myself" in Sterry Hunt's copy of the 1855 edition of *Leaves of Grass*, Bucke realized that in making the poem the poet was remaking himself, that the poem and the poet were inseparable. With the important exception of Emerson, early critics abhorred *Leaves of Grass*. The only other favourable reviews were those written anonymously by Whitman himself. These were egregious, stagey, slightly dishonest, but they described himself as he wished to be seen. Bucke never acknowledged the bad taste these reviews display, for he was never able to see the side of Whitman that was street actor and shamelessly immodest. He responded passionately to the poetry and became one of Whitman's first vocal disciples. The poetry led ten years later to a first meeting of the doctor and the poet, and to the unusual friendship which ended only with Whitman's death.

The letters between Bucke and Forman in 1869 contain many references to Whitman. In contrast to Bucke's unbridled enthusiasm, Forman's is tempered with some criticism. Forman wrote on July 14th:

And up to now it seems to me that the more you read him the more you may, for there is much that a glance makes appear superficial and trite which seems to assume vast meaning as one becomes familiar with it .... Sincerity is stamped on every page —— doubtless ... but bad taste, according to our notions, is stamped on the surface of many pages, and paradox seems to abound.

Although Bucke's approval of Whitman at this time was almost unconditional, a tentative note of bewilderment appears in his letter of 1 April 1870:

But there is no poem of his as far as I know that is not a masterpiece and which will prove itself a masterpiece if it is only read in the right spirit and read until understood, or rather until felt, and in this distinction lies the only piece of criticism I have to offer at present on Walt. It is that he does not appeal to the intellect, or if at all only to a minor degree to the (I was going to write feelings or emotions, but I believe it would be better to say) man himself, and he does it by using the inaudible words of the earth .... What do you make of this "I swear I think all merges towards the unspoken meanings of the earth, towards him who sings the songs of the Body and of the truths of the earth; toward him who makes the dictionaries of the words that print cannot touch", this means something or nothing. If it means something (as I think unquestionably it does) it means considerably more than the same number of words generally do.

Bucke was struggling to release himself from his rationalism, nurtured by his medical training and by the philosophy of Comte. The struggle ended two years later with his illumination, in which he conceded he learned more in a few moments of mystic joy than he had in previous months or years of study.

By the end of 1870 Bucke was exhausted from continuous night calls resulting in little sleep. He recovered temporarily during a trip to England in February 1871, but by the end of May he was back in practice and again overworked. In July, with his health deteriorating once more, he availed himself of an opportunity to cross again to England as a ship's surgeon.

It was after his return to Sarnia a few weeks later that Bucke began to mention his speculations in moral philosophy. Although thirty years later in *Cosmic Consciousness* he would attribute the origin of his moral philosophical ideas to the 1872 illumination, on 11 December 1871, he wrote to Forman:

> It will be nothing less than a new theory of all art and religion and I am sure a *true* one. It will furnish a sound basis for poetical and other art criticism, not but that taste and ability will be needed to work on this basis. It will supply a new theory of the universe and of man's relations to the external universe and which being as a religion as positive as positivism and will supply more hope for mankind and will not shut up men's faculties in the known and present in the same way that positivism does.

Bucke had other speculations in mind as well. He had begun to buy land near Sarnia and had invested in an oil well in nearby Petrolia. These investments so tied up his money that he was unable to pay Forman for books he had ordered. He worried about his brother George's chronic inebriation, and his own health.

> My health has completely broken down again and as I am now satisfied that this is due to the climate here, or rather to the malaria, I have decided to pull stakes and leave Sarnia for good.[5]

Bucke visited England again in March 1872, mainly to see his relatives and the Forman brothers, one of whom had just named his son Maurice in Bucke's honour, but the trip was memorable because of the mystic experience he had while there. Many years later in the introduction to *Cosmic Consciousness* Bucke described it:

> It was in the early spring at the beginning of his thirty-sixth year. He and two friends had spent the evening reading Wordsworth,

Shelley, Keats, Browning and especially Whitman. They parted at midnight, and he had a long drive in a hansom (it was in an English city). His mind deeply under the influence of the ideas, images and emotions called up by the reading and talk of the evening, was calm and peaceful. He was in a state of quiet, almost passive enjoyment. All at once, without warning of any kind, he found himself wrapped around as it were by a flame-coloured cloud. For an instant he thought of fire, some sudden conflagration in the great city, the next he knew that the light was within himself. Directly afterwards came upon him a sense of exultation, of immense joyousness accompanied or immediately followed by an intellectual illumination quite impossible to describe. Into his brain streamed one momentary lightning-flash of the Brahmic Splendor which has ever lightened his life; upon his heart fell one drop of Brahmic Bliss, leaving thence forward for always an after taste of heaven. Among other things he did not come to believe, he saw and knew that the Cosmos is not dead matter but a living Presence, that the soul of man is immortal, that the universe is so built and ordered that without any peradventure all things work together for the good of each and all, that the foundation principle of the world is what we call love and that the happiness of every one is in the long run absolutely certain. He claims that he learned more within the few seconds during which the illumination lasted than in previous months or even years of study, and that he learned much that no study could ever have taught.(CC,7)

Bucke visited his relatives and consulted one of his former teachers, Dr. Jenner, about his health. His special concern about his health is expressed in a letter to his wife:

But my health is very important to all of us and as long as the stay here seems beneficial to me I think it is my duty to stay, for after I will settle down in a new place I must stay there if I want to get a practice and it will not do to have my health failing again within the next four years if it is possible to avoid it.[6]

His uncle, Biggs Andrews, wrote Bucke, now back in Sarnia, on August 4th:

I am sorry you have found it necessary to come over here again, but very good that you had the resolution to come away when you found it necessary for the reestablishment of your health. It was quite right too to see Jenner and I think his report is on the whole satisfactory. It is quite evident you must take things very quietly for some time. You should make up your mind when you get back to Sarnia to restrict your practice within very narrow bounds for a year or two....[7]

Bucke took his uncle's advice. He did not re-open his practice on his return and began considering other possibilities: he wrote to Harry Forman a few months later that he was planning to apply for the position of Superintendent of a new asylum for inebriates.[8] Bucke knew the Provincial Secretary, whose jurisdiction included all the asylums in Ontario, and expected that the appointment would be made the following April or May, and the asylum constructed near Hamilton that summer.

Although in early 1873 the Ontario Legislature passed a bill to build the asylum at a cost of $100,000, Bucke ended up waiting for three more years before the position became available. During that time, he continued his buying and selling of land; in July 1874, he formed a partnership with Dr. A.S. Fraser who had taken over his practice in 1872. During the wait, Bucke was often depressed. Furthermore he was frustrated at his inability to articulate the philosophical concepts that excited him. In a reply to Forman's letter in 1873 which included a copy of his essay, "Music and Poetry", Bucke replied that although he had read the essay, he could not see what Forman was driving at.[9] His own pretensions were not modest:

I think I see a truer and deeper explanation of the function of the arts than that has been propounded yet.[10]

Later that year his discouragement found another source in learning that there was a second applicant with a good deal of support for the asylum position. His mood improved when he re-entered practice with Dr. Fraser a few months later, and on October 28th, he wrote Forman, "I am in excellent health and am making money."[11]

By February, 1875, Bucke was again depressed. He saw no prospect of his book going ahead:

I have just as much faith in its central idea and the light thrown by it on many things in life and literature, yet I see great difficulty in carrying it out logically to its ultimate conclusion.[12]

In a letter Alfred Forman wrote to Bucke at that same time [11], describing his enthusiasm for continuing his translation of "The Ring" and "Tristan and Isolde", Forman expressed his inability to embrace any philosophical system.

Your system I have yet to learn — meantime religion being out of the question, I hold to art.[13]

When Bucke wrote about his 1872 illumination in *Cosmic Conscious-ness*, he referred to being with two friends throughout the evening. The two Forman brothers were the only English friends with whom he would have spent the evening reading "Wordsworth, Shelley, Keats, Browning and especially Whitman". No mention is made of the mystic experience by Bucke or either of the brothers in subsequent correspondence. Yet, later, he incorrectly credited the experience as being the wellspring of his as yet unarticulated philosophical system. Bucke did, however, in 1875, manage to write and publish his first paper since his prizewinning essay as a medical student thirteen years earlier. No copy of the publication has survived, but it was presumably similar to a paper with the same title he published two years later, "The Functions of the Great Sympathetic Nervous System".[14] It derived from an address Bucke gave on 1 June 1877 at a meeting of the Association of Medical Superintendents of American Institutions for the Insane. A year earlier the appointment had finally come through. Bucke was to receive $1600, a house, furniture, fuel, light and food; he estimated it all to be equivalent to $4,000 a year. In March 1875, he left medical practice for good, and moved his family to the new asylum in Hamilton which opened on March 17th, not for inebriates after all, but for lunatics. A new era had begun.

—— Chapter 6 ——

First Encounter With Whitman and Bucke's First Published Book

O N 17 MARCH 1876 the new asylum in Hamilton began receiving patients. Planned originally as a hospital for alcoholics, it was not equipped to handle acute or violent mental cases. By the end of September 1876, the hospital was full. Two hundred and eleven patients had been transferred from the other provincial asylums in Toronto, London and Kingston. Of these, six had died and three were returned to London as unmanageable. Bucke acknowledged in his medical report of September 30th that the building was suitable only for passive, chronic cases. He was initially busy organizing the staff and wrote to Forman two months after the opening:

> The only trouble has been with the Bursar who seems to believe that he is Superintendent but I think he will be disabused before he is much older.[1]

Disabused he must have been because in the September 30th report Bucke praised the Bursar, Mr. Bidwell Way, for his diligence and helpfulness.

Although the hospital was new, Bucke had many suggestions for its improvement. He recommended doubling the size of the hospital to make it more efficient in terms of the patient-staff ratio. He wished to have the land divided into fields for cultivation and to purchase livestock. In spite of the challenges at the new hospital, Bucke never complained of being overworked, as he had so often done during his days of general practice in Sarnia. By November he was able to write to Forman:

> All goes quietly in the asylum, it is pretty dull but not an unpleasant a way of living on the whole ... the work is not nearly so hard as it used to be, but there is still enough work to keep one from going to sleep. One of the worst things about the asylum is that I have to get up at 6 every morning, it is not really necessary except as an example ... the getting up itself is not so bad but it prevents one from spending the evening out.[2]

Throughout the year in Hamilton, Bucke continued his reading. Forman had completed the first of his projected four-volume edition of Shelley's poetry, and Bucke, who received one of the special twenty-five shilling copies, read the text carefully and sent Forman a couple of textual suggestions.[3]

Bucke's period of tenure in Hamilton was brief. On 6 January 1877, Dr. Henry Landor, the first superintendent of the asylum in London, died and Bucke was appointed his successor at the London Asylum, which had opened in 1870. Bucke remained at this post for the rest of his life.

Large events were soon to unfold in two trips Bucke took that year. The first was his address on the "Functions of the Great Sympathetic Nervous System", given in St. Louis in May to the Association of Medical Superintendents of American Institutions for the Insane. It was published in October, and later formed the third chapter of his first book *Man's Moral Nature*. The second event was his first meeting with Walt Whitman.

Bucke had been planning the meeting for some time. On 19 December 1870, he wrote Whitman the following letter from Sarnia:

> Walt Whitman,
>   Dear Sir: Will you please send to the enclosed address *two* copies of "Leaves of Grass", *one* copy of "Passage to India" and *one* copy of "Democratic Vistas". Enclosed you will find $7.25 — $6.75 for the books and $0.50 for postage. I do not know

exactly what this last item will be but I fancy $0.50 will be enough to pay it. I am an old reader of your books, and a very great admirer of them. About two weeks ago I borrowed a copy of the 1855 edition of "Leaves of Grass" and I have a great ambition to own a copy of this edition myself: (wh) would it be possible to get one? Before getting that the only thing I had ever seen of yours was Rossetti's selection. Lately I have got a copy of the 1867 edition of "Leaves of Grass" and I have compared the "Walt Whitman" in that with the same poem in the 1855 edition and I must say I like the earlier edition best.

I have an idea I shall be in Washington in the course of 1871; if I am it would give me much pleasure to see you, if you would not object. I am afraid, however, that, like other celebrities, you have more people call upon you than you care about seeing; in that case I should not wish to annoy you —

> At all events
> Believe me
> Faithfully yours,
> R.M. Bucke[4]

Bucke wrote Forman three weeks later that he was planning a trip to England, and would bring with him a copy of the latest edition Whitman had sent him. He also mentioned that he was bringing a letter he had received from Walt, although there is no other record of such a letter.

In the intervening years Bucke continued to cherish the hope of meeting the poet. This opportunity arose in 1877 when he was asked to visit some asylums in the northeastern United States in October.

While in Philadelphia, Bucke crossed the Delaware River to Camden, N.J. and called on Whitman who was living in his brother's house. He described the meeting to Forman a few days later:

I hardly know how to tell you about W.W. If I tried to say how he impressed me you would probably put it down to exaggeration. I have never seen any man to compare with him — any man the least like him — he seems more than a man and yet in all his looks and ways essentially commonplace ("do I contradict myself?"). He is an average man magnified to the dimensions of a God — but this does not give you the least idea of

what he is like and I despair of giving you any idea at all however slight — I may say that I experienced what I have heard
so much about the extraordinary magnetism of his presence —
I not only felt deeply in an indescribable way towards him —
but that I think that short interview has altered the attitude of
my moral nature to everything....[5]

This was the third critical moment in Bucke's life that related to Whitman, the others being his inoculation by reading *Leaves of Grass* in 1869
and his illumination in 1872 after an evening of reading poetry, "especially Whitman". There was never any diminution of his worship for
Whitman. Bucke became Whitman's most ardent disciple and remained
so throughout his life. His feelings toward the poet, the deep need which
Whitman filled in him and the unusual relationship between these two
men are all crucial to an assessment of this nineteenth-century physician, and will be explored in a later chapter.

Harry Forman, who was very sympathetic to Whitman's poetry,
found Bucke's reaction to Whitman somewhat enigmatic:

Your sketch of this wonderful man has a value of its own, though
the peculiar qualities of the man seem to be often almost intan-
gible and baffling description to a great extent.[6]

Although Bucke had planned a trip to England after the annual May
1878 meeting of mental hospital superintendents in Washington, he had
to cancel it because his assistant superintendent went to the Kingston
asylum to replace the superintendant there who had become ill. Bucke
had had some nervous symptoms and had felt depressed during the winter.[7] He had a recurrence while away at the meeting [8] and consulted some
of the other physicians there. He was advised not to work so hard.

Bucke's paper was well received. Entitled "Moral Nature and the
Great Sympathetic", it was an extension of his lecture to the same association a year earlier; subsequently it became chapters II and IV of his book.

The highlight of the trip, however, was his second meeting with Walt
Whitman on May 11th. Bucke not only pressed an invitation again to
visit him in London, but proffered Jessie's love and hospitality as further inducements. He even gently lectured Jessie concerning the gratitude that she should bestow on Whitman:

I saw Walt yesterday evening for a couple of hours and shall not see him any more as he has an appointment to spend the day today in the country — I asked him when he was coming to see us and I told him that you had sent him your love and that you wanted him to come to London. He has promised to come towards the end of June — I am to go to Niagara to meet him — Walt will stay with us some weeks, perhaps a month; he is not very well and has had some doubts about the prudence of undertaking so long a journey but I persuaded him that it could not do him any harm and would probably do him good — I told him that he would have a comfortable room to himself and that he could stay by himself as much as he chose — he still seemed doubtful about coming until I told him that you had sent him your love and that you were very anxious he should come — this decided him and he said he would come. You will not be able to help liking him for old and broken down as he is by age and illness he is still a most magnificent man — and rough as he may look to you at first he has perhaps the warmest heart that ever beat on this earth — I look forwards to his visit with great pleasure and not only so but I consider it a very great privilege for the children that they may be able to say in after life that they have seen Walt Whitman — besides all this I owe Walt Whitman a large debt of gratitude — and I am anxious to do something wh[ich] may be some return to him however slight for what he has done to me — you too my best darling owe him more than you know — when I come home I shall get you, if you will, to write him a little note to enclose in one of my letters to him.[9]

On the same day, Bucke in a buoyant mood wrote to Forman[10] to report that he had encouraged Whitman to write Forman, adding that it was likely Whitman would send some of his hair at the same time. A few days later in Washington, he wrote this poem to Jessie:

TO MY WIFE

A PROBLEM

by R.M.B.

Why should I love my love so much?
Why should the sight, the sound, the touch
Of her hand, her face, her voice
Make my heart so rejoice?
Why does the thought of her when far away
Brighten the darkest day?
Others are fair as she
Though none so fair to me.
Other hearts may be as true
If I their secret knew.
Others I love — but not as I love
My darling; the stars in the blue vault of heaven above
Are bright till the glorious ray
Of the sun vails[sic] them with day.
Why should I love my love so much
Her beautiful face, her voice, her touch?
This is God's mystery,
Into which may no man see.
This alone I see and know
That with spirits above and near below
On earth around — in heaven above
There is nothing better than love, sweet love.[11]

Bucke ended with the gentle admonition, "Now you little darling scalawag write me some nice letters to pay me for that."

Bucke always took the initiative in correspondence with Jessie and frequently chided her for not writing. But Jessie followed through this time because on May 25th, she replied on hospital stationery:

A GUESS AT THE "PROBLEM"

by Jessie M. Bucke

In his goodness God has given,
Gifts of earth and gifts of heaven,

To his creatures well deserving,
Thus his glory safe preserving.
Ever *just* his blessings falling
On all whom his name's heard calling.
This is why from Heaven above
He's given me to you to love.

Angel spirits meet at His Throne
Some plead for us and some his own.
Natures alike, above or here
All sing "sweet love" and none know fear.

Knowing full well that man would stray
Far from his bright eternal day
If he were left in lonely state
He gave man woman for a mate.

By the sunshine of her sweet smile
Man is saved from earthly guile
Through the power of her "sweet love"
His eyes are turned from earth above.

To the good man God gives the true
And if the one he gave to you
Live constant how plain 'twill prove
Your worth and goodness *my* "sweet love".

And thus "sweet love" to me 'tis clear
Why from Heaven he sent *your* dear
To bring you with me to his Home
Where he will claim us for his own.[12]

It was following this second visit with Whitman that Bucke began to consider writing a biography, and proposed to Forman that together they publish an edition of Whitman in England including a biographical section.[13] Forman doubted that an English edition would pay, but did suggest that Bucke write the biographical part. He cautioned Bucke gently about expressing his boundless enthusiasm for Whitman too extravagantly:

I don't think it would be wise to contend before the public that
Walt is the greatest man living; because even if we cannot our-
selves show one as great it is quite on the cards whether France
or Germany might not show a man at this hour at least Walt's
equal in essentials, and his superior in the not unimportant matter
of art. Victor Hugo and Richard Wagner are huge men.[14]

Bucke sent this letter of Forman's on to Whitman because of its suggestion of publishing an English edition of his works.[15] Whitman would,
therefore, have read the above admonition to Bucke. There is no evidence
that Bucke was embarrassed by this. Whitman would certainly have been
amused by it.

Bucke spent every spare moment over the next few months on his
book *Man's Moral Nature*. He had planned to have Whitman's picture
at the front of the book but was dissuaded from doing so by Forman.
The book was actually completed on November 27th and on that same
day he wrote Forman:

There is one thing about this book that I want to tell you. I think
it is somewhat remarkable from the first moment that the central idea flashed across my mind going home from the P.O. that
night in the spring of 1871 till now. I have never had to alter
a thought that has gone into it, and although I did not see all
its parts that first night the whole book was really revealed to
me then.[16]

Bucke's memory was inaccurate. The illumination occurred in the
spring of 1872, but he had been speculating on the moral issues later
expressed in the book in the autumn of 1871 and had written Forman
that he planned to write such a book.[17,18] It seems curious that in the
years following the illumination, Bucke, in his many letters to the For-
mans, never referred to the transcendental experience although they must
have been the two with whom he had spent the evening which culminated in his vision.

Bucke and Jessie went to New York on December 9th looking for
a publisher. After unsuccessful visits to Appleton & Co., Scribner's and
Henry Holt, Bucke found Mr. Putnam more receptive and he left the
manuscript with Putnam's for review.

From New York they went to Philadelphia where Whitman joined them, meeting Jessie for the first time. Bucke wrote Forman after their return to London:

Jessie used to laugh at me for going on so about him but now she likes him as much as I do and I expect to innoculate [Bucke's spelling] her with his poetry before very long. He has promised to make us a long visit of a month or more next summer "as sure as death and taxes".[19]

The cherished visit was postponed for a year, but a successful inoculation with Whitman's poetry and, indeed, with Whitman himself never did take place, although Bucke remained oblivious to Jessie's antipathy throughout the London visit of 1880. It was only in June 1881 that Jessie expressed her feelings so directly that Bucke was forced to take note.

But in December 1878, Bucke was savouring the heady effects of much labour and planning. He had persuaded Whitman to visit him and he had found a publisher willing to consider his first book. G.P. Putnam agreed to publish the book if Bucke would put up $700. Of the initial 750 copies, 25 copies were to be released by Trubner and Co. in England. Four years later, only 241 copies had been sold. In spite of the large conceptual issues that the book discussed, the abstruse subject matter and the numerous technical terms easily explained its poor sales. Even Whitman never read it through.

Bucke believed that the centre of man's moral nature was located in the sympathetic nervous system. In vertebrates, there are two major components of the nervous system: the brain and the spinal cord with its branches (the central nervous system) control sensory perception and motor activity; the other component, the sympathetic nervous system, consists of a double chain of ganglia with connecting fibres, situated along each side of the vertebral column. The sympathetic nervous system controls movement of viscera such as the intestine, and influences the calibre of the small arteries supplying the various organs of the body. The concept of anatomical localization of emotions had begun earlier in the century with Franz Joseph Gall's theory that man's innate faculties each had a specific localization in the cerebral cortex.[20] Dr. Paul Broca's paper in 1861 gave support to this theory by demonstrating that aphasia was caused by a lesion involving a specific area of the frontal lobe of the brain.[21] Bucke had sought as much information on the sympathetic nervous system as Forman could find for him including Dewey's *The Ganglionic Nervous System, Its Structure, Functions and Diseases*. Together with the realization from Brown-Séquard's earlier publication in 1851 that the sympathetic nervous system influenced regional blood flow, Bucke joined the "localizationists" in postulating the sympathetic nervous system as the anatomical site of the prime emotions that constituted man's moral nature.

Bucke believed that man's moral nature was composed of four basic emotions: love, hate, faith and fear. They were usually combined with the basic elements of his intellectual nature called concepts. These were so-called "simple ideas" — e.g., the idea of the colour yellow or the idea of a mile. Combinations of concepts were called compounds. Man's evolutionary moral progress consisted of increasing his love and faith and diminishing his hate and fear. The sum of the various combinations of concepts and the four primary moral elements constituted a person's character. A good man and a highly moral man were not necessarily synonymous. A good man was one whose combination of concepts and moral elements was similar to those of the society in which he lived. Other men, whose moral state was equally elevated but whose views were not in accordance with the society in which they lived were not described as good. Jesus and Shelley, in Bucke's opinion, would have been in this category.

Bucke concluded that fear of death was not intrinsic or essential; it was an acquired evolutionary protective device. Man with his evolving self-consciousness would have a better chance of survival if he feared and thus attempted to avoid death. At a much later stage of development, man's reasoning faculties began to question the closeness of this juxtaposition of fear and death; in addition, compound states such as patriotism and religious feelings began to replace crude fear. Bucke sought support for his belief in the supposedly greater fear of death among primitive than among civilized societies.

His reasons for believing that the sympathetic nervous system was the site of man's moral nature can be summarized as follows: 1) the languages of all nations refer emotions to the heart, near which are located the largest ganglionic masses of the sympathetic nervous system; 2) emotions are deeper and less easily identified than intellectual expression just as the sympathetic nerves are anatomically more deeply placed than the cerebro-spinal nerves which often lie close to the surface of the body; 3) simple moral states such as fear and love, unassociated with any idea, are less complex than the simplest intellectual concept; therefore, the sympathetic, which is a less complex network than the central nervous system, is more likely related to moral states than to intellectual ones; 4) small men, according to Bucke, were morally but not necessarily intellectually inferior. Inasmuch as the sympathetic nervous system is responsible for nutrition, it follows that a good-sized sympathetic system would result in a man with good-sized moral nature; 5) Bucke concluded his evidence with a syllogism: men who have the best moral teaching live longest, and length of life depends upon the degree of perfection of the sympathetic system: therefore, an elevated moral nature is a function of a well-developed sympathetic nervous system.

Bucke did not support any of the above with experimental verification, such as by noting changes which might result from extirpation of any part of the sympathetic nervous system. He felt that an experimental physiological approach would produce artifact:

> I have quoted very few experiments upon the sympathetic in this essay, for the reason that I put very little confidence in the deductions drawn from them. To divide large sympathetic trunks, or to remove large sympathetic ganglia, must cause a disturbance of the general system which would necessarily mask to a great extent the peculiar efforts flowing from the lesion of the nerves operated on; and any one who has paid attention to the literature of this subject cannot have failed to notice how contradictory are the positions supposed to be established by these means.[22]

Bucke went on to address the question of whether man's moral nature was a fixed quantity. He felt that man's moral nature was gradually improving through history; the amount of love and faith were increasing at the expense of hate and fear. He used phylogenic and ontogenic arguments to show that contemporary man had more love and faith and less hate and fear than ancient peoples. More surprising was his view that children had lower moral natures than adults, and became moral only as they grew up. Bucke observed that children's capacity for affection was "certainly very limited", for example in their absence of grief.

Bucke then attempted to explain how man's moral nature improved. He argued that, by natural selection, individuals with an elevated moral nature would have, through the great sympathetic nervous system, more vigour, would tend to live longer and would pass on these qualities to their descendants. He also believed that individuals with an elevated moral nature would, because of their great capacity to love, more likely marry and reproduce themselves. Finally, children born without a moral nature first developed predominantly the negative qualities of hate and fear; through the influence of their parents they then developed the positive moral elements, learning love mainly from their mothers and faith from their fathers. The role of the intellect in the development of an elevated moral state was secondary, but could serve as a channel for the conveyance of emotion.

Bucke concluded:

The notion that grown-up people or children are made better by rules and catechisms cannot be too soon done away with.[23]

Bucke saw the artistically creative person as one with more love and faith than ordinary men, one whose societal function was to elevate those who came in contact with his work. He saw the intellectual component of the artist's work as of secondary importance; music had no intellectual component. He saw the religious leader as even more morally elevated than the artist, and a yet rarer species. He believed that great religious leaders could not be at first appreciated but, indeed, were necessarily reviled in their own time since they were elevated beyond the level of their own society. When such a leader expressed great love of objects considered useless by the populace he was bound to be misunderstood.

Bucke's conclusion was optimistic. He felt that just as our intellectual nature had advanced over the millennia, so our moral natures were capable of evolutionary development. In this statement lay the seed from which his concept of cosmic consciousness was slowly developing and which would result in his best known book, to be published twenty years later. In *Man's Moral Nature* Bucke had been influenced by Comte in attempting to use the new science of biology to gain understanding. As Comte had written,

The highest progress of man and of society consists in gradual
increase of that mastery which man alone can attain over all his
defects, especially those of this "moral nature".[24]

And:

Henceforth all true men of science will rise to the higher dignity
of philosophies, and by so doing will necessarily assume something of the sacerdotal character, because the final result to which
their researches tend is the subordination of every subject of
thought to the moral principle; a result which leads us at once
to the acceptance of a complete and homogeneous synthesis.[25]

This attempt at a synthesis was also influenced by Whitman, whose
quotation forms the epigraph to the last chapter:

I swear the earth shall surely be complete to him or her who
shall be complete.[26]

Bucke's first book certainly did not sell, nor did it fulfill the author's
original grandiose ambition expressed earlier to Harry Forman that it
would provide a new theory for art, religion and the universe.[27]

However, he had cut his teeth on it, and in mentioning the evolutionary trend toward man's moral improvement he had helped to sharpen
his focus on the later theory of the "cosmic sense". Not a bad beginning.

— Chapter 7 —
Whitman's Visit to London, Ontario

I<small>N MAY</small> 1880 Bucke made another visit to Philadelphia after having attended a medical meeting in New York. He had been ruminating on Whitman and wrote Jessie on May 23rd:

> People do not seem to be at all agreed as to the meaning of him — and as to what the result of his life will be and what its effect will be on the human race — I dare say it will take a hundred years or so yet to settle this question.[1]

At this time Bucke also repeated his invitation to Whitman to visit London. Although it was not yet definitely settled, Bucke wrote Jessie on May 28th that Whitman would be coming home with him, and outlined their travel plans. On May 31st, he wrote again:

> You will of course have the best spare room ready for Walt. I wish we could give him still better accommodations, no palace that ever was built would be quite good enough for Walt, but we must at least give him the best we have and along with that give him our love and he will be satisfied for indeed he is easy enough to please if he feels that he is liked.[2]

Whitman's arrival in London with Bucke by train from Niagara Falls
aroused some curiosity, and a number of citizens were on the platform
to catch a glimpse of the poet. The local interest in Whitman resulted
from a lecture Bucke had given to the East Middlesex Teachers' Association in which he proclaimed him a prophet whose mission was to "produce a moral state superior to anything of the kind already existing."[3]
He went on to say:

Probably no man who has ever lived on this earth was ever loved
so intensely and by so many people as Walt Whitman.[4]

These extravagant claims led to some spirited letters in local
newspapers criticizing both Bucke and Whitman.[5]

Reporters from both local papers interviewed Whitman on his arrival;
in fact the London Free Press reporter scooped his rival by boarding the
train in Paris, Ontario. In the interviews, Whitman talked about his work
in hospitals during the Civil War and about Leaves of Grass, in which he
said the pervading theme was comradeship.[6] He also compared himself
with other contemporary poets:

the fault I have to find with Tennyson, although he is a master
of his art, with Longfellow, Whittier, and all the rest, is that they
are too much like saints. Nature is strong and rank. This rankness is seen everywhere in man, and it is to this strength and
rankness that I have endeavoured to give voice.

On Sunday, June 6th, Whitman attended the church service at the
asylum and wrote his impression in "Specimen Days". In one of the
very few references to people written during his visit, he describes the
patients:

O, the looks that came from those faces! There were two or three
I shall never forget. Nothing at all markedly repulsive or hide-
ous ... strange enough I did not see one such. Our common
humanity, mine and yours, everywhere: "The same old
blood...the same red, running blood" yet behind most an inferred
arrière of such storms, greed for wealth, religious problems,
crosses ... mirrored from those crazed faces (yet now tem-

porarily so calm, like still waters) ... all the woes and sad happenings of life and death ... now from every one of the devotional element radiating .... Was it not, indeed, the peace of God that passeth all understanding, strange as it may sound.[7]

Whitman accompanied Bucke and his wife to Sarnia, visiting Mrs. Bucke's mother and her friends. When Bucke and Whitman returned to London, Jessie remained in Sarnia, and was still there on July 7th, although Bucke had been politely entreating her to return. On July 1st he wrote:

I was a little shocked at your intention to stay until Saturday 10th.[8]

On July 26th, Bucke and Whitman left London for a three-week trip on the St. Lawrence and Saguenay rivers. Letters and diaries attest to the pleasures provided by the scenery. There were periods of ennui, however. Bucke wrote to Jessie, "I shall be more glad to get back than I was to get away."[9]

Two days later he wrote:

I believe Walt is half homesick and would as leave return to London as go on with our trip....I do not know that I am much better myself.[10]

By August 6th, he could say:

Walt is keeping well and I think on the whole he is enjoying his trip very much ... but I think he will be almost as glad as myself to get home.[11]

While they were away Bucke wrote a poem entitled "The Saguenay", and after their return to London Whitman sent a letter to a local newspaper with which he included Bucke's poem. The editor, however, overlooking the attribution, published both letter and poem as Whitman's, referring to the poem as the best he had ever written.[12] Bucke's sense of humour, seldom displayed, enjoyed chaffing Whitman about that grand poem of his on the Saguenay. However, his sense of fun did not encompass an incident that took place one evening after he had, as usual, retired at 10 p.m. Whitman had finished a bottle of whiskey and "was quite well set-up". He suggested that the others (minus the sleeping host) should join him in a procession to bury "the corpse". It was a lovely moonlit evening and Whitman made a fervid oration to the bottle and the moon as the burial took place under a tree, 100 yards from the house. Bucke was rather shocked when his brother related the story in the morning.[13]

Bucke took Whitman as far as Niagara Falls on September 28th, then returned to his responsibilities at the asylum, and to his biography of Whitman begun a few months earlier during Whitman's visit. Indeed, Whitman ended up playing a large part, both as subject and author of the book.

For Bucke, the visit had been a great success. His adoration of Whitman was undimmed. Toward the end of the visit, he wrote Forman:

The three and a half months' absolute intimacy in which we have just lived have made him seem greater to me than he did before, which I hardly thought possible.[14]

Bucke was completely oblivious to Jessie's feelings about the visit, and remained so until the following year when he was planning another visit from Whitman. On 16 June 1881, Bucke wrote Jessie from Toronto, where he was spending a few days at a meeting:

I shall not be sorry to be quietly back in London with you all and if dear old Walt comes we will have a lovely visit together to Kingston and the thousand islands....[15]

Jessie's letter from Sarnia has disappeared, but its content and its effect on Bucke are clear from his reply. This letter is important not only in revealing Jessie's feelings and Bucke's unawareness of them, but also in providing additional evidence of the passion and depth of Bucke's feelings toward Whitman:

I have written to Walt Whitman and have done my best to stop him from coming here without being absolutely rude to him. I wish you had said long ago that you did not want him, but I was under the impression that you liked him — you seemed to, and I knew you had good reason to. Some of our Sarnia friends have been cautioning you against him and you have been weak enough to fall into their way of thinking. You may be sure I shall never try to get Walt Whitman into any house where he is not wanted, and I am more sorry than I can say that he is likely to come here this summer — If he comes now I shall have no pleasure in his visit — at first I thought I would enclose your letter to him but that seemed too hard on you and cruel to him so I have taken a different course and one that I hope will prevent his coming without letting him see that we don't want him for I want him as little as you do now — but Jessie never allow yourself to imagine for a moment that you or any of you can shake my affection for Walt Whitman — if all the world stood on one side, and Walt Whitman and general contempt on the other and I had to choose which I would take I do not think I should hesitate (I hope I should not) to choose Walt Whitman.

Do not be uneasy, you could not make me angry on such a subject but I am profoundly grieved to see that our minds are so far apart upon it.[16]

Four days later Bucke wrote Jessie a letter chatting of a party the children had had and of the medical visitors he was entertaining, but he did not mention the Whitman crisis.[17] However, just one week after writing Jessie of his disappointment in her and his staunch defence of Whitman, Bucke wrote that although Walt Whitman would not be coming to London, he had arranged to meet him for a couple of weeks in Long Island. He went on to say that he would be glad to have her come along, but that the trip would be rather rough at times and he thought Jessie would be lonely. He suggested that Jessie might go with her brother Robert and their eight-year-old son Willie, and stay at Old Orchard Beach on the coast of Maine while he was with Whitman. Afterwards, he would pick them up and return with them to Canada.[18]

On July 14th, Bucke left for Long Island, and must have made a further proposal for Jessie, her brother and his wife Sarah to join Whitman and himself in New York, because on July 27th he wrote from Long Island:

Walt and I have decided we will go to the Astor House so I want you and Robert and Sarah to settle on the same thing — If you get there first on Monday you will choose rooms and if I get there first I will wait until you come ....[19]

Jessie stayed on at her mother's in Sarnia. She was still there on August 23rd when Bucke wrote her from London alternately expressing his devotion and his loneliness for her, and admonishing her failure to return as promised.[20] He received a letter from Jessie on the following day and promptly replied, once again imploring her to return, pointing out that she had been in Sarnia nearly all summer:

My darling, your mother has great claims upon you but we have also and I really think she has had her share of you for this time.[21]

In spite of Bucke's enforced realization a month earlier of Jessie's antipathy to Whitman, he seems not to have really accepted it. On the day following his letter to Jessie entreating her to come home, he wrote Forman,

I hope to have W.W. here the good part of the coming winter.[22]

Rejection of Whitman by Bucke's devoted wife left Bucke's enthusiasm undiminished. He completed his hagiographic biography and continued to visit Whitman intermittently for the rest of his life. He became the poet's physician and senior literary executor. But Whitman never returned to London, nor did Jessie ever see him again.

—— Chapter 8 ——
Bucke Becomes Whitman's First Biographer

O<small>N</small> 22 M<small>AY</small> 1881, Bucke mentioned in a letter to Forman that plans were afoot to form a medical school as part of Western University in London, and that he had been given the job of organizing the medical faculty. He did not seem the least intimidated by the project.

> I think I shall succeed and I will probably take a chair myself.
> If I do, I shall probably take "Nervous and Mental Diseases"[1]

Bucke attended the first organizational meeting at the main local hotel, The Tecumseh House, on May 24th with eight other physicians. On the following day an offer was made by the Chancellor, Bishop Hellmuth, which was accepted at the second meeting two days later. Bucke proposed the names of five physicians who would select the faculty from the community. Events moved swiftly in those non-bureaucratic times and on 1 October 1882 Dr. William Waugh gave the first lecture.

Exactly one year later Bucke himself delivered the opening lecture, given in Victoria Hall to the medical students and open to the public. Anticipating by nearly a century the link between the university and the community in continuing education, Bucke remarked:

It is our confident expectation that not only will those who desire
to make medicine the business of their lives enter our college
and study with us but that large numbers will, solely for the love
of knowledge and for the sake of informing themselves on these
important subjects, take such lectures as they can make it con-
venient to attend, such as those on anatomy, physiology, chemistry and histology — and in this way we hope to do our full share
towards raising the general standard of intelligence and acquire-
ment of the city and surrounding country.[2]

Apart from his participation in the birth and early development of
the Medical School and his responsibilities at the Asylum, Bucke was
occupied during the years 1881-1883 with the development of his philosophy of immortality, the subject of his 1882 lecture to the Association
of Superintendents of American Institutions for the Insane, and with the
completion of his biography of Whitman.

In his unpublished essay "The Question of a Future Life" Bucke put
forth his case for immortality. It echoed the concept of man's evolutionary moral development discussed in his earlier book *Man's Moral Nature*.
As man has become more civilized, the positive elements of his moral
nature, love and faith, have increased at the expense of the negative elements, fear and hatred. As part of this development of faith in civilized
man, has come his belief in an afterlife. Bucke illustrated his point by
reproducing a conversation between Sir Samuel Baker, a nineteenth century British explorer, and an Egyptian savage chief named Commoro.
Sir Samuel is taken aback to hear Commoro enunciate a very materialistic view of life and death.

Sir Samuel interrogates: "Have you no belief in a future existence
after death?"

Commoro replies, "Existence 'AFTER' death! How can that be? Can
a dead man get out of his grave, unless we dig him out?"

Sir Samuel: "Do you think that man is like a beast, that he dies and
is ended?"

Commoro: "Certainly; an ox is stronger than a man; but he dies,
and his bones last longer; they are bigger. A man's bones break quickly
— he is weak."

Sir Samuel: "Is not a man superior in sense to an ox? Has he not
a mind to direct his actions?"

Commoro: "Some men are not so clever as an ox."[3]

Thus the idea of a future life is simply one aspect of man's evolutionary moral ascension. Bucke next brought Whitman forth as a witness, describing the latter's relation to our time as similar to that of the Gautama, Christ and Mohammed to theirs, and quoted long passages from "Song of Myself" to illustrate.

Bucke went on to repeat an idea he had expressed in *Man's Moral Nature*, namely, that fear of death is not inherent in man, but it was an important feeling at a certain evolutionary period in history to protect him from incurring needless risks to his life. It was rather like a mother's fear of her child's crossing an intersection. But Bucke felt that man's fear of death, which had been acquired for pragmatic reasons, was no longer necessary and would become vestigial as his increased faith envisioned an afterlife.

Finally, in an attempt to help those who could not conceive of an afterlife necessarily different from our earthly existence, Bucke used the analogy of a society of unborn babies. A society of foetuses whose world was dark and warm and soft could not imagine a life of breathing air, independent of a placental blood supply.

Bucke developed his theory of man's evolutionary intellectual development in a lecture to the Association of Superintendents of American Institutions for the Insane in Cincinnati in May 1882. He expressed his belief that man's ability to articulate more complex concepts would not have been possible without his refinement of language. He saw fairly recent evolutionary acquisitions such as colour perception as evidence of further development. This led Bucke to make the case for yet untold future intellectual advances of which we are not yet aware. He saw it simply as part of the evolutionary journey to cosmic consciousness, at present the prerogative of the special few including Whitman, but accessible to increasing numbers in future generations. This was the germ of his third book, *Cosmic Consciousness*, which would be published nearly twenty years in the future.

Bucke's view on education had also taken shape by this time.[4] He believed that educators, like physicians, clergymen and lawyers, were convinced that without their special contribution, society would collapse in a morass of ignorance. Although he acknowledged that the professions contributed much, each brought obstacles that diminished their usefulness. He quoted Goethe:

"Ja unser' Thaten selbst sogut als unser Leiden
Sie hemmen unseres Lebens Gang."[5] (Our deeds as much as
our suffering restrict the course of our lives.)

Bucke saw that man in his growth builds creeds, laws and social
orders which seem invaluable at the time, but which eventually imprison
the individual, that man inevitably bows down before the institutions
he himself has created. When the incarceration becomes sufficiently
unbearable the edifice is attacked and destroyed.

School education, Bucke felt, was such an institution which destroyed
the spontaneity of the mind, crowding it with useless information. Most
young men and women considered to be educated had little knowledge
of the most commonplace matters — how their bodies function, how a
steam engine works, etc.

He believed that educators should consider a maxim he had learned
in 1863 as a young postgraduate student in England from his teacher,
Sir William Jenner:

Never forget this, every dose of medicine you give will do harm,
it may do good, it may do more good than it does harm, but
it is *sure* to do more or less harm. Therefore never give a dose
of medicine unless you can see that the good which it will accom-
plish is greater that [sic] injury wh is certain to result from its
administration. The same lesson might be taken to heart by all
teachers. Their injuries are certain, the advantages which are to
balance and outweigh them are not by any means always so certain. It closely concerns the conscience of every teacher to consider well and see that in every case the last preponderates over
the first.[6]

Bucke's reputation by now had earned him, in June 1882, election
to the English Literature Section of the newly formed Royal Society of
Canada. But his principal achievement in 1882 was the completion of his
biography of Whitman.

He had first entertained the idea of attempting a biography of Whitman in 1878.[7] Initially, he had suggested to Forman that they put together
an English edition of Whitman's works to which he would add a short
biography. Forman felt that an English edition would not pay. Instead,

he encouraged Bucke to write a life of Whitman, at the same time cautioning him against excessive praise.[8] Bucke wrote the biography through 1879 and 1880, completing the text in early 1881. Although Whitman always referred to it as "Dr. Bucke's book", his alterations of the manuscript were so extensive that it was as much his book as Bucke's. Whitman had revised the original manuscript by July 1881. Later that year Bucke revised the altered original, and a first amanuensis copied out the new revision. It was then extensively altered by Whitman in February 1882, and copied by a second amanuensis. In March 1883, Whitman made his third and most thorough revision. He changed words, omitted sizeable portions of Bucke's original text, and inserted sentences and paragraphs of his own. The product was a literary hybrid. There were delays in obtaining satisfactory pictures and in finding a publisher, but the book finally appeared in 1883. Bucke wanted a picture of Whitman for the frontispiece and Forman obtained one by the artist Herbert Gilchrist. It was a drawing of the poet in 1864, and was reproduced by the then new process of photo-intaglio. Herbert Gilchrist was the son of Alexander Gilchrist, Blake's first biographer; and his wife Anne was one of Whitman's most passionate admirers. Anne Gilchrist appears in the book as the author of an idolatrous essay published in *The Radical* in Boston in 1870.

Walt Whitman, more hagiography than biography, is in two parts. The first includes a chronological account of the poet's family background and life up to 1880 and a detailed presentation of the poet's appearance and conversation written largely during the three-month visit of Whitman with Bucke in 1880. The tone of the prose brings to mind that used to describe both one's hero, even one's saviour, and one's beloved. It is an important document in understanding the texture of the feeling which Bucke had for Whitman. An appendix to this part of the book contains two long essays on Whitman by W.D.O'Connor, also an ardent admirer of the poet, and one of his closest friends, particularly in the later years.

On 30 June 1865, Whitman was dismissed from a clerkship he had held in the Department of the Interior, by the Hon. James Harlan, Secretary of the Department. The cause of the dismissal was Harlan's view of *Leaves of Grass* as "full of indecent passages". Nine weeks later O'Connor published a passionate and lengthy vindication of Whitman, entitled "The Good Gray Poet". In considerable detail O'Connor describes the dismissal and the unfair accusation of indecency. Bucke reprints the

"Good Gray Poet" in this appendix, along with an 1883 essay by O'Connor. This essay, in the form of a letter to Bucke, contains the same passionate espousal and reiterates Whitman's place in literature:

The grandest book of poetry uttered in the English tongue for over two centuries.[9]

The second part of *Walt Whitman* begins with a history of *Leaves of Grass* from its first 1855 edition through to the suppression of the seventh edition published by J.R. Osgood, who had approached Whitman with an offer in May 1881. Whitman agreed, provided that not a line be changed or deleted. The edition appeared in November 1881. In March 1882, the Boston District Attorney, Oliver Stevens, notified Osgood and Co. that he intended to institute a lawsuit against *Leaves of Grass* and to suppress it under the statutes regarding obscene literature.

Osgood and Co. wrote Whitman asking him if the passages deemed obscene could be deleted. Whitman, of course, refused. Osgood and Co. ceased publication of the book, and it was taken up by the Philadelphia house of Rees Walsh and Co., later bought by David McKay and Co.. The first Philadelphia edition appeared in September 1882 and was sold out in a single day.

Bucke did not appear to resent, generally, his subject's intrusion into his creation. However, in March 1883, when he sent his final revision to Whitman for scrutiny, the manuscript was accompanied by a letter:

I like all your emendations, additions, etc. so far (on the whole) very much, I can see that you are materially improving the book, for wh I feel very gratefull — But dear Walt be very carefull like a good fellow with chap iii of part ii — whatever you do dont slash it up [/] — if you make material changes send me the M.S. with proofs that I may see exactly what they are and consider them — don't fail me in this — that chap is the pivot on which the Book turns.[10]

The part referred to is his analysis of *Leaves of Grass*, presenting his interpretation of the major poem "Song of Myself" and the poems comprising the groups entitled "Children of Adam", "Calamus" and "Drum Taps". Whitman ignored Bucke's wishes and made considerable changes in this as well as other parts of the book. A typical example of Whitman's manuscript alterations is shown in Plate II, which reproduces part of pages 182 and 183 of the published text. In addition to word changes and sentence insertions, Whitman has added a footnote, and deleted three paragraphs following line 30 on page 182 which elaborated Bucke's concept of moral nature.[11]

Bucke saw "Song of Myself" as a religious poem expressing more nobly than any previous work man's faith in himself. The poem celebrates, through Walt Whitman, man himself — everyman, and there is a fusion of poet and reader. Bucke selected several passages for exegesis and concluded that although love was expressed in many forms in the poem, 'the ground work and vivifying spirit of the poem is Faith.'[12]

Bucke next defended the groups of poems first published in the 1860 edition called "Children of Adam" and "Calamus". These celebrate sexuality, including homoerotic love, in some of the most sensuous poems in the language. Soon after its publication, Emerson, Whitman's first champion, attempted to persuade him to delete the poems, not on moral grounds, but on practical ones. The public simply was not ready for such lines as

Limitless limpid jets of love hot and enormous, quivering jelly
of love, white blow and delirious juice;
Bridegroom night of love, working surely and softly into
the prostrate dawn,
Undulating into the willing and yielding day,
Lost in the cleave of the clasping and sweet-flesh'd day.[13]

If the public was unlikely to accept the "Children of Adam" poems, it was certain to reject the "Calamus" poems, with lines such as

When I saw the full moon in the west grow pale
and disappear in the morning light,
When I wander'd alone over the beach, and
undressing bathed, laughing with the cool waters,
and saw the sun rise,
And when I thought how my dear friend my lover
was on his way coming, O then I was happy,
O then each breath tasted sweeter, and all that

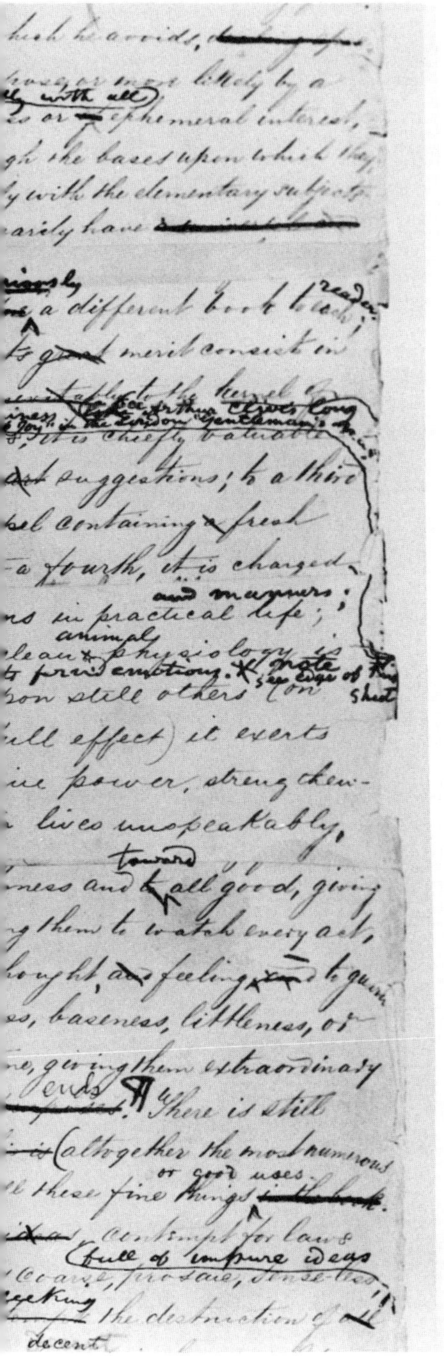

PLATE II — from pages 182 and 183 of Bucke's biography of Whitman showing Whitman's alteration of the text.

day my food nourish'd me more, and the
    beautiful day pass'd well,
And the next came with equal joy, and with the
    next at evening came my friend,
And that night while all was still I heard the
    waters roll slowly continually up the shores,
I heard the hissing rustle of the liquid and
    sands as directed to me whispering to congratulate me,
For the one I love most lay sleeping by me under
    the same cover in the cool night,
In the stillness in the autumn moonbeams his face was
    inclined toward me,
And his arm lay lightly around my breast — and
    that night I was happy.[14]

Although Whitman respected Emerson highly he valued his own artistic integrity more. Bucke felt that the "Children of Adam" poems were important in removing the shame and guilt commonly associated with the heterosexual act. In his defence of the "Calamus" poems, which celebrate homoerotic relationships, Bucke interprets these platonically as "an exalted friendship, a love into which sex does not enter as an element".[15]

To Bucke, *Leaves of Grass* was the bible of democracy and the instrument through which Whitman as prophet could liberate nineteenth century American citizenry. He expressed its meaning in the terms of his conception of man's moral nature: *Leaves of Grass* would enable those who read it with an open mind, and who read it as an emotional and not an intellectual experience, to further their own moral elevation. In Bucke's terms, that meant to increase the amount of love and faith and, perforce, to diminish the amount of fear and hate. He saw the process in Blakean terms, as enabling man to recognize the divinity that resided within his breast, and to discard "church-going, bible-reading, creeds and prayers".[16]

Bucke, then, was among the first to see the genius erupting out of *Leaves of Grass*, which spoke for its age with all its turbulence, vitality and confidence. Man need not shrink from the cosmos, nor from himself — he could be glorious, strong and unfettered in both mind and body. Bucke understood that excitement and wanted desperately to share it.

The last section of the biography, the appendix to part 2, consists of a collection of some forty-five reviews, letters to editors and short poems, including two letters by Bucke himself. Most of these had been published in various newspapers and periodicals between 1855 and 1883 and commented on *Leaves of Grass* or on Whitman himself. The box score is thirty-five favourable and ten critical or frankly vituperative. One of the earliest, a description of Whitman in unrelieved superlatives, appeared in the Brooklyn *Daily Times* on 29 September 1855. Part of the text reads:

> Of American breed, of reckless health, his body perfect, free from taint from top to toe, free forever from headache and dyspepsia, full-blooded, six feet high, a good feeder, never once using medicine, drinking water only — a swimmer in the river or bay or by the seashore of straight altitude and slow movement of foot — an indescribable style evincing indifference and disdain — ample limbed, weight a hundred and eighty-five pounds, age thirty-six years (1855) — never dressed in black, always dressed freely and clean in strong clothes, neck open, shirt-collared flat and broad, countenance of swarthy transparent red, beard short and well mottled with white, hair like hay after it has been mowed in the field and lies tossed and streaked — face not refined or intellectual, but calm and wholesome — a face of an unaffected animal — a face that absorbs the sunshine and meets savage or gentleman on equal terms — a face of one who eats and drinks and is a brawny lover and embracer ....[17]

It was unsigned, but was written by Whitman himself. This was not an isolated example of Whitman's manoeuvring for publicity. In fact, he even included these anonymous reviews in a curious anthology which he published to accompany the 1860 edition of *Leaves of Grass*, calling it "Leaves of Grass Imprints". Nor did Whitman ever desist from this practice. As late as December 1888, he sent to the *Post* a brief autobiographical summary of his later years and, without asking the author, the copy of a letter from Bucke describing Whitman's latest edition as "the volume of the future for the next thousand years".(WWC, 3,97) Although Bucke was aware of this practice of Whitman's, he does not acknowledge the above review as Whitman's in this appendix. This egregious staginess has often offended Whitman's admirers, but Bucke never expresses disappointment at such breaches of propriety. He would not permit himself to see any fragment of clay in his god's feet.

One of the most passionate pieces in the second appendix was written by Mrs. Anne Gilchrist in England, and published in 1870 by *The Radical* in Boston. It begins:

> I had not dreamed that words could cease to be words, and become electric streams like these.
>
> I do assure you that, strong as I am, I feel sometimes as if I had not bodily strength to read many of these poems. In the series headed "Calamus", for instance in some of the "Songs of Parting", the "Voice out of the Sea", the poem beginning "Tears, Tears", etc., there is such a weight of emotion, such a tension of the heart, that mine refuses to beat under it, — stands quite still, — and I am obliged to lay the book down for a while.[18]

Mrs. Gilchrist had first read *Leaves of Grass* in 1869, the same year as Bucke. It seemed to her a love-call, and she began writing Whitman offering her love. Whitman did not reply to her first letter but responded with a brief note to her second. She continued to send him long, passionate letters to which he replied perfunctorily from time to time. In August 1875, for whatever reason, Whitman sent her a ring. A few months later she informed him that she was coming to America and bringing her two youngest children. Whitman proved himself adept at deflecting her advances, but visited her regularly.

A review of Bucke's book appeared in the *Nation,* and was unfavourable both as to its contents and to *Leaves of Grass.*

> This is an unadulterated eulogy by a man of very little culture or critical ability; and there is not much in it that was not better said by Mr. Burroughes a dozen or more years ago. Dr. Bucke has included, however, a long and amusingly vehement letter by Mr. W.D.O'Connor that enlivens his otherwise dull pages immensely. Dr. Bucke himself describes Whitman's moral nature as "perhaps the highest that has yet appeared". He tells us of his unbounded humanity and of a mysterious and, indeed, miraculous power that works upon people he comes in contact with like champagne or falling in love.[19]

Bucke never refers to the adverse comments his biography received. With the confidence that accompanies an unshakable belief in having discovered a Messiah and his liberating message, there was little point in brooding over some journalist's unenlightened views. Moreover, Bucke's hours and days were filled to overflowing with duties and responsibilities as superintendent of a large asylum and father of seven children. He was involved with the organization of a new medical school, busily maintaining his epistolary friendship with Harry Forman and others, such as his classmate John Harkness practising near Cornwall, Ontario, and developing new ideas both philosophical and pragmatic. The latter included the marketing of a water meter being developed by his brother-in-law, Robert Gurd. Bucke planned to form a company to distribute the meter. He hoped to make Harry Forman's brother, Alfred, the British agent. Alfred Forman was a writer, who had translated both the "Ring of the Nibelung" and "Tristan" into English to the satisfaction of Wagner. Forman wrote to Bucke:

My opinion certainly is that this "Ring" looked at as a whole (poetry — music and performance under the man's own direction) will be the greatest *single* act-work of a single brain that the world has seen.[20]

Alfred sent Bucke the translation and Bucke commented on it a month later in a letter to Alfred's brother:

I have not read Alfred's translation but have dipped into it a few times. I think from what I have seen of it that I shall find it dry reading though I dare say it is a good translation.[21]

Bucke saw only one of Wagner's operas, "Gotterdammerung", in New York, and Whitman reported:

Doctor thought it a revelation — was filled with it for days and days.(WWC, 4, 427)

Yet Whitman had remarked in a conversation with his young friend Horace Traubel four months earlier:

"Maurice never seems very fertile in esthetic suggestions: that is a talent that has been neglected in him." I (Traubel) said "Maybe it goes along with his utter failure to enter into musical things." We assented: "I shouldn't wonder: in fact it seems almost necessarily true."(WWC 3, 210)

Alfred Forman had married a young actress named Alma Murray, who later achieved a considerable reputation on the London stage by playing the original part of Raina Petkoff in Shaw's *Arms and the Man* in 1894.[22] However, Forman remained largely impecunious, and Bucke saw the water meter as a means of helping his friend while at the same time liberating himself to spend more time on his metaphysical and literary activities. Whitman was sceptical of the whole water meter venture, his scepticism and disapproval being based less on understanding of it than on suspicion of Bucke's inflated hopes of becoming rich.

Thus, by the end of 1883 Bucke had become a member of a royal society, helped inaugurate a medical school, published a second book and had a plan for patenting and marketing a water meter that could make him rich. All this in addition to his professional duties at the asylum and his uxorious life at home. He was in full stride.

—— Chapter 9 ——

Increasing Concern Over
Whitman's Decline

IN MAY 1884, the young Canadian physician William Osler, then at
McGill, was offered the chair of Clinical Medicine at the University of
Pennsylvania. Osler had grown up in Ontario and had graduated from
McGill in 1872, a decade after Bucke. He was without peer in the medical world of his day and was the model for all physicians in the English-
speaking world throughout the first half of the twentieth century. At
thirty-five he began his ascent in academic medicine, spending five years
in Philadelphia before taking the chair in medicine at Johns Hopkins in
1889.

It is not surprising that Bucke, who knew Osler, asked him to see
the ailing Whitman in consultation not long after Osler's arrival in
Philadelphia in October 1884. Osler became, with Bucke, physician to
Whitman and made frequent visits to Camden. In a long reminiscence,
he recalled in his memorable prose his first consultation, as well as his
impression of Bucke's idolatry:

> Not long after removing to Philadelphia a telegram came from
> my friend Dr. Maurice Bucke of London, Ont.: "Please see Walt
> and let me know how he is." — to which I had to answer: "Who
> is Walt and where does he live?" It was very stupid of me as

I should have remembered that a few years before when Dr. Bucke had been a guest at one of our Club dinners in Montreal he had startled us into doubts of his sanity by extravagant praises of one Walt Whitman, a new seer of a new era, whom he classed with our Saviour, Buddha, and Mahomet. Then I remembered, too, to have seen notices of a book he had written about Whitman; but I had no idea where the prophet lived. The next morning I had the answer: "Mr. Walt Whitman, 328 Mickle Street, Camden". In the afternoon I crossed the Delaware River ferry and in a "clean, quiet democratic street" I found the little, old-fashioned two-story [sic] frame house. A pleasant middle-aged woman answered the door, to whom I showed Dr. Bucke's telegram. "He will be glad to see you — anyone from Dr. Bucke. Mr. Whitman is better to-day and downstairs." The door opened into what appeared to be a room, but I had no little difficulty at first in getting my bearings. I have seen what the tidy housewife calls a "clutter", but nothing to compare with the front room, ground floor of No. 328 Mickle Street. At the corner, near the window, the head and upper part of a man were visible — every-where else, covering the floor, the chairs and the table, were, to use his own description, "heaps of books, manuscripts, memoranda, scissorings, proof-sheets, pamphlets, newspapers, old and new magazines, mysterious-looking literary bundles tied up with stout strings". The magazines and newspapers, piled higher than the desk, covered the floor so completely that I had to pick my way by the side of the wall of the room to get to the desk. I thought of Prof. Teufel's room in "Sartor Resartus". After a hearty greeting, I had some difficulty in explaining that I did not come directly from Dr. Bucke, but that he had sent me over from Philadelphia to find out how he was. There was nothing serious the matter — a transient indisposition which had passed away. With a large frame, and well-shaped, well-poised head, covered with a profusion of snow-white hair, which mingled on the cheeks with a heavy long beard and moustache, Walt Whitman in his 65th year was a fine figure of a man who had aged beautifully, or more properly speaking, majestically. The eyebrows were thick and shaggy, and the man seemed lost in a hirsute canopy .... My visit was made without any of that preparation — that expectation, upon which Gideon Harvey dwells as influencing so profoundly our feelings. I knew nothing of Walt Whitman and had never read a line of his poems — a Scythian visitor at Delphi!...That evening at the Club after dinner I opened the volume of "Leaves of Grass" for the first time. Whether the meat was too strong, or whether it was the style of cooking — 'twas not for my pampered palate, accustomed to Plato and Shakespeare and Shelley and Keats. This has been a common experience; even Dr. Bucke acknowledging that "for many months I could see absolutely nothing in the book", and would even "throw it down in a sort of rage". Whitman himself has expressed this feeling better than anyone else, speaking of his "strange voice", and acknowledging that critics and lovers of poetry may well be excused the "chilly and unpleasant shudders which will assuredly run through them, to their very blood and bones" when they first read him, and exclaim:"If this is poetry, where must its foregoers stand?"...At this time, of the two men, Bucke interested me more. Though a hero-worshipper, it was a new experience in my life to witness such an absolute idolatry. Where my blurred vision saw only a fine old man, full of common sense and kindly feelings, Bucke felt himself in the presence of one of the world's great prophets. One evening after dinner at the Rittenhouse Club with Dr. Chapin, Dr. Tyson, Dr. J.K. Mitchell and a few others who I knew would appreciate him, I drew Bucke on to tell the story of Whitman's influence. The perfervid disciple, who talks like [Chaerephon] in the [Apology] is not often met with in these matter-of-fact days. It was an experience to hear an elderly man—looking a venerable seer — with absolute abandonment tell how "Leaves of Grass" had meant for him spiritual enlightenment, a new power in life, new joys in a new existence on a plane higher than he had ever hoped to reach. All this with the accompanying physical exaltation expressed by dilated pupils and intensity of utterance that were embarrassing to uninitiated friends. This incident illustrates the type of influence exercised by Whitman on his disciples — a cult of a type such as no other literary man of our generation has been the object ....[1]

The house at 328 Mickle Street, Camden became the focus of much of Bucke's energies over the next seven years. Whitman had been able, in March 1884, to buy the small, two-storey wooden house, the first he had ever owned. As Osler had observed, it was filled with a cluttered disarray of books, trunks and wooden boxes. Although Whitman, who had always dwelt nomadically in rooming houses, had now come to moorings, the atmosphere was still Bohemian, as though he might depart at any time.

Whitman not only did not depart, but over the next few declining years became increasingly incarcerated by his physical disabilities. He had suffered a stroke in 1873 which left him lame, and during his years in Mickle St. he gradually became unable to get about, especially after a second stroke in June 1888. His medical advisers, in addition to Bucke, included the celebrated Osler, until he left Philadelphia for Johns Hopkins in 1889, and Dr. Daniel Longaker, who remained Whitman's physician for the rest of his life.

Whitman's health and comfort were a constant source of worry to Bucke during these years. His distance from the scene encouraged his epistolary propensity, and many letters were exchanged between Whitman and himself dealing largely with daily accounts of symptoms, bowel function, diet and medications.

Mickle Street became a court where Whitman's admirers came to pay homage, some famous, such as the actor Henry Irving and the writer and critic Edmund Gosse.[2] Many were simply devoted pilgrims seeking confirmation of their idealistic dreams personified by the imposing presence of the poet. The inner circle, in addition to a housekeeper, Mrs. Davis, included a young clerk named Horace Traubel, his brother-in-law, Thomas Harned, a lawyer, and Bucke, who made the long trek from London, Ontario at every opportunity.

In addition to the worries about Whitman's health, Bucke was chronically anxious about Whitman's financial difficulties. He had always been impecunious. His only income came from the sale of books and articles; in the last half of 1885 his royalties amounted to $20.[3] His English editor, Michael Rossetti, brother of the pre-Raphaelite painter, organized a subscription in England that year which yielded $500. Another source of income was the lecture Whitman gave on each anniversary of the death of Abraham Lincoln, the 15th of April. It was an opportunity for his friends to make a donation, and in 1887 he spoke in New York to an audience of three hundred, the evening bringing in $600.[4]

By 1888, a more continuing method of support was organized with a list of people who would send a monthly cheque. Bucke contributed $3 a month, sent quarterly. It was a substantial sum for him, financially burdened by the cost of a large family and dependent upon a civil servant's salary. He worried considerably about his own financial matters, but was buoyed intermittently by hopes of becoming a millionaire from the invention by his brother-in-law, Robert Gurd, of the water meter which was to be marketed by the Gurd Water Meter Co., of which Bucke was a director.

In 1885 Bucke became involved in a historic event. On 15 July 1885, during the celebrated trial of Louis Riel, he left for Regina to be one of the medical witnesses for the defence.[5] Riel had been charged with treason for leading the Metis in the North West rebellion. There are no extant letters by Bucke describing his trip or his experiences in Regina, but it is known that he did not testify at the trial, apparently having arrived too late.[6] There were four medical witnesses for the prosecution at the trial, two of whom felt that Riel was insane and not responsible for his actions, and two who believed he was of sound mind.[7] The medical witnesses were criticized for a lack of thoroughness,[8] and a two-man commission was appointed for a post-trial assessment of Riel's sanity. This was a political sop to Quebec, furious over Riel's conviction. In fact, neither of the post-trial physicians was a psychiatrist, and in the end they disagreed on the issue as to whether Riel was an "accountable being".[9] Despite this difference, the Cabinet decided for hanging, which was carried out on November 16th.

It is difficult to understand why Bucke did not give evidence. On July 21st Judge Richardson granted a one-week delay for the defence to prepare its case, enough time for Bucke's arrival if he had left London as planned on July 15th.[10]

The day after the hanging Bucke was interviewed by a reporter from the *London Free Press*.[11] He dodged the central issue of whether Riel was insane or not. He said he had observed him carefully and that "the common phrase 'wrong headed' would hit him off". Bucke then expressed some sympathy with phrenology in conceding that "Riel's was, in a word, what phrenologists would call a criminal head and to persons long accustomed to study criminal physiognomy he stood a confessed criminal."[12]

Bucke seemed, thus, to attach little importance to the case, dismissing the journalist's questions in a rather cavalier fashion and never, as far as I was able to discover, mentioned in subsequent letters to Whitman, Forman or others one of the most celebrated trials in Canadian history.

Bucke was not feeling well that summer. He had sought and been granted a three-month leave of absence. He intended to go to England in late October but was prevented by the illness of his deputy, Dr. Beemer.[13] In January 1886, he lamented to Forman,

> As regards my own health, I am of course poorly, feeling pretty miserable a good part of the time; have been in this state for over a year in fact nearly for quite two years. But I got very bad last summer and autumn. Lately I am not suffering quite so much, don't seem to have any disease, just tired out, poor appetite, and low spirits.[14]

Bucke was obviously depressed, but part of it was related to his worry about the ailments of his family. It is a typical catalogue of nineteenth century illnesses: his daughter Clare had peritonitis; his wife and son Maurice were ill with typhoid; his sister-in-law, who was staying with the Buckes, suffered some sort of uterine trouble; and her six-year-old son had contracted typhoid in the Bucke household. All this was in addition to the prolonged illness of Dr. Beemer and to typhoid contracted by Dr. Fairchild, who had been sent to replace him.[15]

By mid-April 1886, Bucke was able to get away and, as always, he was restored by an ocean crossing.[16] He visited the Forman brothers in London and saw a production of Shelley's Cenci in which Alfred Forman's wife Alma, played Beatrice.[17] He sailed from London to Aberdeen, visited three asylums in Scotland, then returned to London and sailed for America on July 4th, feeling entirely well again.[18]

But there was a small thorn that pricked him increasingly and became an obsession over the next few years. Bucke's hopes of shedding his financial yoke lay in the manufacture and sale of the water meter. He saw this project as the only way he could liberate himself to devote all his energies to proselytizing Whitman's ideas. When Bucke arrived in New York on July 16th, he was irritated that Gurd, who met him there, was not nearly ready to begin manufacture of the meter. It was not his last annoyance with his brother-in-law or the "meter business". His dream of its success and the recurring nightmares of delays gradually dominated his ruminations, taking second place only to his chronic anxiety about Whitman's illness and disability.

By September 1886, Bucke was in high spirits about the meter. The prototype was finished and he estimated it could be manufactured for less than $5. The cheapest competitor on the market was selling for $75! Bucke wrote Forman that the City Engineers of London had said that the city was prepared to take a thousand.[19] It seemed a simple matter to secure the necessary patents, and his mood was brighter than it had been earlier that year.

During 1887 Bucke was busy as usual with his regular asylum responsibilities. He was also successful in building up Forman's Whitman collection, acquiring a copy of the 1856 edition of *Leaves of Grass* for him. During this time he endured continuing delays in the progress of the water meter project. In September he visited Whitman, found him surprisingly well and felt "encouraged to hope that we shall have him with us yet for some years."[20]

But 1888 marked a heightening of Bucke's concern about Whitman. In February, Bucke went to Florida by himself for a vacation to rid himself of fatigue. He visited Whitman en route both ways and found him unchanged. At the beginning of June, while on a commission visiting an asylum in New Jersey, he arrived unexpectedly at Camden. He and Whitman had a drive together and Whitman seemed all right, but on the following day suffered a stroke. Osler was summoned. Whitman's condition remained precarious and on June 10th Bucke thought he was dying. He learned from Whitman that he had not made a will, so Harned drew up a rough draft. Whitman rallied, and on June 29th signed his will making Bucke one of his three literary executors along with Harned and Horace Traubel.

Traubel, a thirty-year-old clerk who had grown up in Camden, first met Whitman when the latter came there in 1873 to live with his brother George. This casual friendship ripened, and by 1888 Traubel was a daily visitor at 328 Mickle Street, where he began to record every sentence Whitman uttered. He was an indefatigable if untalented biographer, and his worship of Whitman rivalled Bucke's. He became a close friend of Bucke's and the illness of June 1888, which marked the beginning of Whitman's last decline, brought them all closer together. From then until Whitman's death Bucke's waking hours were filled with concern not only for the patient's comfort but apprehension for the funeral service which he thought would not be far away. During the ensuing three and three-quarter years hundreds of letters were exchanged between Bucke and Whitman and Bucke and Traubel.

By July 7th Bucke was writing Traubel with his suggestions for the funeral service. He thought that the opening should be a short address by John Burroughs.[21] Burroughs was a Whitman admirer who, in 1867, had published *Notes on Walt Whitman as Poet and Person*, a work on which Whitman had collaborated shamelessly.[22] He was to be followed by O'Connor reading from "The Good Gray Poet", his vehement attack on Whitman's dismissal from his post in the Civil Service in 1865 when it was discovered that he was the author of *Leaves of Grass*. Then would come the Rev. Clifford, pastor of a church in Germantown, who would read some passages from the Psalms, *Leaves of Grass* and the New Testament as the body was lowered into the grave. Then Bucke himself proposed to speak for twenty to twenty-five minutes.[23] He also suggested that the whole service be printed in a little pamphlet to be sold and distributed widely.

Bucke was very concerned that the format be appropriate for what Whitman stood for and he was aware of his great responsibility. A few days earlier he had written his young friend Traubel:

I would not say it to anyone but you but we are in the same boat and must sink or swim together, but we must brace up and go through with it — millions of eyes in the future will watch our actions to-day.[24]

He was surprised and annoyed to learn that Burroughs declined to take part in the service as proposed by him. Although Burroughs had said he didn't care much for Bucke's book, his objection seemed to be that Whitman's family, not Dr. Bucke, should be making the funeral service arrangements.[25] But Bucke knew that George and Mrs. Whitman had been approached with the plan and had agreed. He suspected that Burroughs wanted an orthodox funeral. He was aghast that one of the few who had proclaimed Whitman "the Saviour and Redeemer of the modern world" was willing to hand the funeral over to a Methodist for a "respectable" burial. Bucke believed that Burroughs feared being laughed at by the ordinary townspeople if Bucke's funeral plans were carried out. His passion and certainty burst forth.

> Have they not laughed at W. and L. of G. for forty years? Who are we that we should not also be laughed at and hooted? The thing is, what is *right*?[26]

Although Whitman had ups and downs, he did not become critically ill again in the next few months; the funeral-format theme faded from the correspondence. In addition to his chronic frustrations with the meter, two other issues irked Bucke at this time. Most salient of the two was his desire to raise money for Whitman, both for ongoing expenses and funeral costs. Thomas Donaldson, a reporter and future biographer of Whitman, had taken on the task but seemed to be doing nothing. Bucke felt a sense of urgency and of helplessness, being several hundred miles from the action.

The second, a more general despair and one known to all devout followers, was the indifference of people generally to the Great Cause.

> It makes me mad sometimes, as mad as damnation to see the Americans so apathetic about by far the greatest man the country has so far produced.[27]

However, the ardent disciple's enthusiasm was undiminished and his energy in promoting Whitman in the autumn of 1888 was focused on the latter's preparation of his *Collected Works* for publication. Whitman, with admirable courage and tenacity, still forced himself to write, whenever he felt well enough. After a seven years' silence, he published *November Boughs*, a mixture of prose and poetry, and later in the year the *Complete Poems and Prose*. Bucke had anxiously followed the preparation of these, particularly the latter, and in letters to Traubel had fussed about the cover:

> I wish I could take part in deciding on the cover for "C.W". I do hope you will strike on something *good* for it — but you will consider it all and not doubt it will be right when settled.[28]

Two weeks later Bucke again wrote Traubel about the cover. After admitting that he was not competent to advise about it, he went on to suggest that it should be green with some characteristic design stamped over the words "author's edition"; more specifically, that it should preferably be a white vellum cover with green designs.[29]

Bucke had earlier been nudging Whitman frequently with suggestions for the book, encouraging him to make each copy an autographed one and to sell them for not less than $10 each.[30] Whitman, fond as he was of Bucke, tended not to take Bucke's suggestions in non-medical matters too seriously. Characteristically, he commented a few days later to Traubel:

Maurice lives in a small town and sends me large advice.(WWC, 2:209)

Finally, the large book of 900 pages arrived in Bucke's mail on December 17th.[31] He scrutinized it quickly; by December 20th, Whitman had Bucke's comments:

An impromptu criticism on the 900-page Volume, "the Complete Poems and Prose of Walt Whitman", first issued December, 1888.

It is grander, grander than even I had hoped. It is the volume of the future for the next thousand years, and after that (superseded by even greater poems) to live as a grand classic for ever. It is a gigantic massive autobiography, the first of its kind. (though the trick had been tried before by Goethe, Rousseau and others; but even Goethe could not do it). The title page is perfect — I cannot conceive anything finer — and the little notes (opening and closing) are (to my notion — though you seemed so doubtful about them) just right.

Dear Walt, you have had a hard fight, but we may say of you to-day that you have won the battle. If you have fallen at the end, (though I trust even yet you may still have before you some good days) but even if you are to fall now, your fame is safe beyond all peradventure. Your work is well done: and here or elsewhere. (I do not know that it matters much which - except for those you leave a little while behind you), you will live and be honored always. Yes, and loved always.

R.M. Bucke

Whitman must have been impressed because he arranged to have the letter printed. It appeared twice, printed as broadsides on 27 December 1888 and 2 January 1889.[32]

There is an interesting textual mystery in the second sentence after the title. In the first edition the sentence reads as above, but in the second the word "volume" is replaced by "bible": "It is the bible of the future for the next thousand years." Lozynsky speculates that Bucke actually wrote "bible", but that even for Whitman it was a bit heavy, so he changed the text before circulating the letter to his friends including Bucke. Bucke picked up the change and re-inserted "bible". Whitman then had a second edition printed using the word "bible", but sent the copies only to Bucke.[33] Bucke felt that no praise of *Leaves of Grass* or its creator could be excessive. Whitman himself had mixed feelings about Bucke's public idolatry of him — part of him knew full well it was excessive, but the egocentric in him welcomed it. Certainly Traubel was aware of Whitman's views on Bucke's idolatry.

Whitman did not take to Bucke's suggestion that the collected works should be priced at $10. The book sold for $6 which rankled Bucke who believed, not incorrectly, that it would be worth $100 in twenty-five years.(WWC, 4:50)

Whitman, who understood Bucke very well, replied to Bucke who had commented about this to Traubel and Harned:

No doubt everything would have been different, Maurice, if you had had your way: but thank God you didn't have your way. We're not making this book for faddists, collectors, curio hunters: no: we're making it for people, readers: nor are we making it for nineteen hundred and twenty five: nineteen hundred and twenty five will take care of itself: we're making it for eighteen eighty-nine: that's as far as we've got — maybe as far as we'll ever get.(WWC, 4:50)

But Whitman's understanding of Bucke also included a complete acceptance of his character. When Harned replied, "Walt., ain't Bucke a trifle extreme?" Whitman replied at once, "No doubt. So was everybody I ever liked. Why, you're extreme yourself, Tom — and sometimes more than a trifle."(WWC, 4:50)

Bucke regarded *Leaves of Grass* as Holy Writ and, as such, misread the poems, the central message of which is not only a plea for democratic, individual liberty, but also the rejection of all cant and formalized ritual.

— Chapter 10 —

Bucke Misunderstands His Hero

Rivalling Bucke's concern for Whitman's health at the end of 1888 was his pre-occupation with the development and promotion of the Gurd Water Meter Co. of which he, his brother-in-law, Robert Gurd, and a friend, John Nesbitt, were partners. The delays in the development of the water meter prototype had seemed endless, but by January 1889 Bucke was planning to apply for patents in Canada, Great Britain, Western Europe and the United States. His optimism and enthusiasm were high. Scarcely one of the dozens of letters to Traubel and Whitman in the early months of 1889 failed to provide the latest bulletin on the project. Bucke's exasperation at the repeated delays and unreliability of Gurd was balanced by his faith in the honesty of both partners. By January he seemed confident that the tests had found the meter accurate, and that it would be cheap to produce and durable.

By early February, Bucke had formulated further plans. He wanted to include Thomas Harned in the project. Harned was a lawyer in Camden with business connections in Philadelphia. Bucke needed not only an American patent, but also an infusion of capital of which he, Gurd and Nesbitt had very little. He shipped the prototype to the Export office in Philadelphia, while he and Gurd arrived in Camden on February 26th.

In addition to the excitement of furthering the meter project and of seeing Whitman again, Bucke was planning to give a lecture in nearby Germantown. Traubel had written him three months earlier with this suggestion, and Bucke had agreed to give a lecture in Rev. Clifford's church on the evolutionary concept of immortality, a theme which he was to develop subsequently in *Cosmic Consciousness*.[1]

Bucke entered 328 Mickle Street to find Whitman being helped from the back hall by Ed Wilkins, a Canadian male nurse from London, Ontario whom Bucke had sent to Camden the preceding November.[2] Traubel recorded these moments:

> "W said: 'Well — the family is reunited at last!' Bucke and W said little at the start. They gazed at each other. They both looked serene."

They may have looked serene to Traubel, but Bucke was sizing Whitman up clinically, and within moments was examining his abdomen where he had pain; Bucke was relieved to find only an enlarged spleen! Although Bucke was chronically anxious about Whitman and wanted everything possible done for him, he was very candid with him. In those initial few minutes Bucke told his patient:

> I'll be honest with you, Walt: I know I couldn't deceive you if I wanted to — and I don't want to: I don't think your status anything to brag of. (WWC, 4:224)

Whitman apparently took this calmly and told Bucke he appreciated being told the truth (WWC, 4:224), but like all patients he wanted to be left a chink of hope, as is illustrated by a conversation eight days earlier when Traubel had asked:

> Did not B differ from doctors generally in his frankness with patients? "Yes, he does: radically: Doctor believes in telling the truth at all times: he is more moralistic than I am." If I thought it would help a sick man I'd lie the top of my head off.(WWC, 4:170-171)

Bucke was not given to subtle nuances but used a frontal approach to everything. There was nothing tentative about him. His views were extreme, passionate and honest. Whitman was completely aware of these qualities and quick to defend Bucke.

After the first joyous moments of reunion and the clinical assessment of Whitman's health, the conversation inevitably turned to the "meter business". Bucke was obsessed with the possibilities of the meter project. Surprisingly, and surely out of politeness, Whitman opened the subject by asking about the meter. Bucke replied fervently:

> Oh Walt! we've got a big vast thing there: no one can tell what it will not do for us: we'll all be millionaires quicker'n it takes you to say Jack Robinson!(WWC, 4:225)

Whitman answered perceptively:

> "Do you say that Maurice, because you don't believe it or because you do believe it?" Bucke replied: "I believe nothing, Walt: I know!"(WWC, 4:225)

Traubel showed considerable understanding of Whitman by interjecting:

> I was only thinking that you, Walt, would have said that thing the other way about: you would have said: "I know nothing Maurice: I believe!"(WWC, 4:226)

Whitman attempted to defuse the situation by saying:

> You see Doctor, Horace is trying to humble us both with his transcendental epigrams!(WWC, 4:226)

But Bucke was piqued, and in a rare instance of anger with Whitman the following conversation occurred as recorded by young Traubel:

> "Walt, I don't believe you want the meter to go, damn if I do." W. was good natured, yet emphatic: "I don't want you to make a million dollars, Maurice, damn if I do!" We all laughed. Bucke said: "You'd rather see me poor than rich." W. assented. "If you have to be either I'd rather you were poor .... I'm afraid to have anyone I love make money: I'd rather he'd make

anything else than money: I don't want to see you rich, Maurice:
I'd rather see you mostly as you are: I'm simply afraid — yes
afraid: you sort of scare me when you come here and talk of
millions, millions: though as for that" — here he laughed quietly
and put his hand gently on Bucke's knee — "as for that I don't
think there's any danger impending: I feel it in my bones that
you are never to be tested." Bucke cried: "Do you mean that
you feel in your darned bones that the thing'll all go to smash?"
"I didn't say smash, Maurice: I only said I felt it in my bones
that you'd never be tested." Bucke still vehement: "You're cute,
you're stubborn: I don't know how to take you: I never saw you
before in the role of kill-joy." W. looked straight at B. "Oh
Maurice, won't you understand? It's not kill-joy: it's kill-grief:
I feel that success in this thing will only bring you sorrow." Bucke
was mystified "Why? Why?" W. was not disposed to continue.
"I'd rather not argue it, Maurice: you asked the broad question
— I gave you the broad answer: let it pass at that." I said: "Walt
and I have taken the vow to poverty!" B. regarded us with gen-
ial contempt: "You fellows do as you please: but as for me —
well, watch me." The meter talk stopped here. But when we
were out on the street alone afterwards Bucke said to me: "Did
you ever hear anything so extra-ordinary as the way the old man
went on about the meter? Why, I felt as if he was kicking my
ass out of the house!"(WWC, 4:226)

Bucke continued to be puzzled by Whitman's lack of enthusiasm
about the meter. Two days later he admitted to Traubel:

I took it for granted he'd be keyed up to it but it rather seems
as if he didn't care a rap what came of it.(WWC, 4:252)

Bucke was simply unable to see that Whitman's feelings about the
meter project expressed his concern as to what deleterious effect wealth
would have on him, and had nothing to do with wishing failure upon
Bucke. Although Whitman was tolerant of Bucke's obsessional views,
he knew that they skewed his vision.

On February 28th, in thinking about his lecture on Whitman the
following Sunday in Germantown, Bucke asked Whitman for some

suggestions. Whitman replied that he had already supplied enough.
Bucke objected:

"How can we evangelize for you, Walt, if you won't help us?"
"I don't want you to evangelize for me, Maurice: neither you
nor anyone: I'd rather not have anybody evangelized into a belief
in Leaves of Grass."(WWC, 4:242)

The conversation continued with Traubel's observation:

"Walt shrinks from the idea of conversion even to himself: he'd
rather have enemies than converts." Bucke was dubious. "That
sounds like nonsense to me," he said. W. was of the opposite
opinion." It does not sound like nonsense to me, Maurice:
Horace hits the nail on the head." "I don't think so Walt: I can't
reconcile myself to some of his transcendental fol-de-rol." W.
laughed, sticking his forefinger at B.: "Oh Maurice! Maurice! Will
you never understand Leaves of Grass!"(WWC, 4:242)

Thus Whitman understood his friend's deep need for certainty, and its
handmaiden, proselytism.

Bucke's proselytizing propensities were exercised broadly on March
2nd at the Rev. Clifford's church in Germantown, where twenty-six people, including Traubel, heard his lecture. The following morning Traubel
and Whitman had this conversation:

" How did the Doctor sing his song?" "O.K. I had no criticism
to offer. Except," I said. He looked at me. "Except what?" he
asked. "Except his superlatives," I said: "he claimed too much
for you." W.: "I shouldn't wonder: that's the Doctor's failing."
I said: "He talked too much about your superiority to everybody
through all time." W.: "I don't like that: it does not help us any
— rather retards."(WWC, 4:270)

Others in the audience shared Traubel's opinion of Bucke's lecture.
One of them had remarked to Traubel:

"Why didn't he stop sooner? he went up and up till he was out
of sight."(WWC, 4:288)

Another remarked, upon hearing that a future speaker was planned:

"If he's another crank like that Doctor Bucke, I won't go: for he was enough, with care, to last a lifetime!"(WWC, 4:345)

Whitman read Bucke's lecture and agreed that it made too large a claim for him and too dogmatic a claim for *Leaves of Grass*. Although he seemed pleased that Traubel had expressed his dissatisfaction for Bucke's position he defended Bucke, concluding that Bucke's evangelical espousal was perhaps necessary to counter the detractors.(WWC, 4:292-293)

One day, Bucke made mention to Whitman of something being a miracle. Whitman replied:

"Miracles are dangerous affairs, Maurice." B.: "You may not be a believer in miracles, Walt, but you are a worker of miracles." W. said: "You are a liberal interpreter, Maurice: you construe me far beyond what I am or could be — far beyond what I want to be." Yet he also said: "What greater miracles than the telegraph, telephone — all the wonderful new mechanisms of our day!" At the same time he said he always "wanted to be 'quoted against the theological miracles'." Bucke's insistence that there was a background for it all, W. said, did "not explain the case." W. added: "The whole miracle dogma business has been swung as a club over the head of the world: it has been a weapon flourished by the tyrannical dynasties of the old world."(WWC, 4:352)

Bucke did not really understand this point of view. He reflected on his own tendency for the extreme view:

"Walt, when I say radical things about you, I get into a hell of a scrap." W.: "Is that so, Maurice? Why, then, do you say the radical things?" "I can't help it, Walt: they sort of say themselves." W. then: "Take my advice: shut up!" B. said: "I can't: you are a disturber of the public peace: you get your friends in trouble as the sparks fly upward."(WWC, 4:353)

But Bucke had a need for the extreme view, the absolutist position, not confined to his idolatry of Whitman and *Leaves of Grass*. He had become an ardent teetotaler, he was obsessed by the water meter project, and he was developing a burgeoning interest, soon to become a passion, that Bacon was the author of the Shakespeare plays, and that there was a cipher to prove it. Indeed, Bucke claimed to have discovered a cipher in Whitman's volume *November Boughs*.(WWC, 4:454) Whitman dismissed it with humour:

In a case like that a man can find anything he is determined to find: What he wants is always there — infallibly.(WWC, 4:454)

Bucke's visit ended abruptly and unpleasantly on March 8th. He had a disagreement with Harned over the shares in the meter business, spoke briefly with Whitman, then departed, spent a day in New York and returned to Canada. Harned later told Whitman that Bucke was hopeless as a promoter, that the machine was imperfect, and that Philadelphia backers refused to put up the money without adequate protection.(WWC, 4:481)

Bucke had hoped to return for the celebration of Whitman's seventieth birthday on May 31st, but the annual hospital ball prevented his leaving London. He sent $5 for a ticket and a letter to be read at the dinner. The birthday dinner was held in Philadelphia at Morgan's hall, attended by local dignitaries and Whitman admirers. The most distinguished guest was Richard Watson Gilder, editor of the *Century Illustrated Monthly Magazine*, who, in the course of the evening in private conversation with Harned, referred to Bucke as "that Canadian crank".(WWC, 5:265) The speeches of the evening as well as the letters were subsequently published, including the one from Bucke. In it, Bucke quoted an unidentified writer as having said to him, "Walt Whitman is the Saviour, the Redeemer, of the modern world,"[3] and went on, "Walt Whitman has (as I believe) lived the highest life yet."[4]

When Whitman heard of Gilder's remark to Harned, he defended Bucke as usual:

Bucke is no crank at all — he is simply individualistic.(WWC, 5:265)

In this same letter Bucke alluded to the concept that was to become the theme of *Cosmic Consciousness*: that the heightened sense of consciousness that had characterized the greatest men in the past, and which Walt Whitman embodied most completely, would become accessible to increasing numbers of people as an evolutionary process in the fullness of time.[5]

The rest of 1889 passed uneventfully for Bucke. He confided that he hoped his burdensome annual Superintendent's Report in September might be his last, that wealth from the meter project would liberate him. His optimism was unshaken by the collapse in March of promised financial support from Harned's American friends. However, the year ended on a wistful note. At the end of a letter to Traubel on December 31st, after discussing several matters pertaining to Whitman, Bucke wrote:

For my part I think I shall like to join W. as soon as I can get settled up after he is gone.[6]

Chapter 11

Whitman's Last Birthday Party

W ILLIAM OSLER had left Philadelphia in May 1889 to become Professor of Medicine at Johns Hopkins in Baltimore. Later that year Bucke, concerned that Whitman was not receiving the close medical attention he deserved, mentioned the possibility of Whitman's going to live at the Johns Hopkins Hospital.[1] Whitman was non-committal at the time but seemed more inclined to the idea in January 1890.[2,3] Bucke then wrote Osler, who replied that Whitman could go and that $25 a month would look after all the expenses. Bucke sent Osler's letter on to Whitman and asked Traubel to try to get a commitment from him.[4] Bucke realized that this move would require more money than was available, and offered to increase his own contribution from $3 to $5 each month. On March 6th, Bucke wrote Traubel to let the hospital matter rest. Whitman never did go to Hopkins; presumably he rejected the idea.

In May 1890, two events pertaining to Whitman occurred. The first was the publication of Bucke's essay "Leaves of Grass and Modern Science".[5] It is Bucke at his most extravagant. He acknowledges that Whitman is not a scientist, but feels that Whitman's intuitive knowledge is as great; though not an Egyptologist, Whitman knows as much as the experts, and in spite of the lack of training in zoology he had foretold of evolution before Darwin:

He knew why the animals reminded him of himself. That he
had passed that way huge times ago....Note the field he covers.
How he touches upon or dips into all conceivable subjects, and
never (as far as I know) strikes a false note.[6]

The second event was Whitman's seventy-first birthday. Having
missed the previous celebration, Bucke planned to take a cottage on Cape
May on Delaware Bay in May and stay on until after the party on the
31st. The birthday dinner was held at Reisser's Restaurant in Philadelphia. Thirty people were present, including Colonel Robert Ingersoll, who
gave the birthday salutation with a much admired forty-five minute
address. Ingersoll and Whitman had had a long friendship but met only
infrequently, and Bucke had not met him before this occasion. He was
a celebrated orator, a passionate humanist, vehemently opposed to religious orthodoxy, and a fervid disciple of Whitman's. Both Bucke and
Whitman admired him, although his disbelief in immortality was in contrast to theirs, especially Bucke's, who had a more personal view of
immortality than Whitman. After the speech Ingersoll, sitting opposite
Whitman, had a long discussion on the subject with Whitman while
reporters scribbled shorthand as they debated.[7]

Bucke returned to Canada to prepare a lecture on sanity, which he
gave at a medical meeting in Niagara Falls on June 10th. He began by
saying to his colleagues who were, like himself, superintendents of mental
hospitals, that although they thought a good deal about insanity and spent
most of their working hours with insane people, they gave little thought
to sanity, rather taking it for granted. If asked about the nature of sanity,
they would likely dismiss the subject by simply saying that sanity consisted of thoughts and feelings which were in accordance with the truth
of things.

Bucke challenged this view by pointing out that in several important
areas the perceptions of the so-called sane person were *not* in accord with
reality. His first example was our distorted perception that we, our houses
and our surroundings are stationary objects on a stationary earth una-
ware of our movement through space. Then, echoing a theme from *Man's
Moral Nature*, he referred to the average sane man's fear of death, which
Bucke felt is now irrational but which once served man as a means of
self-preservation. Another belief not in accordance with the true nature
of things is the sane man's preference for his own children above some-

one else's, even when to an outsider they seem less worthy. This too could be explained historically as a means of preserving the family against outside threats, and was grounded in natural selection and heredity. Reiterating a concept he had presented twenty years earlier,[8] Bucke discussed what a long journey man had made from his primeval state which was characterized by fear and lack of faith and in which mountains, thunder and darkness held him captive through dread, to his present state in which he could truly enjoy the glories of nature. But nature had not changed through those millennia, so man's perception must have been erroneous. In contrast, many insane individuals imagine themselves flying with incredible speed through space, have no fear of death, and some — maniacs and neurosyphilitics — believe themselves to be living in a world of fabulous glories and beauties in which they have a supreme power.[9] Bucke, then, in a year when Van Gogh was languishing in the mental hospital at St. Remy, was aware of the difficulty and arbitrariness of defining sanity.

Whitman made two public appearances in 1890. The first was his annual discourse on April 15th commemorating the death of Lincoln. Bucke was unable to be present but had sent some new Canadian cloth which was made into a suit for Whitman. Dressed in his new suit, Whitman set out in a carriage for Philadelphia where, sitting in a wheelchair on stage, he delivered his address.[10]

The second event, which was to be Whitman's last public appearance, also took place in Philadelphia. On that occasion, October 21st, Whitman was seated on stage while Colonel Robert Ingersoll gave his magnificent oration, "Liberty in Literature", celebrating the genius of Whitman as liberator and prophet.[11] Bucke had been involved in the planning of this fund-raising event at which $869.45 was collected.[12] The arrangements did not run smoothly. Initially Bucke had hoped that Mrs. Bucke would accompany him, but Mrs. Bucke once more declined the pilgrimage.[13] A major technical difficulty was finding a hall that would allow Ingersoll, an atheist, to speak. Bucke had suggested hiring the largest theatre in Philadelphia, in which to inspire the citizens "if they have any manhood left in them".[14]

The Academy of Music refused to rent its hall, prompting a vitriolic attack in the October issue of the *Conservator* by the clergyman John Clifford, in whose church Bucke had given his hyperbolic lecture on Whitman a year and a half earlier.[15] Rev. Clifford decried the narrow-mindedness that would prohibit an atheist an opportunity to speak. In a companion article, Bucke, certainly no atheist himself, lamented bitterly that such a great country should disregard both its great poet-prophet and its great orator-spokesman. He concluded the article:

Oh, poor, sick America! How long, O Lord! how long?[16]

But the obstacles were at last overcome, Horticultural Hall was obtained and during the evening before the lecture Whitman wrote in his journal:

The prospect for the Ingersoll meeting to-morrow night looks well — Horace has worked like a beaver — Dr. B is here — I feel in the midst of my staunchest friends.[17]

Traubel accompanied Bucke back to Canada, staying in London for several days. The Ingersoll lecture remained on Bucke's mind, and shortly after Traubel's return to Camden he wrote him that the great value of the lecture was that it attracted

the extreme — "Naturalists" — shall I call them? those who believe in and rest in the objects of sense... will cause thousands of these people to look into Whitman's writings who otherwise would never have done so being repelled by their mysticism and spirituality and when they once begin to peruse in earnest these wonderful pages we may feel certain of the result. That "L of G" must eventually attract and captivate the better class of believers in the beyond and the hereafter (however much it revolts them at first) I have never doubted and now I feel equally sure that it will do as much for those who fancy that they are living, and can live, exclusively in the here and now.[18]

In his lecture Ingersoll, though unconvinced of man's immortality, leaves the door open:

And is this all? Will the forthgoer be lost, and forever? Is death the end? Over the grave bends Love sobbing, and by her side stands Hope and whispers: We shall meet again. Before all life is death, and after all death is life. The falling leaf, touched with the hectic flush, that testifies of autumn's death, is, in a subtler sense, a prophecy of spring.[19]

Bucke was ruminating on his own future, with encouragement to Traubel to keep up his notebook:

I can fancy myself an old, old man and you a middle aged one, W. gone from us years ago, living on these notes then printed — reading them and discussing them — never tiring of them — and how many hundreds, thousands, millions after you and I are dead and gone and but for our connection with W.W. forgotten![20]

As 1890 drew to a close Bucke's thoughts inhabited familiar themes. The Gurd Meter Co. Ltd. had capital stock of $45,000. Bucke estimated a rise in the stock of 1000% over par after manufacturing began, which he expected in a few weeks.[21] He received, all duly autographed, a trunk load of books he had sent off to Traubel to have Whitman sign. He praised, perhaps not extravagantly, a lovely poem published in November as the best of Whitman's later work. This poem, "To A Sunset Breeze", was later much admired by a more discerning critic, Ezra Pound. Bucke's anxiety about Whitman's health was unrelieved, for Whitman had had a return of his abdominal pain, and Bucke correctly suspected that "some serious condition underlies and causes this pain"[22] though a correct ante-mortem diagnosis was never made.

On Christmas Eve, Bucke had a fall that dislocated his left shoulder which, however, did not prevent the relentless correspondent from writing Traubel on Christmas Day and, stoically, again on the last day of the year, chiding both Traubel and Whitman for worrying too much about him.[23]

In the following year, 1891, Bucke's life was shaped by four events: the last of the three birthday parties for Whitman, a trip to England, his lecture to the McGill Faculty of Medicine and his last visit with Whitman. It was to be a momentous year.

By April, Bucke was fussing over the format of the May 31st birthday party. Although he had enjoyed the preceding year's party and

Colonel Ingersoll's speech, he thought a repetition of the function would be anti-climactic, and with candor added:

> And then I detest these formal dinners — but I do not know that our hide-bound social ideas permit anything better. Horace I suppose you know that we live lives of the most contemptible slavery — driven with whips along a narrow road by the ghosts of our ancestors! It is enough to make one sick just to think of it.[24]

As it turned out, Bucke must have been pleased with the birthday party arrangements. It took place at 328 Mickle St. where, in addition to Warren Fitzinger, who had replaced Ed Wilkins as Whitman's nurse, some thirty-one guests assembled for dinner, including Traubel's new wife, Anne, and three other women. Whitman had not been well that day, and was carried downstairs to the table. He sat next to Mrs. Harned, who plied him with champagne; he was able to converse and question the guests, and genuinely be the star of the evening. Letters of greeting and adulation from absent admirers were read out, and each of the guests was asked by Whitman to say something.

When Bucke spoke, his message was more accurate and penetrating than his usual excessive chants describing the poet and his work. He expressed the mystery and the beauty of both Whitman and the *Leaves* in accommodating opposites:

> While you are good you are also evil; the godlike in you is offset by passions, instincts, tendencies that unrestrained might well be called devilish; if on the whole you have lived well and done well yet none the less you have had in you, though subordinated, the elements of a Cenci or an Attila. This side of you is little realized, and therefore I have said and say that no one has yet understood you.[25]

Whitman was very complimentary to Bucke. When one of the guests commented that he had never seen anything written about Whitman that captured the man, Whitman referred to Bucke's book and said that Bucke had understood him and his work better than almost any other critic.[26] This was his usual view although, as we have seen, in an exasperated moment after Bucke's excessive Germantown lecture fourteen months earlier, Whitman had charged Bucke with not understanding *Leaves of Grass*.

A little later in the evening one of the guests, in praising Whitman, asked him obliquely why he had not married. Whitman dodged this by saying that Dr. Bucke

> who, I think, knows me better than anybody, and has sort of intercalated and found out, partly by his own instigation and partly because he feels it to do. I leave a large — a very, very large explication of that and all other questions to Dr. Bucke.[27]

This obfuscating response was even more evasive than the one he had given Bucke when he asked him the same question during his Canadian visit in 1880. Bucke never surmised the possibility of homosexuality in Whitman, nor saw the blatant homoeroticism in his Calamus poems.

One of the other contributors to that birthday party did see the homoerotic content. John Addington Symonds was an English writer who, though married and a father, was fundamentally homosexual. He was a great admirer of Whitman's and had first written him in 1871, enclosing a poem of his own inspired by "Calamus". He continued to write, hinting at and asking obliquely if the poems were homosexual, hoping in vain for some suggestion of confirmation. Ten months before the birthday party he wrote again, but more directly:

> In your concept of Comradeship, do you contemplate the possible intrusion of those semi-sexual emotions and actions which no doubt do occur between men? I do not ask whether you approve of them, or regard them as a necessary part of the relation. But I should much like to know whether you are prepared to leave them to the inclinations and conscience of the individuals concerned?[28]

The disappointment and disillusionment on reading Whitman's reply must have been very painful. Although it began casually, it responded to Symonds with anger:

> Ab't the questions Calamus pieces etc: they quite daze me. L of G is only to be rightly construed by and within its own atmosphere and essential character — all of its pages and pieces

so coming strictly under that — that the Calamus part has even
allow'd the possibility of such construction as mention'd is terrible — I am fain to hope that the pages themselves are not to
be even mention'd for such gratuitous and quite at the time
entirely undream'd and unreck'd possibility of morbid inferences
— wh' are disallow'd by me and seem damnable.[29]

The pain of Whitman's denial is not apparent in Symond's thoughtful birthday letter, sent from England and read aloud to the gathering
by Whitman. In his reply to the letter Whitman said that evening how
fond he was of Symonds, though they had not met, and referring to their
correspondence said:

About every three months he writes me, O the most beautiful
splendid letters; I dare not show them to anyone hardly, they
are so like those tete a tete interviews with your chum, your mate,
your comrade, who throws off everything — and that is the kind
of fellow Addington Symonds is.[30]

Another tangential method of homosexual denial which Whitman
used was his references to his children. Unprompted by any question-
ing by Bucke, Whitman in a letter to him just a week before the birthday
party, in mentioning his plans for his own burial house, added:

I wish to collect the remains of my parents and two or three other
near relations, and shall doubtless do so — I have two deceased
children (young man and woman — illigitimate of course) that
I much desired to bury here with me — but have ab't abandoned
the plan on acc't of angry litigation and fuss generally and dis-
interment f'm down south....[31]

In Bucke's reply, written a few days before he left for the party at
Camden, no mention is made of the above astounding disclosure. In a
life regarded by Bucke as the epitome of purity and moral elevation, such
a revelation would have been too upsetting so he simply blocked it out.
No corroborative evidence has ever been discovered that Whitman did
in fact sire any children.

When Bucke left for Canada after the party, he was accompanied by Traubel and Anne, his bride of two weeks. The Traubels stayed in London until June 14th, while Horace and Bucke discussed plans for another book on Whitman. Bucke also received the good news that his son and namesake, Maurice, had been appointed to a geological survey at $60 a month.

But, even more exciting was the progress with the "meter business". In February, the first machine-made meter had been assembled and seemed to work perfectly. Bucke subsequently sent by express several meters to England, and on June 18th he received a telegram that the meters had arrived and that arrangements were pending for testing them. Upon receipt of this news, he immediately began to make plans to go to England.

There were also other reasons for the voyage. Two of Whitman's most ardent disciples, who lived in Lancashire and who saw Bucke as Whitman's emissary, had extended a warm invitation to him to visit them. Dr. Johnston, a general practitioner in Bolton, Lancashire, had made the pilgrimage to Camden a year earlier. J.W. Wallace, who lived near Chorley, a few miles from Bolton, was planning to pay a visit to Whitman at the time of Bucke's return to America at the end of that summer.

A few years earlier, in January 1885, Wallace, then a thirty-one-year-old unmarried assistant architect, had lost his mother. They had had a close, essentially oedipal relationship. Her devotion and self-sacrificing goodness to her only son remained undiminished throughout a painful and debilitating malignancy, which gradually made her too weak to walk. When her husband was home he would carry her upstairs to her bed, otherwise she would crawl up the stairs, not permitting Wallace to carry her up for fear of his hurting himself. Eventually she became so weak that, in her husband's frequent absence, she had to allow her son to carry her; thereafter he always carried her. Her parting from him each night was almost more than he could bear.

Eleven days before she died Wallace went out to a late birthday party after having taken his mother upstairs. The same night he was awakened by his mother knocking on the wall, calling for water. He obliged, but inwardly grudgingly, and did not offer to get anything else for her. Thus guilt was added to the recipe of sadness and forlornness as the days passed. He spent more time with her than did her husband through this period, and was alone with her in the minutes before her death. Wallace then called his father, who arrived at the moment of death. Wallace cried out, "Thanks be to God that giveth us the victory."(CC, 340). It seemed to him that his mother's spirit nodded assent. He felt momentarily to be in the presence of an Infinite Love, and this illumination affected the rest of his life.

In the weeks that followed his friends dropped in to see him, and gradually began to make a practice of coming on Monday evenings. They decided to turn these evenings into discussions, not of current events, but of philosophical and literary interests.

Several of these young men were admirers of Whitman and they frequently read his poems and presented papers about his work. In 1887, Wallace and Dr. Johnson wrote a letter to Whitman, enclosing a small gift of money for his birthday. Whitman replied, and over the next few years the correspondence ripened, Whitman finally becoming the patron-saint of this group which referred to itself as "The College".

Whitman frequently forwarded these letters on to Bucke, and by 1890 Wallace and Bucke were corresponding directly. Wallace had given a paper to "The College" on the illumination he had experienced in the moments following his mother's death.(CC,340)

The meaning and the importance of this experience seemed to have escaped most of the members of "The College" [32]; it did not escape Bucke, to whom Wallace sent the "Address":

I *know* what you say is true — I have been myself for one instant (long ago and under entirely different circumstances) in the same divine presence and that instant did more towards lighting up my life than all the rest of my experiences put together — the value of W.W. is that he, more than any other man ever born, has had a more or less continuous life in that wonderful region — it pervades his book through and through.[33]

When Wallace learned that Bucke was planning to visit Lancashire in July 1891, he wrote Whitman that he considered the visit

a consecration of the life you have lived — an apostolic visit to the small church planted here. May God's blessing rest upon his visit and his Spirit be poured out upon us.[34]

Bucke was not disappointed at his reception. After disembarking at

Liverpool on July 17th, he took the train to Bolton, where Johnston and Wallace met him. He accompanied Dr. Johnston as he made some house calls, and after dinner they returned to Dr. Johnston's home where some fourteen men were waiting to greet him. The evening was spent in talks, songs and recitations; Bucke said he laughed and enjoyed himself.[35] Well he might, for these Lancashire disciples saw him as their link with the great man. It was a pep rally such as Bucke had never experienced before. They had even written words to the Welsh national air which they sang with the fervour of the committed. Entitled "The College Welcome to Dr. Bucke", it went:

> Comrade-stranger! Glad we greet you,
> One and all are pleased to meet you,
> Cordial friendship here shall treat you,
>   Whilst with us you stay.
> Friend of Walt! Be that the token,
> That enough our hearts to open,
> Though no other words be spoken
>   Friends are we always.
> Friendship let us treasure,
> Love to greater measure,
> Comrades true our journey through:
> Life's thus made a pleasure.
> Hail! to Whitman, lover's poet!
> Here's his portrait, all well know it,
> To the world we gladly show it —
>   Proud his friends to be.
> Doctor Bucke! Walt's brave defender,
> Thanks to you we gladly tender,
> Noble service did you render
>   To our hero's fame.
> You, his chosen "explicator",
> "Leaves of Grass's" indicator,
> You, his life's great vindicator —
>   Honoured be your name!
> Health to Walt and glory
> Long live the poet hoary
> Noble life through peace and strife,

Immortal be his story!
Let us cherish his example,
Kind, heroic, broad and ample,
Be our lives of his a sample,
Worthy friends prove we![36]

On the following day, several of the College's members went into the country for a picnic. In pastoral surroundings Bucke read them an essay on Whitman which he had written. Wallace responded with a speech in praise of Bucke. There were more conversations and visits, and on July 19th and 20th letters arrived from Whitman and Traubel. These were read aloud before Bucke departed for London by train with a promise to return to Lancashire for a few days before sailing home.

In London, Bucke stayed with Buxton Forman and his wife Laura at their home in St. John's Wood, and occupied himself with attempts to promote the meter business. Nothing definite was accomplished, but Bucke was philosophical and saw the visit as paving the way for future deals. He spent some time preparing a lecture he was to give at McGill in October, and worked at the British Museum with one R.M. Bain translating a Danish essay on Whitman into English; this was subsequently published as part of a collection after Whitman's death.[37]

But the highlight of this part of his trip was Bucke's visit with Lord Tennyson at his home, Aldworth, in Haslemere, Surrey. When Bucke mentioned to Whitman this hope of meeting the poet-laureate, Whitman sent Bucke on June 26th an introductory letter:

If you are feeling well enough and in opportune mood let me introduce my good friend and physician Dr. Bucke — He is Superintendent (Medical and other) of the big Insane Canadian Asylum at London, Ontario — is an Englishman born but raised (as we say it) in America. I still stick out here in the land of the living but pretty tough pulling most of the time....[38]

At the time Bucke was spending the weekend with friends, Robert Pearsall Smith and his wife, who lived only a few miles from Tennyson. On Sunday, August 9th, Mr. Smith and a driver delivered Bucke at Aldworth at 4:00 p.m. A footman answered the door and took Bucke's letter of introduction. A few minutes later the footman directed him into a reception room where Hallam Tennyson, the poet's son, appeared. Hallam was friendly and asked Bucke if he would wait until Tennyson awakened after his afternoon nap. Bucke, of course, said that he would, and after a few desultory remarks Hallam asked if he would like to meet his mother. After the expected assent he led him into another room where the valetudinarian Lady Tennyson lay on a couch. They talked about Canadian politics, including the death of Sir John A. MacDonald. Lady Tennyson, an unabashed Conservative, noted that Sir John A. had not replied to a telegram Tennyson sent him on the occasion of his last successful election. Bucke was tactful in suggesting that Sir John might not have been well, but certainly he did not reveal his own Liberal allegiance.

Bucke was soon led into another room by Hallam and introduced to the poet. The latter was perusing Whitman's note of introduction, turning it in his hand, puzzled by the heading:

From the Boston Evening Transcript, May 7, 91.

— The Epictetus saying, as given by Walt Whitman in his own quite utterly dilapidated physical case, is, a "little spark of soul dragging a great lummux of corpse-body clumsily to and fro around".[39]

Bucke held back an impulse to laugh. Tennyson wondered why Whitman used such note paper and thought it very American. That was the closest they came to humour, and almost the closest they came to the subject of Whitman. In a most uncharacteristic way, Bucke did not steer the conversation to Whitman or to *Leaves of Grass*. Tennyson did comment later, "Whitman is still unlabelled: that's a good thing about him;" and "Whitman is immense but I cannot make him out."[40]

Bucke felt that if Tennyson had been asked within ten minutes of the beginning of their conversation why Bucke had been received, he would not have known.[41]

Tennyson had a copy of Carpenter's *The Permanent Elements of Religion* sitting on the table beside him. When asked about it, the poet said he had not yet read the book, and that perhaps the author, who had visited him a few days earlier, had left it.[42] This led to a discussion of immortality, a subject dear to Bucke's heart. Tennyson seemed more uncertain about it and asked Bucke several times, "So you feel sure — quite sure — do you?"[43]

The conversation turned back briefly to Whitman when Tennyson asked, "Do you tell me that Whitman himself is quite convinced that he will survive this life with his identity preserved?"[44]

Bucke replied, "Quite, quite. I never knew any man more firmly convinced of anything."[45]

Tennyson took it up, "How extraordinary! How fine!"[46]

This visit with the most famous literary figure of the day gave Bucke wings, later commenting that he needed no carriage to take him back to the Smiths.

On August 24th he arrived back in Bolton and related his Tennyson experience to Dr. Johnston. In the evening, the College met at a restaurant, where there was another round of readings, culminating in a twenty-minute speech by Bucke, described as "by far the most important and the weightiest he has yet delivered himself of here."[47] Finally, there were songs to bid farewell to Bucke and bon voyage to J.W. Wallace, who was also going to America to pay homage to Whitman. The enthusiastic acolytes sang out these words to Bucke, who must have begun to feel his dream starting to come true.

> Glad are we Canadian frien'
> Once again yer face to see;
> Fain is ilka college boy
> Once again tae welcome ye.
> Fast draws nigh the fatal day
> When alas! We'll pairted be;
> When between us braid we'll roll
> League on league o' billowy sea.
> *Chorus*: Will ye no' come back again?
> Laith are we tae let you gang;
> Sweet tae us has been yer stay;
> Cherished will its memory be
> In oor herts for mony a day
> Oh! may gentle, favoring winds
> Waft ye o'er the ocean vast!
> May Good Fortune ye attend,
> Land ye safely hame at last!
> Soon ye'll see oor frien o' friens,
> Soon ye'll in his presence stand,

Gaze upon his noble face,
Grasp him warmly by the hand.
Tak tae him the warmest love
O'oor herts, devoted true!
Be oor messenger o' cheer,
And God's blessing gang wi oou!![48]

On August 26th, Bucke and Wallace were accompanied to the train station by most of the admirers in "The College". Some, including Dr. Johnston, went on to Liverpool and saw them embark. Wallace had been unable to get a passage on the *Majestic* with Bucke, but sailed the same day on the *British Prince*. Bucke considered his trip a great success, in spite of the lack of any real progress in promoting the meter. So enthralled was he with the overwhelming admiration of this Lancashire pocket of disciples that he wrote Traubel while there:

I am more than ever (if that is possible) convinced that we are right at the centre of the largest thing of these late centuries. It is a great privilege and will be ages from now a great glory to us.[49]

The *Majestic* docked in New York on September 2nd. After spending a day with his New York patent lawyer, John Dane, Bucke travelled to Camden. When the *British Prince* arrived in Philadelphia on September 8th, Bucke, together with Traubel and Whitman's nurse, Warren Fitzinger, were waiting for Wallace. Traubel departed for work, Fitzinger returned at once to Camden to inform Whitman of Wallace's arrival, while Bucke took the new visitor to dinner in Philadelphia.

After dinner they took the ferry to Camden, then a cab to Mickle Street. They found Whitman upstairs. Wallace, like Bucke thirteen years earlier, was about to have one of the most important experiences of his life.

Whitman satisfied some deep need in his admirers. His composure, his personal magnetism and, indeed, his interest in those who surrounded him, flattered his coterie of followers who often came in times of personal crisis, already inspired by the liberating message of *Leaves of Grass*. Wallace was certainly no exception. Although his illumination at the moment of his mother's death had given him a sense of peace, he had not resolved his feelings about her and continued to be troubled.

After the initial friendly greetings, Bucke and Traubel began a prolonged conversation about Canadian politics. Whitman, who seemed tired, did not take part in it, but sat quietly and seemed pre-occupied. During this period, Wallace was free to gaze upon his hero and soak himself in his impressions of Whitman's appearance, which he described as noble and pensively majestic:

> One who has had long and intimate experience of all human sorrows and full of a profound and wistful tenderness and compassion; but it was also that of one who is visibly clothed with immortality, sharing to the full the limitations of our mortal life and yet ranging in works beyond our ken.[50]

While so absorbed, Wallace found himself taken by surprise:

> But quite suddenly there came into my mind what I can only describe as a most vivid consciousness of the presence with us of my mother, who had died six and a half years before. I seemed to see her mentally with perfect clearness, her face radiant with the joy of our realized communion and with more than its old expression of sweetness and love, and to feel myself enwrapped in and penetrated by her living and palpitating presence. I record it here because it seemed equally indubitable that Walt was somehow the link between us, and as if his presence had made the experience possible.[51]

The identification of his feelings toward his dead mother and his living hero, the prophet-poet, was therapeutic for Wallace, as similar feelings had been for many others, including Bucke. It is not difficult to understand the profound effect of meeting an idealized guru, whose literary message had the exhilarating power of emancipation, and finding him capable of satisfying the deep longing for love and acceptance.

Bucke himself had made a great impression on Wallace. He had come to the group in Lancashire as Whitman's disciple and had acquitted himself well, catalyzing their enthusiasm for Whitman. In the opening moments of Wallace's first meeting with Whitman, he found himself comparing the two:

Walt himself was hardly more simple and unaffected in his inter-
course with all classes of people than was Bucke. It was very
interesting to see them together. Bucke tall and powerful in physique, robust and virile, easy and unaffected in manner, and
direct almost to bluntness in speech, his voice strong and slightly
harsh, and addressing Walt, for all his profound reverence for
him, with the careless ease and frankness of an equal comrade.
Walt, originally robust and powerful as he, now grown old and
feeble, presented a striking contrast with Bucke's more exclusively masculine nature by his exquisitely delicate sensitiveness,
his gentleness and refinement of speech and manner, and also
by his deep and sympathetic tenderness, ''maternal as well as
paternal''.[52]

On September 10th, after a two-day visit, Wallace travelled with
Bucke to London where he stayed for eighteen days. They were met at
the station by Bucke's son Pardee, Dr. Beemer, Bucke's assistant administrator, and Mr. Sippi, the business manager of the asylum. When they
reached the asylum in the moonlit evening, a band was playing on the
lawn and a crowd of friends and relatives were waiting to welcome Bucke
home. He strode from group to group shaking hands for half an hour
until the band played the National Anthem and the family went inside.

Any small disappointment Bucke may have felt at the negligible progress in the marketing of the water meter in England was erased by the
triumphs of his reception by ''The College'', his interview with the poet-
laureate and his visits with Whitman, whom he thought looked better
than he had for three years.[53]

Wallace spent much of his visit with Bucke going on ward rounds,
driving into town to see the fledgling operations of the Gurd Water Meter
Co. and getting to know the Bucke family, of which all seven children
with the exception of Maurice were at home that September.

Wallace left on the 28th for a second visit to Camden before returning to England, while Bucke with his wife journeyed to Montreal, where
he was to give a lecture to the McGill Faculty and medical students on
October 1. The subject, the ''Value of the Study of Medicine'', was as
thoughtful and stimulating then as it is nearly a hundred years later. This
was one of Bucke's wiser addresses and unique in its lack of any reference to Whitman apart from a short, apt and unnamed quotation. He

began with warm reminiscences of some of his professors when he had sat in those same seats for the first time nearly a third of a century earlier. He said, with considerable insight, nourished by his previous mystical experience, that although medicine would continue to advance, it would never get any nearer to absolute knowledge than it had been from the beginning. But the struggle would always continue:

urge and urge and urge
Always the procreant urge of the world.[54]

Conventional belief, Bucke said, saw the value of the study of medicine in enabling the physician to cure the few diseases that could be cured, to ease the suffering caused by those that could not be cured and to guide the patient through disorders that were self-limiting; it was from the last that the physician derived his income and his reputation. All of this, Bucke went on, was but trivial compared to the value of the study of medicine in preventing disease. He gave as examples the control of plague, cholera and smallpox. He prophesied that in the course of the next century the bacterial infectious diseases would be eliminated in all civilized countries. He also felt that as knowledge of anatomy and physiology increased, certain harmful social customs would be eliminated. The two he mentioned were alcohol and lacing. Although tight lacing of women's dresses and the use of corsets gradually disappeared, it was not because of a greater awareness of supposed harmful effects but because of changes in fashion. Replacement by cosmetics and hair dyes would have been unlikely to please him.

But there was an even more important function of medical science than the prevention of disease. Man is naturally indolent, he said, and had he not been driven by fear of disease and death, he would have remained as ignorant of himself and the world around him as he had been ten thousand years ago. Although man's immediate purpose has been to detect disease, he has achieved something far more valuable than what he was seeking; he has come to understand himself and, by extension, the world in which he lives. For example, to understand the eye in order to treat its diseases, he has to understand the laws of optics, which involves the study of light. Further, as man is the highest form of life, and since ontogeny recapitulates phylogeny, the study of man must include the study of all lower forms of life. Thus, anatomically, physiologically and biochemically the study of medicine had been, and would continue to be, a study of all life and the forces surrounding it including, of course, the mental and emotional.

But the main value of the study of medicine is yet something else. In the closing part of his lecture he considered the hierarchy of sciences which as a young man he had learned from Auguste Comte. Mathematics, the foundation, precedes astronomy, as astronomy must precede physics; then come chemistry, biology and psychology. The mind is an offshoot of the body and depends upon the body for its existence, so the laws governing the former must have some kindred relationship with the laws governing the latter. Similarly, psychology has led to the new science of sociology. Medicine is the key to understanding these last two disciplines, which Bucke believed to be the most interesting and important branches of human knowledge. They had led to important changes in the way human beings were treated, two examples being the insane and criminals. Bucke was a determinist in his views of these two categories. Their afflictions were inherited so that they were not responsible for their behaviour. Just as great progress has been made in the treatment of the insane — they were no longer tortured or mocked — so too in the future would criminals be treated more humanely. A criminal simply had a moral defect; he was no more responsible for his actions than a colourblind person was for his inability to distinguish red from green, or an idiot for his inability to add or subtract. Bucke foresaw the day when gallows, whip and jail would be obsolete, and society would find more humane ways of protecting itself from criminals. Medicine, therefore, through the Comptean historical hierarchy is

the origin and source of human enlightenment. It has been one of the principal agents in the enfranchisement of human thought. It has more than perhaps any other agency tended to and assisted in the ennoblement of man.[55]

Bucke concluded the address by exhorting the young medical students to join in the great work of his honoured profession:

Take off your coats then and buckle to it. The labor is great but not greater than the reward. Does it seem impossible to master so much and then advance beyond? Never think so. Resolve to achieve and you will achieve. Resolve to conquer and the victory is half won. At the least work, work while it is yet day with you; join in the good fight, the war for the liberation of the human soul. The enemy is not far to seek, he is close at hand, his name is ignorance, prejudice, superstition, it is for you, come fortune or misfortune, sorrow or joy, honor or dishonor, to spend your days in hand to hand strife with him.[56]

Thus Bucke's conception of the value of the study of medicine included the traditional view of the physician as healer, but it was grander than that. Medicine was a discipline that fostered the pursuit of the knowledge of man and his relationship with the world in every possible aspect — the view of the pure scientist; its noblest expression, however, would be to cultivate man's enlightenment in his relationship with other human beings, be they physically, emotionally or morally defective.

Creek Farm, the Bucke homestead in the 1840s — a sketch by Bucke's older brother, Dr. Edward Bucke

Dr. and Mrs. R.M. Bucke — wedding photograph, September 7, 1865

R.M. Bucke, circa 1879

Horace Traubel, circa 1888

Harry Buxton Forman, English editor and Bucke's longtime correspondent, circa 1892

Walt Whitman, London, Ontario, 1880

— Chapter 12 —

Whitman's Death

DURING THE remainder of 1891 Bucke's anxiety about Whitman's condition continued to mount. His virtually daily letters to Traubel expressed repeated concern for Whitman's suffering and his own feelings of despair and helplessness, intensified by his distance from Camden. He made occasional medical suggestions, such as advising a water bed to lessen the patient's discomfort. Bucke was also worried over the arrangements Whitman had made concerning the tomb for himself and several members of his family.[1,2]

Whitman had engaged Reinhalter & Co. to construct a tomb in Harleigh Cemetery just outside Camden. The agreed-upon price had been $4000.[3] Whitman had paid $1500, but upon completion of the tomb on October 27th the company requested the remainder of the money. Whitman felt that $3000 was realistic, and both Traubel and Harned believed that the company's demand was exorbitant. The controversy was eventually settled in Whitman's favour the following February.

Bucke was not downcast by these concerns about Whitman, however. He wrote Traubel:

I am fighting along — lectures, meter, sick doctors, work, work, work but I seem to thrive on it.[4]

He also was persuaded by his daughter Clare, twenty-one, to give a ball, and on November 13th over 200 people were entertained until three in the morning. "It was generally allowed to be the prettiest and most enjoyable party ever given in London."[5]

In spite of the demands made on him, lecturing regularly to the medical students, carrying out his routine administrative duties and his almost daily correspondence with either Traubel or Whitman, Bucke continued to read material on the Bacon-Shakespeare controversy. Referring to Francis Bacon's *History of Henry VII* and Shakespeare's *Henry VIII*, Bucke said in a letter to Whitman, "I will bet money the same man wrote them both."[6]

After Whitman replied to Bucke to "hold y'r horses ab't the Shakespear-Bacon point,"[7] Bucke reassured Whitman in a most uncharacteristically tentative way:

In this S-B matter it is the *speculation* that I enjoy — I am not too anxious to be sure — in one sense to be sure would spoil the fun.[8]

Bucke may simply have deceived himself it was the speculation he enjoyed, and that lack of certainty would not trouble him. Certainly he was not deceiving Whitman about his need for absolutes, which Whitman sometimes found exasperating.

It was during this hectic autumn of 1891 that Bucke began to formulate more concretely the theme of *Cosmic Consciousness*: that the cosmic sense has been accessible to a few men over the centuries, that it is part of our evolutionary potential and that Whitman represented its highest expression to date.

When Bucke visited Camden on December 21st, Whitman was too ill for talk. He had developed the clinical signs of bronchopneumonia, he had "the death rattle" and Bucke felt the end was imminent. Bucke remained in Camden over Christmas. Miraculously, on December 27th Whitman's condition improved, and Bucke reluctantly left for Canada. His clinical diagnosis, based on Whitman's left-sided abdominal pain, his wasting and the difficulty with his bowels, was cancer of the descending colon[9]; the pneumonia was simply a complication resulting from feebleness and chronic illness.

During the next three months Bucke wrote Traubel nearly every day, though his correspondence with Whitman had ceased. In every letter he asked Traubel to remind Whitman that he was never out of his thoughts and that his gaze was fixed steadily on Camden.

In January a Mrs. Keller, who helped Warren Fitzinger look after Whitman, bypassed Traubel and wrote to Bucke, perhaps because he was a physician, concerning the dreadfully unsanitary state of the patient. There were bed bugs and nothing was clean, and she asked what could be done. Bucke suggested to Traubel that they raise $500 to clean up and renovate the room,[10] but was worried whether they could afford to pay Mrs. Keller as well. By February 4th Bucke had given up and settled for just soldiering on to the end, which he felt could not be far off.[11]

Bucke was still anxious to have Whitman's opinion about his concept of cosmic consciousness. He wrote to Traubel with many questions to be asked of Whitman: which year had Whitman become aware of the cosmic sense and had its arrival been accompanied by a sensation of physical illumination? Bucke went on to describe his sensations accompanying the arrival of cosmic consciousness, asking Traubel to find out from Whitman what he thought about it.[12]

Although the idea that "cosmic sense" might be a part of man's evolutionary equipment had been mentioned in a letter to Traubel a year earlier, presumably it was not discussed in Bucke's last real conversation with Whitman in September.[13] It seems strange that they had not raised the whole subject of mystical insight before. Had that been the case, many of the questions posed in the March 20th letter would have been unnecessary. It seems as if Bucke now felt a desperate need to do so as Whitman was fast fading. Whitman, of course, was far too ill to discuss philosophical matters or, indeed, anything else.

The long awaited telegram arrived on March 26th:

Walt has just died — 6:43 — come at once.[14]

Bucke took the next train to Philadelphia and stayed on until after the funeral. An autopsy, for which Whitman had given consent some months earlier, was carried out on March 27th. There were surprises. A huge left pleural effusion containing three-and-a-half quarts of fluid was found. The left lung was completely collapsed and the right upper and middle lobes were completely consolidated. The cause of these findings was clear from the tubercles found, including a tubercular abscess

which had eroded the left fifth rib and one in the breast bone which had
burrowed into the adjacent pectoralis major muscle. In addition, there
was widespread tuberculous peritonitis, which accounted for the long
standing abdominal pain.[15] Dr. Longacre, who had been Whitman's main
physician, was very honest in admitting that he missed such a large
pleural effusion. He gave two reasons for the error: the lack of complaint
of pain and his disinclination to disturb the patient with a really thorough examination. The heart was enlarged but there was no valvular disease; perhaps hypertension had caused the 1873 stroke. Since the
sphygmomanometer was not yet in clinical use, the cause of the old stroke
remains uncertain.

Bucke's wish that the funeral be non-denominational was carried out.
Whitman's body was offered for public viewing at 328 Mickle Street after
11:00 a.m. In the afternoon the carriages made their way to Harleigh Cemetery where the coffin was deposited in a tent with the sides rolled up.
Those who were to speak sat on a raised platform. Quotations from Con-
fucius, Gautama and Jesus were read, and eulogies delivered by Harned,
Bucke and Colonel Ingersoll.

Bucke's address extolled Whitman's greatness and his own gratitude
to Whitman for the vision vouchsafed him:

This universe is not the hollow nutshell containing the rotten
kernel that so many make it. It is vital and infinite ("In vain I
try to think how infinite"). Infinite not in one way, or two ways,
but in an infinite number of ways. What! the universe not capable of satisfying our needs? On the contrary, we are capable of
feeling but a fraction of the wants that it is able to satisfy.

In this faith, learned from the friend whom we mourn, I rest
satisfied and at ease.[16]

Bucke did not mention the pain of his bereavement. In fact, he said:

That I am not overwhelmed and crushed, either by our loss or
by the gravity and greatness of the occasion, that I can stand
here and speak calmly of our great friend who is gone — is cause
of astonishment to myself, as it well may be to you.[17]

Thus ended a most unusual relationship between physician and poet, pupil and teacher, disciple and prophet, lover and beloved. It had begun in the winter of 1867-8 when Bucke had heard from his friend Sterry Hunt about Whitman.[18] Bucke acquired a copy of *Leaves of Grass* and struggled with it for several years, having difficulty understanding it, but absolutely convinced that those words had a message for him. Heroes may be disappointing in the flesh, but Bucke's admiration for the author during the first visit in 1877 exploded with a sudden transition from friendship to love. Whitman's vision had excited Bucke when he was a tired young practitioner living in intellectual isolation in a small town. Then, one spring evening three years later in England, Bucke had had a mystical experience, his only one, in which he believed he learned more in a few moments than during his previous years of study. This moment had occurred after an evening of reading poetry, especially Whitman. The triggering factors of such experiences are unknown, but most occur in solitude: Bucke's occurred while riding home in a carriage.

The emotional impact of *Leaves of Grass* and the mystical experience was catalytic. The third ingredient in this intoxicating recipe was the initial encounter five years later. Bucke's recollection of that first meeting had all the overtones of a blossoming love affair.[19]

I remember well how, like so many others, I was struck, almost amazed, by the beauty and majesty of his person and the gracious air of purity that surrounded and permeated him.... A sort of spiritual intoxication set in which did not reach its culmination for several weeks, and which, after continuing for some months, very gradually, in the course of the next few years, faded out.[20]

But unlike most love affairs, Bucke's needs were so completely filled that the affair never lost its intensity. There were other differences as well. Whitman was unaffected. Until his last years, Bucke was the irrepressible suitor and Whitman remained simply the flattered idol of a circle which increasingly included Bucke.

The relationship changed somewhat as a result of Whitman's three-month visit with Bucke in the summer of 1880. Bucke was by then writing his biography of Whitman, with the latter close at hand and willing to make substantial changes in the text. Whitman enjoyed the hospitality and in his recollections of that summer writes of the scenery, the asylum and his trip with Bucke up the Saguenay. Nearly a decade later, in his conversations with Traubel, he spoke fondly of his summer in Canada with Dr. *and* Mrs. Bucke, but by then his friendship with Bucke had deepened.

So enamoured of Whitman was Bucke that summer that he failed to notice Mrs. Bucke's lack of enthusiasm for the poet. It is unlikely that Jessie spoke directly of her antipathy, but her frequent and prolonged absences during that summer might have aroused at least the curiosity, if not the actual displeasure, of her husband. But we know that Bucke had not the slightest inkling of her feelings until her letter a year later. That important letter was written when she learned that her husband planned to have Whitman back for another visit. Bucke's reply, (*please see Chapter 7*) informs us of three important facts: Jessie did not wish Whitman to return, Bucke reluctantly acquiesced to that wish, at the same time explicitly ranking his primary allegiance to Whitman.[21]

Of the source of Jessie's feelings about Whitman we have no direct evidence. We do know that she, like most people of that time, did not appreciate his poetry. Her daughter Ina recalled years later her mother's comment to Bucke:

> Maurice, I cannot see all the beautiful things in Walt's writings that you see. It is the sweetness of your own mind that prevents you from seeing what is unpleasant in them.[22]

We don't know whether she found the style inaccessible or whether the sensuous passages were offensive. We don't even know how much she read — did she read "Calamus"? Would she have recognized the homoerotic content? Certainly some had, and with varying reactions. For many there was revulsion at the homosexual overtones, but for a few, such as the English writer John Addington Symonds, himself a despairing, repressed homosexual, they represented a hope that his own clandestine, tortured sexuality could find a legitimate outlet in the concept of comradeship expressed by Whitman in these poems. It was a forlorn hope, cruelly and dishonestly dashed by Whitman in the letter to Symonds, who had asked the poet obliquely about the scope of meaning of the term comradeship in the "Calamus" poems.

If Jessie's hypothetical objection to these poems was because of the sexual allusion to male comradeship, it is extremely unlikely she would have discussed this with her husband; the topic was simply not within the lexicon of Victorian marital discussion. But even if she had, the objection would have been deflected because Bucke himself was unable to see the homoerotic dimension of these poems. He certainly saw and approved of the healthy celebration of heterosexuality in the "Children of Adam" poems, though these too may have been offensive to Mrs. Bucke. We can only conjecture as to whether there was any conversation on this subject, but it is my opinion that there was not.

Perhaps Mrs. Bucke simply resented her husband's obsession with Whitman. She may have felt Whitman an intruder, absorbing much of her husband's precious time and energy. Or she may have sensed with a woman's deep intuition some hint of a sexual flavour in the relationship between the two men. Certainly this was never articulated, nor even perceived at a conscious level, but it may have smouldered far below her reach as an unrecognized dislike. And there is nothing to suggest her feelings were born simply of antipathy to Bucke's literary interest, because he had been a bibliophile long before he knew Whitman, indeed, before his marriage.

There is no evidence to suggest that Jessie's feelings resulted from an actual or perceived dislike of her by Whitman. When asked by Traubel several years later what he thought of Mrs. Bucke, Whitman replied,

She gives me the ideal of maternity. While not a striking woman in what are called intellectual matters she is a great mother — a noble mother. Do you know anything in all this universe superior to a noble mother? I have seen Mrs. Bucke and a group of children going about together there in London, and the manner of it all was to me most beautiful, convincing.(WWC, 2:66)

In the end we simply do not know. But we do know that Bucke, initially dumbfounded to learn of Jessie's wish not to have Whitman back, subsequently ignored it, and repeatedly mentioned to her that perhaps Walt would be coming later this year or next, and issued open invitations to him.

Does this tell us that Bucke did not care what Jessie thought and felt, and insensitively did just as he pleased? In most matters between them, Bucke seems to have been a considerate, solicitous husband who cared very much for his wife's happiness as far as he, constrained by the nature of a Victorian marriage, was capable. Certainly all the plans for holidays, except for the visits to her family in Sarnia, were made by him.

The Whitman coterie, with a very few exceptions like Mrs. Gilchrist, who was herself in love with the poet, was entirely male. But in an era characterized by men's clubs exclusive male friendships were common, and Bucke's failure to include Jessie in the Whitman circle may have been just part of the social custom. We can assume he invited her to join him on his frequent visits to Camden, as he suggests in letters to Whitman. The obvious conclusion is that Jessie refused to go.

Bucke's failure to take his wife's feelings into account where Whitman was concerned did not reflect a general insensitivity to her needs beyond the social norm of the day. It meant that she came second, fond and adoring husband that he was. Faced with the choice between her and the poet-prophet, in Bucke's estimation perhaps the greatest who had ever lived, it is certain Bucke would have cast his lot with eternity. After Damascus, family and personal matters seem trivial. But to become rich through the success of "the meter business" he saw as a means of liberating him to use all his energy in hastening the day when the world would be enlightened by Whitman's vision.

Far from diminishing, Bucke's long apprenticeship as a disciple grew more firm and resolute. This was partly because the balance of the relationship changed during Whitman's last years. Incarcerated by infirmity at his home, he felt dependent on Bucke who became not only his physician but an increasingly relentless correspondent and not infrequent visitor. Thus the balance of the friendship changed from the earlier days when Bucke was the pursuer. Although the prophet-disciple relationship remained unaltered, Whitman needed and appreciated Bucke more than in the early days. Bucke became less sycophantic towards Whitman, and of all the acolytes who surrounded the poet in his last years, Bucke could be the most candid with him.

The other reason for Bucke's tenacity of purpose in these last Whitman years was his increasing awareness that he, together with Traubel, would be immortalized as first generation disciples, perhaps as the earlier twelve were. Next to being the Messiah himself, there can be little else as heady as the knowledge that one has grasped the Message, not only from a first edition of the sacred text, but from the prophet himself. That sense of destiny was in Bucke's thoughts in the last years of Whitman's life, alloyed, however, with his anxiety over the poet's day-to-day physical miseries, his own uncertain future, and the equally uncertain future of the Gurd Water Meter Co.

Of the sexual texture of his feelings toward Whitman, Bucke's was not unlike the feelings of Alcibiades for Socrates, with the important difference that Alcibiades was aware of the sexual component of his total feelings for his hero while Bucke was not.[23] Nothing is known concerning his opinion on homosexuality, but it is likely he would have taken a negative view. He accepted the Victorian view that sexual activity outside of marriage was immoral and harmful, and he advocated physical measures to prevent male asylum patients from masturbating, believing the vice contributed to and aggravated their mental illness.[24]

Very little was written on the subject of homosexuality in the late nineteenth century medical literature. Havelock Ellis was to write a few years later in the preface to *Sexual Inversion*:

We may remember, indeed, that some fifteen years ago the total number of cases recorded in scientific literature scarcely equalled those of British race which I have obtained, and that before my first cases were published not a single British case, unconnected with the asylum or the prison, had ever been recorded.[25]

Thus it is not surprising that Bucke would remain oblivious to the sexual component of his feelings toward Whitman. But the shading was still there when, two years after Whitman's death, at the same restaurant in Philadelphia where he had given an address at Whitman's penultimate birthday party, he spoke at the organizational meeting of the Walt Whitman Fellowship:

When I think how many dozens of times, all seasons, for fifteen years, I afterwards crossed the same river, with the same purpose — to hold that hand, to look at that face and to listen to that noble and musical voice — and that now that is all over and past, forever gone; when I think of these things, I sometimes feel as if I should die outright, and end the matter, but that far down in me, somewhere, below clear consciousness, below thought, almost below feeling, there is a something that, speaking with absolute conviction, with supreme mastery over all

all the so-called facts of science and experience, tells me that when the right time comes I shall cross another Delaware and land at another City, and that then and there I shall take the same hand, look into the same eyes and listen once more to the same voice.[26]

These are the words of a bereaved lover, whose grief is mitigated and made bearable only by an unshakable belief in personal immortality. It was this same conviction of immortality which was to become central to his concept of cosmic consciousness. It was also this belief which sustained him seven years later following the tragic death of his oldest son Maurice.

—— Chapter 13 ——
Renewal of Interest in Silver and Gold

O N 30 MARCH 1892, the day of Whitman's funeral, Maurice Andrews Bucke came home from Toronto hoping for some paternal advice about his future. Learning that Bucke was in Camden, he wrote the same day asking his father whether he should go to British Columbia as a mining assayer.[1]

Young Maurice had graduated in mining engineering from the School of Practical Science in Toronto in the spring of 1890. He subsequently completed a course in assaying at the same school and had spent three summers as an assistant to a Mr. Ingall, Director of the Bureau of Mines, in Ottawa. The latter had encouraged him to go either to Kootenay or to the United States; Sudbury was a third possibility.

His decision made, by the middle of May, Maurice was in Nelson, British Columbia, looking for a location to set up shop as an assayer to the miners in the area. He was discouraged to learn that there were already two assayers in Nelson, two in nearby Ainsworth and one a few miles away at Slocan. He decided on Ainsworth and remained there for three months, living in a rented shack and obtaining the occasional assay. His food and rent cost $20 a month, which was more than he earned, so that he reluctantly included in his frequent letters to his father a request for $10, which was willingly sent along.

By August, Maurice had moved to Kaslo where the prospects seemed better, and as time passed he involved Bucke increasingly in decisions concerning investments in mining sites.

Bucke's enthusiasm was whetted by a letter from Maurice when he mentioned an assay containing substantial silver. Bucke replied:

> That assay you mention 15% silver 4364 oz. to the ton is wonderful. Never heard of such ore. Surely those fellows, whoever they are, have a big thing? But may be there is not much of it? In Nevada they used to think more of the WIDTH of the vein and the ease with which it could be mined than the richness — but 15% is wonderful.[2]

But Maurice found that in spite of frugal habits he could barely pay his room and board from the fees charged for sporadic assays. He was well aware of the mining possibilities in the area but, although he depended on his assay work to pay his bills, increasingly his energies were devoted to speculation.

The first excitement was the Golden Eagle Mine, 80 miles up the Duncan River, discovered in September 1892, by William Hazelton and six other men in the party. Another assayer in Nelson estimated the ore at $1170 per ton. One of the seven partners later gave Maurice a sample from near the Golden Eagle claim; it contained only $140 in gold, which slightly puzzled him. His scepticism was allayed when the partner said it was the poorest rock they could find in the whole ledge of the Golden Eagle.

Maurice became a partner in the mine when one of the original investors in a drunken state sold his seventh to a Tom Shearer for $10. Shearer, who needed money badly, sold the share to the eager young assayer for $200. Maurice soon had offers for his share but, upon hearing that Hazelton the discoverer would not sell his seventh for $15,000 decided to hang on. In fact, Maurice increased his holding by buying another seventh interest in January for $500. He wrote his father the next day asking him to send the money. Bucke was eager to comply and over the next several months followed every minute detail of Maurice's mining interests. In addition, he persuaded some other men in London, as well as Robert Gurd, to invest. Maurice was always completely honest with his father and the other "London men", and never recommended an investment which he did not believe to be sound.

The Golden Eagle group met and decided they should try and sell as early as possible in the coming season for $100,000 to $500,000, and agreed that no one would sell without the others.[3] By February 1893, Maurice was considering giving up assaying, as there was so little money in it. Bucke was very supportive of his son's speculations, both financially and philosophically. He was always able to straddle without difficulty the chasm between the mystic vision embodied in *Cosmic Consciousness*, on which he was then working, and the pragmatic focus of the capitalistic entrepreneur. His financial schemes, such as the water meter, were imaginative, but he declared simply and honestly that his motive was to make money. On 8 March 1893, he wrote Maurice:

I hope you will succeed in making money — for the possession of money (especially if made by oneself) has a great effect in bracing a man up. The money itself is a good thing but the effect on character is still more important. Taken wrongly money simply damns a man and is a curse to him.[4]

The Golden Eagle began its plummet on May 6th, when 20 or 30 lbs of ore brought back from the ledge were assayed and found to contain only a trace of gold. Maurice, as well as the others, hoped the sample had been taken from the wrong site. But in early June the group returned with another sample, which Maurice assayed and found without gold. He speculated to his father about what had happened. The initial sample found a few months earlier had been taken by a Blair Reno back to Kaslo for assay. He had stopped at the same hotel as a man named Abbey, described by Maurice as a "damn scoundrel". Abbey had brought rock into town which he claimed came from the nearby Duncan River, but which Maurice believed had come from California, and which was high in gold. Abbey was simply pumping interest in the Duncan River area. Maurice believed that Blair Reno unwittingly had the Abbey specimen assayed, believing it to be from Golden Eagle. He believed Reno was innocent because Reno subsequently turned down an offer to sell his share.

Bucke was again supportive and wrote Maurice on June 16th:

It looks as if the bottom had fallen out of G.E. You must not be discouraged. Keep up your spirits Old Fellow.[5]

The disappointment in Golden Eagle was mitigated by another promising speculation and into which Bucke invested money. In September 1892, three of Maurice's friends were staking claims in the Whitewater Basin area. Each staked a separate claim. McKenzie named his Whistler, McDonald's was Honeycombe and the third man Rice, who had sprained his ankle, had his staked for him and called it Snow Bird.[6] The tangled sequence of events that followed engulfed both Maurice and his father, who followed every turn in the flow of letters from Kaslo.

Not long after their return to Kaslo, Rice, his ankle now healed, went back to the Basin alone and claimed to have picked up a piece of rock from the Snow Bird ledge, which was assayed at 763 ounces of silver to the ton.[7] The Snow Bird ownership, besides Rice, included McKenzie, McDonald and a real estate man named Horrocks, who was also a friend of Maurice.

Maurice became interested in acquiring ownership upon learning that his close friend Martin McKenzie was confident they could obtain a $200,000 bond for Snow Bird. He learned that Rice, who had gone to Vancouver, was willing to sell his 11/48 share for $2000. The terms included immediate payment of $250, another $250 as soon as Bucke could raise the money in the east, $500 on July 1st and $1000 on October 1st. Maurice advised his father to take the deal himself, and by June to bring in outsiders from London to add the $1500 for the last two payments.

Bucke made a correction of the intent in Maurice's letter of January 26th, in which he had written, "Believe I can sell 1/2 my S.B. interest at $2000."[8] Bucke crossed out "my" and substituted "our", and quite correctly, too, as he had dispatched a cheque for $1000, half of which was for the first two instalments of $500 on Snow Bird, and half to pay for the additional seventh share Maurice had acquired of Golden Eagle in January 1893, a few months before its demise in May. Bucke himself had put up $333 and his brother-in-law and a friend the remaining $666. Maurice then manoeuvred to protect his father's investment. He traded 1/16 of his 2/7 share of Golden Eagle to Martin in exchange for 1/16 of Snow Bird. He then hoped to sell that 1/16 of Snow Bird together with his own 1/16 to a man named Hirsch for $2000 which would pay off the $2000 initial investment in Snow Bird and still hold a 1/8 share in the mine. By June 27th Bucke had sent another $500 for the next installment of Snow Bird. By that time Maurice had begun an attempt to find the Snow Bird ledge. In early June the snow was too deep, but in August he explored the Whitewater Basin for two weeks and was unable to find the ledge. Maurice also failed to track down Rice, whom he thought in desperation might have helped locate the site of the original sample. Repeated samples obtained subsequently by Martin and McKenzie from where Snow Bird was thought to be yielded very disappointing assays.

Maurice decided to return to London for a visit. Although his assay work had increased, his profit was small and the whole economic scene was volatile. Everyone seemed to feel that the next year would be better, but by the next year the mining action had often shifted somewhere else. Maurice knew a man who had built four different houses, but now could not sell one of them.[9]

In his letters to Maurice, Bucke described his own activities, including brief comments on the other children, his labours with *Cosmic Consciousness* and the undulating fortunes of the Gurd Gas and Water Meter Co.. Maurice was pessimistic about the company, frequently suggesting his father drop the whole matter and not invest any more of his money in it.[10] But in October 1893, Maurice was discouraged enough about his own prospects, with marginal assay profits, the collapse of the fraudulent Golden Eagle, and the elusive and slowly fading likelihood of success at Snow Bird, to ask Bucke to give him first refusal if a job should become available at the meter company.

Maurice arrived home on December 14th. It may well have been the happiest Christmas the Bucke family ever had. Bucke, recovering from Whitman's death, was busy at his book; Jessie had all the children home. Clare had returned from a visit to England in July. Will, aged 20, was at Huron College in London. Pardee, who had won a scholarship, returned home from Upper Canada College in Toronto to find many invitations to Christmas parties waiting for him.[11] The three youngest, Ina, Harold and Robert, were still at home. It was to be the last Christmas they were all together.

Maurice spent three and a half months in London, some of it in trying to merchandise the meters. The first order was placed, but apparently the meters were not ready, and Maurice seems to have shared Bucke's long-standing frustration with Robert Gurd's procrastination.[12] By mid-April he was back in British Columbia.

After Maurice's departure, Bucke began work on two important addresses he was to give in May in Philadelphia. The first was a lecture to the American Medico-Psychological Association on May 18th entitled

"Cosmic Consciousness". It contained his theory of the cosmic sense as a part of man's evolutionary equipment and gave several examples of men who had attained it. It was Bucke's first public utterance of the concept which he developed further in his last book, *Cosmic Consciousness*.

One of the examples he gave illustrating the characteristics of the illuminating moment was that of Saint Paul. Bucke was criticized by the Rev. M.P. Talling of London, Ontario, not for the theory itself, but for the analysis of the details. The example he took exception to was Saul's conversion. Among Bucke's criteria for defining an illumination was an inner sense of a bright light by the beholder. Rev. Talling pointed out that in the moment of Saul's illumination the light came from heaven, was objective, and was seen but not understood by the others accompanying him. Rev. Talling felt that the examples given by Bucke, such as Whitman, Dante and Shakespeare of the *Sonnets*, were men who possessed remarkable intellectual gifts, but that "intellectual illumination gives not knowledge of a different kind, but of the same kind, different in degree."[13]

Thus Rev. Talling demonstrated his inability to comprehend that illumination, as described by Bucke, brought knowledge of quite a different kind.

The second address was given on May 31st at the inaugural meeting of the Walt Whitman Fellowship, an association which embraced all persons interested in the life and work of Walt Whitman. Fifty-one people were present, and Bucke was elected one of the vice-presidents. He entitled his talk quite simply, "Memories of Walt Whitman". It was a résumé of his friendship with the poet, and contained the amatory paragraph quoted earlier which bespoke of his deep love for Whitman.[14]

Bucke attended several of these annual meetings and was elected president in 1897. In 1895 his paper, "Was Walt Whitman Mad?" was read in his absence by Thomas Harned, and subsequently was published three times.[15,16,17]

In the 1895 paper he began by listing his credentials. The audience was reminded that he had been Whitman's physician and had known him intimately, that he was the administrator of a large lunatic asylum and had made a special study of insanity. The approach he used was to describe the characteristics of degenerative insanity, and then to analyze whether Whitman exhibited any of them. The nine markers were 1) imperfect growth or evolution of the body, 2) asymmetry of parts of the body, 3) defects in the sense organs, 4) hallucinations, 5) defect of the intellect, 6) delusions, 7) defect of moral nature, 8) perversion of the moral nature and 9) lack of inhibition. An interesting list, which groups the psychoses with mental defective states, some of the latter well-known to be associated with congenital structural anomalies. In going through the characteristics, Bucke described Whitman as the handsomest man he had ever seen, and then added, surprisingly, that out of five thousand lunatics he had examined there was not a single handsome man or a beautiful woman. Schizophrenia does not in fact have any definite relationship with appearance, but it may have been that by the time Bucke's patients were psychotic and institutionalized their neglect of personal care obscured any favours nature might have bestowed. Pursuing the list, item by item, Bucke refuted the objection.

He concluded by observing that the truly great, such as Jesus, Blake and Balzac, were *often misunderstood*, in contrast to the merely great, such as Goethe, Milton or Wordsworth. The latter belonged to epochs, but the former made them.

Although the poet Edgar Fawcett did not attack Bucke's defence of Whitman's sanity, the published lecture led to Fawcett's asserting in the pages of Traubel's *The Conservator* that Whitman was not a poet at all.[18] A good, clean, healthy and attractive man, but not a poet. Naturally, Bucke jumped into a flurry of correspondence about Whitman's poetic merits. He retorted:

> Mr. Fawcett does not see in Whitman what we see.... We are differently made. That is all, and I should be sorry to claim that I am better made than Mr. Fawcett or any other honest man.[19]

Three months later Bucke felt compelled to pursue his rebuttal. He did so at two levels; the first, an amplification of his contention that aesthetic standard is a matter of taste. He quoted these lovely lines, though for some reason omitting a line:

> Each is not for its own sake;
> I say the whole earth, and all the stars in the sky, are for Religion's sake;
> I say no man has ever yet been half devout enough;
> [None has ever yet adored or worship'd half enough;]

None has begun to think how divine he himself is and how
certain the future is.
I say that the real and permanent grandeur of these
States must be their Religion;
Otherwise there is no real and permanent grandeur;
Nor character nor life worthy the name, without Religion,
Nor land nor men or women without Religion.[20]

If, claimed Bucke, Mr. Fawcett couldn't see the poetry contained in
those lines, so be it.
He then approached the difference in a more distinctly Buckean way.

But suppose ... the pupil comes to understand the master —
comes to see that he has means of knowing not possessed by
us all .... Then it may dawn upon him that passages such as
this have an extraordinary value — a value comparable, for
instance, to the splendid flashes of insight in the Epistles of Paul.[21]

So Fawcett's failure was not only an inadequate aesthetic lens, but
an even more severe deficiency, a failure to recognize something immeas-
urably greater than mere poet, that is, poet as prophet.
After Maurice's return to B.C. in the spring of 1894 Bucke, in addition to preparing the two Philadelphia lectures, was, as usual, absorbed
in many other ways. His views on the monarchy were expressed at that
time in a letter to his Bolton friend J.W. Wallace.

Should I live ten years longer I look to see immense changes
— the Lords must go — almost at once — the throne will soon
follow, the church must be disestablished *everywhere*. These
changes *will introduce* the revolution. When this really comes we
shall [see] nationalization of the mines, railways, land — the present useless and worse than useless drones who have too long
lived on the labor of others and have rewarded these others —
their betters — by affecting to look down upon them, — these
drones must work or die.[22]

A corollary of this theme, together with the long-confessed self-
abnegating tendencies of Canadians, formed the message of another let-

ter, a public one, written within a month of Britain's imperial zenith, Queen Victoria's diamond jubilee in 1897. Bucke chastized the periodical *Saturday Night* for feeling aggrieved that the Countess of Aberdeen, wife of the Governor General, looked down on Canadians.[23] Bucke exclaimed that Canadians deserved to be looked down upon as long as they believed that they had not among them as wise and noble men and women as are found in plenty among the English aristocracy. To admit inferiority was bad enough, but then to complain that the person set above us looks down upon us was surely stupid.

Actually, Bucke and Lady Aberdeen had been linked previously in the celebrated Shortis murder trial in the fall of 1895, when she demonstrated her ability to manipulate not only Canadians but the Governor General himself. (*Please see chapter 14.*)

Bucke's professional and recreational interests required great energy, but he was able to find a necessary respite on an island in Muskoka he first visited in 1892. It was in an inlet on the Severn River known as Gloucester Pool. It had been called Camping Island, but Bucke re-named it Liberty Island, and the house he built upon it, Liberty Hall. Quick to make use of whatever interested him, Bucke described the joys of nature and the superb fishing in a letter which appeared in the *London Daily News* on August 23rd, and which, four days later, he included in a letter to Maurice. The house itself was begun in 1894 by Will, Bucke's second son, then aged 21 and soon to become engaged (against his mother's wishes). Will and several carpenters built the house which was completed the following summer. Bucke had invited James Coyne, his St. Thomas friend and subsequently his first biographer, to Gloucester Pool in 1894.[24] However, Coyne was ill and didn't go, but Ann Traubel and her children spent the summer with the Bucke family in London and at Liberty Island. Following the vacation in August 1895, Bucke wrote a long article in *The Globe* once again describing the pleasures of life at Gloucester Pool. In addition to extolling the enjoyment of tales around the campfire on the shore and identifying the birds and insects, he was busy reading Whitman, Shakespeare, Dante, Plotinus and the philosopher Jacob Behmen. These names embraced three themes in which he was actively engaged: his Bacon-Shakespeare research, the search for historical figures who had achieved cosmic consciousness and his continued Whitman scholarship, soon to produce two volumes of which he would be editor. He ended the article with an echo from Ulysses' sailors who sang:

We will return no more; we have had enough of action; let us
swear an oath, and keep it, to live here always, like gods together,
careless of mankind, for surely this life of ease is more sweet than
toil; we will return no more; our island home is far removed from
the pains and miseries of life; let us rest, dear friends, we will
not labour more.[25]

It was reminiscent of his mood 33 years earlier when, as a young
physician doing post-graduate work, he abandoned himself to the romantic vision of *Westward Ho!*

At Gloucester Pool, Bucke continued his correspondence with
Maurice, following every detail of his son's varied successes and failures.
After his return to British Columbia Maurice had attempted to visit Snow
Bird but, due to the snow, he had to abandon the attempt; he never
returned. He obtained a job with Noble Five Mines for $75 a month and
board, to be responsible for assaying, surveying and sampling. His other
two mining interests at that time were Isis and Muzakadoka. He acquired
a half interest in the former and a quarter interest in the latter.[26] In September 1894, Maurice was exalted about the possibilities of Isis, two ledges
having been discovered carrying silver; he described them to Bucke in
technical detail.

When Maurice became ill in September he was hospitalized in New
Denver.[27] In describing his illness to his father his handwriting is weak,
he reveals his depression to his father, confessing his boredom with life
in Kaslo.[28]

Maurice was not in the least melancholy by nature, so that the
debilitating illness and the frustration of his unsuccessful speculations
fuelled his dark mood. By February 1895, Noble 5 Mines had closed down
and Maurice was out of a job.

Meanwhile, during 1894 and 1895, the stagnation of the meter business continued as a *leitmotif* to Bucke's distress over Maurice's failures.

—— Chapter 14 ——

The Shortis Trial

THE MONTH of relaxation Bucke enjoyed in August 1895 would be needed in October to meet the demands of the Shortis murder trial at which he gave evidence for the defence.

Valentine Shortis was the twenty-year-old only son of a wealthy Irish couple who had been sent to make his way in Canada. After drifting for a year he obtained a job in July 1894 in Valleyfield, near Montreal, as an assistant to Louis Simpson, who was the manager of the Montreal Cotton Co.. After a two-month trial period, Simpson was not impressed with Shortis' work and found another assistant, but allowed Shortis to stay on as an unpaid employee to learn more about the cotton business.

In December 1894, Shortis was arrested and brought before the same Mr. Simpson in his capacity of Justice of the Peace, for shooting at and frightening two mill workers. He was found guilty and fined $5. In January 1895, Shortis, at a meeting with a Bob McGuiness, an enemy of Simpson, offered to kill Simpson, if McGuiness would provide an alibi by saying that Shortis had been with him all evening. McGuiness declined.

On Friday, 1 March 1895, Shortis visited the cotton company where on alternate weeks a large shipment of money arrived for distribution to the employees the following Monday. In the office were four men sorting out the $12,000 into pay packets, when Shortis knocked on the door.

164

The men knew him, and he sat chatting with them as they continued their work. There was a loaded revolver in the drawer of the desk and Shortis, who was very fond of guns, asked if he could look at it. The man in charge said no, but Shortis persisted, saying he wanted to check the serial number. The man removed the shells and handed the gun to Shortis, who cleaned it and gave it back. The shells were replaced by one of the men, and they continued sorting the money. Suddenly Shortis grabbed the gun and fired at one man. Another ran for the telephone, and was shot dead. The remaining men jumped into the safe and closed the door. Shortis lit a fire and tried to smoke them out. The night watchman soon appeared on his normal rounds and Shortis killed him. By the time the police arrived two men were dead, one seriously injured, and two had saved themselves by hiding in the safe.

The trial took place in October in nearby Beauharnois; the issue was whether Shortis was responsible for his actions. He pleaded not guilty by reason of insanity, and Mr. Greenshields, his lawyer, said

That at the time of the commission of the act alleged in the indictment the prisoner was labouring under natural imbecility and disease of the mind to such an extent that rendered him incapable of appreciating the nature and quality of the act and of knowing that such an act was wrong; and was at the time suffering from unconsciousness and disease of mind by which a predetermination of his will was excluded; that he was in a state of madness and was insane.[1]

The defence had hired four psychiatrists, all well known, three of whom, including Bucke, had been called to give evidence for the defence ten years earlier at the trial of Louis Riel. The first witness was Dr. James Anglin, Assistant Medical Superintendent of the Verdun Protestant Asylum. His conclusion was that Shortis had all along suffered from a congenital imbecility which later became a "delusional insanity".

Macmaster, the prosecution lawyer then asked Anglin what he thought of this definition of an imbecile, and read from a book he had in front of him:

The idiot has not even animal intelligence. The imbecile is a step higher in the plane of instinct and knowing, but is little, if any, higher in these than a dog, elephant or chimpanzee, and is held not to be accountable because of mental deprivation.[2]

Dr. Anglin concluded that that definition would not cover Shortis, and that by that definition Shortis was certainly not imbecilic. Macmaster then let it be known that the definition was in a book written by one of the other defence psychiatrists, Dr. Daniel Clark.

Bucke was the last of the four to testify, and entered the witness box on Friday, October 18th, the sixteenth day of the trial. He had visited Shortis three times in his cell, and had written his daughter Ina a few days earlier:

Oct 13, 1895

Sweet Birdie

Your dear mother, sweet Johnie and your darling self will think "the old man" is never coming back again but he is after a while if he has any kind of luck. This Shortis case is the biggest fight I have ever seen in a court. Mr. Shortis is going to spend in the neighbourhood of from $30,000 to $50,000 to try to prevent the wretched boy being hanged not so much for the boy's sake (for he cares nothing about it and it really matters nothing at all to him whether he is hanged or not) but to avert the disgrace of having a murderer in the family. Just think if one of our boys had killed two men by accident (it really comes to that for Val Shortis knew nothing of what he was doing) and was likely to be hanged for it — think what we would all do to save him. Of course, the thing is not the same for Val S. is a hopeless imbecile and a lunatic — still our feeling in the matter would be very much the same as the feeling of Mr. and Mrs. Shortis now. I have become very much interested in the trial and while (of course) I shall not say a word beyond what the facts warrant I am very anxious that the poor wretch should not be convicted if it can be prevented by legitimate means.

I am, sweet birdie
Your loving father
R.M. Bucke.[3]

Bucke's evidence was similar to that of the other three psychiatrists. He felt that Shortis' hallucinations and delusions were expressions of imbecility, both moral and intellectual. Then, using terminology from *Cosmic Consciousness*, he said that Shortis had committed the murders in a state of simple consciousness, that is, in a state that precedes self-consciousness. He added, to the embarrassment of the defence:

> I attribute the killing only in a limited sense to impulse.[4]

On the strength of this gratuitous opinion Macmaster then cornered Bucke into conceding premeditation. In speaking of Shortis' delusion of persecution by Simpson, Bucke said:

> "I think Shortis would have liked to kill Mr. Simpson and also anyone he thought under Simpson's influence."
> "Then there was premeditation?" interposed Macmaster.
> "Undoubtedly there would have been," Bucke replied.[4]

Bucke also said that Shortis' inability to love his mother was an indication of moral imbecility. Both Mr. and Mrs. Shortis had come to Canada for the trial. Mrs. Shortis wept daily in court, but Shortis throughout the trial showed little emotion, did not look at her, and in response to a newspaper reporter who asked him how he was being treated, he replied:

> Splendid, but what a damn farce this is. I want some Pears soap. The soap I get here is all right for washing clothes, but not fit for a Christian.... By the way, will you send the Herald [newspaper], and tell mother, if you can get a word with her, to send me some more soap.[5]

Bucke testified later during the defence attorney's rebuttal, and reiterated that Shortis was insane and would never recover.

Once again Macmaster cross-examined Bucke and referred to Shortis' plot to kill Simpson; the interrogation went as follows:

Macmaster — "Assuming that Mr. McGuiness' evidence be true that the prisoner intended to shoot Simpson, and that he asked McGuiness to help him prove an alibi, what does it indicate to your mind?"

Bucke — "It indicates a certain amount of cunning."

Macmaster — "Do you think it indicates that the prisoner wanted to escape punishment for the crime?"

Bucke — "Yes, in case he committed the crime."

Macmaster — "Assuming the statement by Mr. Brophy to be true, that Shortis asked Brophy not to tell Hachette [the guarantor] the real character of the post office money order transaction, what inference would you draw from that circumstance?"

Bucke — "I consider that he saw it might have an unpleasant consequence, not necessarily that he knew it was wrong."

Macmaster — "Would not the natural inference be that he knew he was doing wrong?"

Bucke — "Yes, if the man was fully equipped mentally, it could only bear that construction."

Macmaster — "Do you think that when Shortis proposed to fill Simpson full of cold lead and asked McGuiness to swear an alibi that he knew that the killing of Simpson was murder?"

Bucke — "He probably had some suspicion of that kind."[6]

Thus, Macmaster in brilliant cross-examination introduced doubt in the jurors' minds that Shortis was incapable of appreciating the nature and quality of the act of homicide, and that he knew the act was wrong, the two prongs of the ruling in the Criminal Code at that time. Macmaster's final shot at Bucke brought up Dr. Clark's definition of imbecility again, and Bucke had to confess that he did not agree with his colleague's conception of that term.

It is surprising that such a brilliant lawyer as Macmaster did not attempt to further discredit the reliability of Bucke's evidence by bringing up some of the physician's most cherished beliefs. What would twelve ordinary citizens of Beauharnois think of someone who believed that an American poet was truly a Messiah, and as great or greater than Jesus Christ; or that Bacon wrote Shakespeare; or even the concept of cosmic consciousness itself.

Although in 1895 Bucke had not yet published on the Bacon-Shakespeare question, his views on Whitman and the theory of cosmic consciousness would have been available to Macmaster, who had read at least some of Bucke's writings. In his summary, Macmaster quoted from Bucke's 1891 address to the McGill medical faculty in a successful attempt to weaken the credibility of the psychiatrists' evidence in general, and of Bucke's in particular:

> In the first place, gentlemen, you know that Dr. Clarke, of Kingston, said that this man was a moral imbecile, and he described what a moral imbecile is. Dr. Bucke came into the box and said the same thing, that a moral imbecile had no morals, and he put the prisoner down as a moral imbecile. But what did I do? I picked up the lecture that he had delivered at McGill College in Montreal and I showed him where he had put down a man of the same description, as a criminal, and I read this passage from his own lecture: "a criminal [speaking broadly and roughly], is simply a person who was born with a defective moral nature".... Gentlemen, when a doctor comes down from London and delivers a lecture, an inaugural address before the learned men of McGill College in Montreal, and says that a man lacking in the moral sense is a criminal, not an imbecile, how can he come into this court and say he is an imbecile?[7]

When Bucke had delivered that lecture four years earlier, his intention in the above quotation was not to differentiate a criminal (a moral defective) from an imbecile (an intellectual defective) but to show in the conventional wisdom of that day the importance of heredity in the genesis of mental disease. He referred to both criminals and imbeciles as expressions of atavism, or reversion to a more primitive state and he drew the analogy of colour blindness as another example of the same phenomenon. The linking of heredity to insanity was the conventional psychiatric wisdom of that time, but it was the end of an era. In the following year, the German psychiatrist Emil Kraepelin published his new classification of mental disease and described the features of dementia praecox, later called schizophrenia. Moreover, Freud had analyzed his first dream in July 1895, and psychoanalysis was about to be born with its strong emphasis on environmental influences in the development of mental disease.

Shortis was clearly a case of paranoid schizophrenia. But, nearly a hundred years later, the outcome of murder trials involving a schizophrenic still hinges on whether the accused at the time of the murder was capable of being responsible for the crime.

Bucke did not stay for the jury address by the defence counsel, but returned to London exhausted, not only by the rigours of the trial, but by two days of sleepless travel. His arrival home was delayed when his horse ran away at the train station and smashed the buggy while his luggage was being collected.

The trial may have been over for Bucke, but it was certainly not over for Valentine Shortis. After the jury addresses by the prosecution and defence counsels and the charge to the jury by Judge Mathière, the jury found the prisoner guilty. In typical schizoid behaviour, Shortis showed no emotion and when the judge, his voice choked with feeling, announced the death sentence of hanging to be carried out on January 3rd, the Irish Shortis responded in a cockney accent:

> I wish to thank you, my Lord, for the kindness and considera-tion you have shown to me, and all the people connected with this honourable Court have given me whilst I have been here.[8]

With that, Shortis smiled broadly and walked calmly back to his cell.

But that drama was far from over. The next day the defence counsel announced his intention of petitioning the Minister of Justice, Sir Charles Hibbert Tupper, for commutation of the death sentence to life imprisonment.

Sir Charles Hibbert Tupper, son of Sir Charles Tupper, Bt., one of the Fathers of Confederation, had become a close friend of Lord Aberdeen, the Governor General, and his wife. Lady Aberdeen, who dominated her husband, was in favour of life imprisonment, but the decision was one to be made by the Cabinet. The Prime Minister, MacKenzie Bowell, was weak and indecisive and had had much difficulty in keeping his cabinet together. The cabinet met on December 24th with ten members present including the Prime Minister. The vote was split five to five, with both Bowell and Sir Hibbert voting for execution. Bowell appealed to the Governor General to make the decision but the latter was reluctant, and Sir Hibbert felt that Lord Aberdeen should cable London for constitutional advice, stating Sir Hibbert's view that the law should be allowed to take its course.

On December 28th, the cabinet met again with the original ten plus two additional members, one of whom was known to be in favour of commutation and one who would support Sir Hibbert. The vote was seven to five in favour of execution, so that one of the original ten had changed his mind in the interval.

On the following two days, December 29th and 30th, Lord Aberdeen talked with each of the cabinet ministers and with the Prime Minister. He attempted to persuade the ministers to change their mind. He succeeded in convincing Bowell to place a memo in front of the cabinet at a final meeting on Monday, December 30th, by which time the hangman had arrived in town to erect the scaffold. The memo asked for a recommendation to be made to Lord Aberdeen to commute the sentence to life imprisonment.

Lady Aberdeen also intervened directly by writing a note to Sir Hibbert the same morning, asking him to visit her and stating that

> there is an aspect of the matter which I want to lay before you in a very few words and so as friends, I ask you to come and hear this.[9]

What was said between Lady Aberdeen and Sir Hibbert is not known, though officially he had not changed his mind in the note he wrote as Minister of Justice later that day to Lord Aberdeen.

The cabinet met for the last time on the issue that evening. The vote came out six and six. Someone had switched from execution to life imprisonment. Whether it was Sir Hibbert, privately persuaded by Lady Aberdeen, is not known. But Bowell, after the locked vote, informed Lord Aberdeen, who made the decision to commute the sentence to life imprisonment.

Lady Aberdeen's crucial role in the Shortis affair had not ended and, indeed, would not be over for more than forty years. Although she left Canada in 1898, she returned more than once, having started a number of voluntary organizations in Canada, including the Victorian Order of Nurses and the National Council of Women.

In 1912 she wrote Mackenzie King, whom she had met in 1894 when he was a student at the University of Toronto, asking him if he could arrange to have Shortis transferred from the penitentiary to an asylum. After much investigation and correspondence Shortis was transferred in 1915 to the new asylum in Guelph. He was subsequently in Burwash, then back to Guelph, then to Penetanguishene and finally back to Kingston in 1936.

For some time after his conviction and imprisonment, Shortis' mental condition deteriorated, and by 1905 he was flagrantly psychotic with paranoid delusions. Gradually, however, over the years these and the other manifestations of his psychosis receded, and by 1936 he seemed perfectly sane and had been an exemplary inmate for some time.

Several people had lobbied for Shortis' release, including his mother, who visited him nearly yearly from Ireland until her death in 1907. Other friends wrote politicians, Ministers of Justice and Prime Ministers over the years. During these years, Lady Aberdeen's friendship with Mackenzie King deepened, in part due to their common interest in spiritualism, and they met in Canada and Britain from time to time. In January 1937, Lady Aberdeen passed on to Mackenzie King a long letter written to her asking her to support Shortis' release. King gave the letter and Lady Aberdeen's comments to Ernest Lapointe, the Minister of Justice, who recommended to the Governor General, Lord Tweedsmuir, that Shortis be released.

On 3 April 1937, after more than forty-two years of continuous confinement, Shortis was free. He lived in Toronto, exhibited no further signs of mental illness, and was successful in joining the Queen's Own Rifles regiment, where he must have felt very proud to have marched past King George VI and Queen Elizabeth during their visit to Toronto in 1939.

Thus Lady Aberdeen played a significant role in Canadian affairs intermittently for nearly half a century. In 1897, *Saturday Night* openly criticized her do-gooding efforts, such as raising money for the Victorian Order of Nurses, not because the project was not deemed worthwhile but because

> Success has been made difficult by the fact that the countess has shown that she must always be promoting something or emancipating someone.[10]

It was this carping editorial to which Bucke somewhat facetiously replied in the following issue (*Please see chapter 13*).

As for Bucke, he returned home from the Shortis trial exhausted; he sent a form letter to his many correspondents explaining his protracted absence, and letting them know that it might be weeks before he could give much attention to his private affairs. He must have been disappointed at the verdict of guilty, and one wonders how significant the skillful cross-examination had been in weakening the effect of the medical witnesses. Macmaster succeeded in establishing a lack of consensus among the psychiatrists as to what constituted moral imbecility, and planted serious doubt in the jurors' minds as to the alleged impulsive and unpremeditated nature of the murder.

Bucke must have been pleased when he learned of the commutation of the sentence to life imprisonment. But had he lived a hundred years he would have been absolutely astounded that Shortis by the time of his release had not exhibited any evidence of mental disorder for several years. Paranoid schizophrenia has a deservedly bad prognostic reputation; and very seldom does a patient abandon entirely his delusional system. Bucke and the other psychiatrists quite understandably described the patient's insanity as hopeless. Without the possible benefits of psychotherapy or psychotropic drugs, and with a good part of the four decades spent incarcerated in appalling conditions, Shortis' madness had gradually burned itself out.

Bucke would also have been surprised to know that Lady Aberdeen, whom he had criticized for her condescension to Canadians, had been instrumental in persuading her husband to commute the sentence, and that she may have influenced the Minister of Justice to change his vote, influenced the authorities to remove Shortis from a penitentiary to an asylum and, finally, more than four decades later, played a part in persuading Mackenzie King, then Prime Minister, to arrange for Shortis's freedom.

—— Chapter 15 ——

Death of a Son

In 1896 Bucke's energies were devoted to a continuation of familiar themes. On March 9th he wrote Harry Forman:

> The Gurd meter is to be made in the Eastern States almost at once — in the course of this year it should be on the market in America. As soon as it is I shall send samples to England. I fully expect to find Alfred out of the hole by means of it inside of a year or two. I dare say you will smile at these hopes and put them down as half crazy notions but you may find that there is a method in my lunacy and that I have not been working and worrying thirteen years without having SOMETHING ahead to work for.[1]

At the end of May, when he participated in the annual Walt Whitman Fellowship meeting in Boston, he was still in an optimistic mood about the meter; he said he expected his patent lawyer John Dane in New York to get some rich Americans interested in helping to finance the venture. At the annual Whitman reunion Bucke presented a paper entitled "Further Memories of Walt Whitman", which consisted of his recollections of Whitman in his last illness.

Work on his other two avocations continued; he pursued his collection of cases of cosmic consciousness and he began publishing articles in his attempt to prove that Bacon wrote the works of Shakespeare.[2]

The assertion that Bacon wrote Shakespeare originated in 1769 when Herbert Lawrence published an allegory, *The Life and Adventures of Common Sense*.[3] Bacon was really launched as Shakespeare in 1856 when Delia Bacon (no relation) wrote an article and followed it a year later with a 543-page volume devoted to the subject.[4]

Bucke was an outspoken Baconian and during the last decade of his life became increasingly involved in the controversy. In the end he felt he had made an important literary discovery. In his Bacon-Shakespeare endeavours he exhibited the qualities of a true believer; passionate espousal of the cause, a diligent and ongoing search for evidence to support the cause and adroit methods of refuting evidence not supporting the cause. Bucke exhibited these qualities most flagrantly in his use of Bacon's cipher to detect the hidden clues in Shakespeare's works that revealed Bacon as the author.

Bacon had devised his cipher as a young man in 1605 but did not give a detailed description of it until 1623.[5] Bucke interpreted this long period of silence as evidence that Bacon had not wished anyone to recognize his Shakespearean authorship until 1623, the year Shakespeare's first folio was published. Bucke spent countless hours after his day's labours poring over Shakespeare's works, including the cryptic dedication of the Sonnets and the inscription on Shakespeare's tombstone to find evidence that the cipher would unlock Bacon's secret as author of the whole Shakespeare *oeuvre*. He found what he had a need to find but in so doing he violated the two cardinal rules of cryptography: rigid avoidance of arbitrariness in decoding the cipher and refusal to accept a decoded message that was not absolutely clear and unambiguous. Not surprisingly, Whitman showed great understanding of Bucke when he mentioned to Traubel Bucke's obsession as a Baconian; "That's a little like Maurice — over emphasis is his failing — going off half-cocked as we say." (WWC,4:169)

Ultimately Bucke came to believe that Bacon was also the author of the works of Marlow and Montaigne. Even Harry Forman, for once, parted company with Bucke and disappointed the latter by chiding him for his attempt to show that Bacon was responsible for the whole canon of Elizabethan literature.[6]

But all of this did not diminish the intensity of Bucke's interest in Maurice's activities in British Columbia which he followed and participated in avidly with frequent letters. At the beginning of 1886 Maurice was employed by the Slocan Star Line Co. and had worked over Christmas which he celebrated with a Christmas pudding sent by his mother and his sister Clare.[7] His speculations now centred on a property named Isis which he and two others, Mackenzie and Horrocks, had purchased and subsequently leased to three other men. Horrocks had never paid for his share, so Maurice and Mackenzie re-staked the ground without him.[8] When Horrocks learned that the lessees had struck ore he demanded his share and threatened a court case. Maurice was optimistic about making a profit and stood to get 10% of the ore from the lessees, according to the arrangement, at no cost.

In the spring, Maurice learned that Kaslo was planning to introduce an electrical system and new water works, and that the mayor was considering offering him the position of engineer to the project.[9] The project was delayed, and when Maurice was actually offered the job in July he turned it down, as by then he had been approached by the English-owned British Columbia Development Company to work for them at $200 a month. He accepted the offer, and by September had set out on pack horse to explore property in East Kootenay and in the area near Spokane, Washington, travelling some 400 miles altogether.

By late October the season for searching for new mining property was over. The company suggested that Maurice stay on as superintendent of property it owned in the Okanagan Valley at $125 a month. He rejected this offer because the salary was low, and also because he found the British too slow.[10] He acquired a partner in November named William Trethewey who, as he advised his father, had more money than he could place. Although Bucke and Trethewey were both assayers, their primary interest was to find property for people interested in mining investment. Maurice had planned to return home for a visit he hoped would include Christmas. As it happened, he arrived in January 1897. He enjoyed long chats with Bucke about his future and spent some time looking both in London and Toronto for investors.[11]

But Bucke's letters to his son would have included much more than the latter's investment plans. His labours in attempting to prove that Bacon wrote Shakespeare were now public, and in 1897 he published six articles and letters on the subject;[12,13,14,15,16,17] some of these he subsequently sent to Maurice in British Columbia. He had also just finished editing a collection of letters which Whitman had written to Peter Doyle between the years 1868 and 1880.[18] The book was published in the spring of 1897 under the title *Calamus*, after the collection of poems which had appeared in the 1860 edition of *Leaves of Grass* celebrating, in some of Whitman's best poetry, comradeship in homoerotic imagery. Bucke did not allow himself to see the sexual dimension in these poems, nor did he see anything but Whitman's huge capacity for warmth, affection and compassion in the letters to Peter Doyle.

A great irony in Bucke's relationship with Whitman touches on this. Bucke, who was certainly heterosexual, was blind to the erotic component in the total texture of his feelings toward Whitman and was equally blind to the erotic flavour of Whitman's feelings to other men such as Peter Doyle. Whitman, on the other hand, homosexual though not confessed as such, displayed no trace of sexuality in his friendship with Bucke.

Bucke's preface to the letters consisted of two parts. The first, a repetition of innumerable previous speeches and writings, was his description of his first meeting with the poet and the impact the latter had had on him. The second part of the introduction was Peter Doyle's recollections of his friendship with Whitman, revised by Traubel, and derived from an interview Bucke and Traubel had had with him in 1895. Bucke prefaced Doyle's account by summarizing the Whitman-Doyle relationship from his own perspective:

> That the friendship existing between Walt Whitman and Peter Doyle was, as compared with the average sentiment that passes under that name, exceptional and remarkable there can be no doubt, but it does not seem at all clear that there was anything about it which was out of the regular and ordinary course when considered as a fact in the life of Whitman. The present editor possesses series of letters by the poet to other young men evincing nearly as great if not as great affection on his part, and that section of the Leaves named Calamus (written long before he knew Doyle) proves the existence of previous friendships at least equally warm and tender.[19]

Peter Doyle, in Traubel's version of their 1895 interview, then related how he had met Whitman in 1866 when he, an uneducated horse-car conductor in Washington, had had the poet as a passenger on a stormy night:

He was the only passenger, it was a lonely night, so I thought I would go in and talk with him. Something in me made me do it and something in him drew me that way. He used to say something in me had the same effect on him. Anyway, I went into the car. We were familiar at once — I put my hand on his knee — we understood. He did not get out at the end of the trip — in fact went all the way back with me.[20]

Whitman's concern and love for Peter Doyle are evident through out. For example, in 1869 Doyle had been suffering from an obstinate ringworm infection of the face which was resistant to the cauterization with silver nitrate. In a moment of despondency Doyle declared life with such an affliction was not worth living. Whitman wrote at that time:

My darling, if you are not well when I come back I will get a good room or two, and we will live together and devote our-selves altogether to the job of curing you, and making you stronger and healthier than ever. I have had this in mind but never broached it to you.[21]

The reviews of *Calamus* were mixed but generally favourable. One reviewer exclaimed that Whitman's executors had made no mistake in authorizing the publication of the letters, stating that it was scarcely neces-sary to add that Dr. Bucke's editorial work was well done.[22] Another reviewer, after acknowledging Bucke's disavowal in the preface that the letters "possessed none of the unusual merits belonging to the published specimens for this form of composition,"[23] went on to say that the book failed to offer the treat Dr. Bucke had promised, and was perhaps suc-cessful as a curiosity but was otherwise uninteresting.

Bucke was also preparing another volume of letters by Whitman, these written to his mother and brother from Washington between late 1862 and June 1864. Whitman had gone to Washington to see his brother who had been wounded in the cheek; he was unemployed at the time and had undertaken to act as a volunteer dresser at the hospitals in which some 50,000 soldiers lay sick and ill-cared for. For nearly two years Whitman visited the soldiers, writing letters for them to their families, bringing them cookies, books, plugs of tobacco and his own warmth and encouragement. The letters, describing the sick and Whitman's work, form the core of the collection which Bucke entitled *The Wound Dresser*. Most reviews were favourable, for example:

> [Whitman] did the things for them which no nurse or doctor could do and he seemed to leave a benediction at every cot as he passed along. The lights had gleamed for hours in the hospital that night before he left it, and as he took his way toward the door you could hear the voice of many a stricken hero calling, "Walt, Walt, Walt, come again."[24]

The one vitriolic review of *The Wound Dresser*, which appeared in *The American*, was brief and unkind:

> Dr. Bucke, one of the poet's literary executors, prefaces the ramshackle collection with candid avowal that the letters made no pretensions as literature. Their publication is as cruel to his literary repute as to the reader who is asked to feast on their compost of twaddle and "agonies".[25]

During Bucke's work on *The Wound Dresser*, Maurice left for the West, after having successfully raised some $50,000 for mining and property investment from a Toronto syndicate.[26] Maurice seemed better able to raise support for his projects than Bucke could muster for the meter company. Bucke was further frustrated to learn from John Dane in New York that he seemed unable for some reason to get an American patent.[27]

Bucke was named to two presidencies over the next three months. In March 1897, he was appointed President of the section of Psychology of the British Medical Association which was to meet in September in Montreal. On May 31st he was elected *in absentia* President of the Walt Whitman Fellowship at its annual meeting in Philadelphia.

Harry Buxton Forman was in America at the time for his long-planned trip which may well have taken him to Philadelphia. He spent the month of July initially at the London asylum, later on Liberty Island. The whole Bucke family with the exception of Maurice was there. Forman must have

form than substance, nevertheless occupied much emotional energy. Another obsession, the rapidly intensifying commitment to the Baconians in their assault on the Stratfordian faction in the authorship controversy, never led to a presidency. Had Bucke lived long enough, however, it is not unreasonable to believe he would have tried to gather the Baconians under a single roof.

Bucke's correspondence at this time included an angry open letter published in the June issue of *The Conservator*. It was directed at Edgar Fawcett, who had previously charged that Whitman's admirers did not "flock about him as he lay dying" in Camden in 1892.[37] In his reply, Bucke felt compelled to quantify the amount of support and concern Whitman received by listing the number of letters one of Whitman's friends, who lived in Camden, wrote to another friend who lived at a distance.[38] Bucke reported that he had written 214 letters in 1888, 148 in 1891 and during the last three months of Whitman's life, 176 letters. He added that the replies "from the distant friend" were just as numerous. Bucke ended the letter with a grandiose comparison which he would use when fervidly defending or extolling Whitman:

I could tell you of men and women who never saw Whitman, who knew nothing of him until his death, who love him with the same passionate affection that was bestowed upon him by his personal intimates. The men and women of whom I speak are not numerous as compared with the rest of the inhabitants of the earth, but they are as numerous, I will venture to say, as were the lovers of Jesus six years after *his* death. I will not say that Whitman's lovers are likely one day to be as numerous and powerful as are at present those of his crucified predecessor, but I will say that as far as I am able to see, and reasoning from one like instance to another, it seems to be probable that the modern poet will eventually have as large and as passionately affectionate a following as has today his elder brother.[39]

Bucke was also corresponding regularly at this time with Charles Nathan Elliot, an American writer and photographer, who lived in Ohio. Elliot had first written Bucke on 8 March 1897, telling him that as an admirer of *Leaves of Grass* he wondered if Bucke would send him an autographed note in a copy of his biography of Whitman. Bucke replied graciously the very next day and was soon sharing his excitement about the Bacon-Shakespeare controversy and his hopes for *Cosmic Consciousness* with his new friend and admirer, whom he later met in 1899.

But Bucke's most regular correspondence throughout this period was with his son. Although the Isis mine claim, of which Bucke was part owner, was found to be filled with water and its lease was given up by the Hazelton group, Maurice's fortunes were beginning to rise. He was asked to be consulting engineer to a mining company in Revelstoke [40] as well as acting foreman to the Slocan Star Mine.[41] He and his partner opened an office in Vancouver; it failed and the partnership with Trethewey was subsequently dissolved.[42] Maurice felt prosperous enough to send his father $100 which he suggested tentatively could be invested in meter stock but, as if on second thought, he rather encouraged Bucke simply to put it to his credit in a personal account.[43]

Maurice came east at the beginning of 1899, partly to visit his family but partly to raise money for mining speculation. He visited Toronto, Montreal and Saint John; he found a syndicate in New Brunswick upon which he could call for $100,000, after reporting on Bear Gulch mine in southwest Montana.[44] While in New Brunswick he also tried unsuccessfully to raise money for the meter company. Otherwise, his good fortune continued, and by June he was assured of the job of manager of all the working mines at or near Bear Gulch. His syndicate became part owners of the Bear Gulch Mining Company in Jardine, Montana. The major owner was a successful entrepreneur named Bush, who visited Dr. and Mrs. Bucke in October 1899, while on a trip East. Bucke found him very unstable, thought he might be paranoid or even suffering from neurosyphilis, and warned Maurice to be careful. Maurice took his father's advice, but respected Bush's ability to generate money and invest it successfully.[45]

Bucke had managed in 1899 to edit and publish his third Whitman book in as many years. As one of Whitman's literary executors, he had inherited large numbers of old boxes containing notes and fragments, some representing preliminary ideas or rough sketchings later incorporated into *Leaves of Grass*. He felt, quite rightly, that they might be of interest to future readers and scholars of Whitman's works. A request for subscriptions to defray the printing costs resulted in a poor response,[46] so in the end Bucke had 225 copies printed privately; the book was entitled *Notes and Fragments left by Walt Whitman*.

But all the events of 1899 were eclipsed by the sudden and tragic death of Maurice on December 8th. Only five days earlier he had written his father optimistically about his future and had enclosed a cheque for $100 for presents for his mother and his sisters, Ina and Clare.[47] While Maurice was travelling by coach in Jardine to catch a train back to Kaslo, the horse bolted and he was thrown out of the coach, struck his head, and died soon thereafter. Bucke's grief is not difficult to imagine. He managed to write a few lines to Forman three days later while still waiting for the body to arrive:

> He was as nearly perfect as a human being could be — loving — kind — gentle — wise — with a standing in his profession that old men might have envied.[48]

In October of that year, Bucke's new epistolary friendship with Charles Nathan Elliott ripened when the latter, with his little daughter Romaine, travelled from their home in Cincinnati to visit with the Buckes. Romaine was subsequently very ill with typhoid fever. A glimpse of Bucke's character shines through his letter of December 16th to Elliott:

> I cannot write much, my heart is very heavy. I want you to send me word every day or two (if it is only a P.C.) how Romaine is — tell your wife that she has my deep sympathy in this trial.[49]

After signing his name, Bucke added as a postscript, "We buried Maurice yesterday". He was never quite the same again, though he carried on stoically. His experience was similar to the crushing blow his old friend Osler would receive eighteen years later with the death in the battle of Ypres of his beloved son, Revere. Bucke was sustained by his belief in immortality and the conviction that he would be reunited with Maurice, poignantly expressed in the dedication to his son of his book *Cosmic Consciousness* exactly one year later.

Although Osler did not share Bucke's source of solace in a firm belief in reunion with his dead son through personal immortality,[50] they both found work a great anodyne. Moreover, Bucke's passionate interest in Bacon as the author of Shakespeare's works had been gaining momentum in the preceding six or seven years. On November 8th, exactly one month before Maurice's death, it reached a peak when, most unexpectedly while riding on a train, he discovered what he believed was the clue to the cipher needed to unlock the mystery of Shakespeare's dedication of the Sonnets.[51] Using the cipher, he was able to extract the name of Francis Bacon twice. Bucke interpreted this as meaning that Bacon dedicated the Sonnets to himself. This encoded message would seem like gibberish to the scientific cryptographer, but Bucke, with the biased eye of the committed, saw with great excitement that it fitted a part of the puzzle and led him to the continued scrutiny of all of Shakespeare's works for further evidence of hidden authorship.

Chapter 16

Bucke's Career as Psychiatrist

In 1877 Bucke had succeeded Dr. Henry Landor as the second superintendent of the new London asylum which had opened seven years earlier. He remained there until his death, and during those twenty-five years he introduced many changes in the management of the insane, some conventional and adopted concurrently elsewhere, but some highly controversial.

Although Bucke had consumed alcohol as a young man and had even occasionally been intoxicated, he abandoned its use personally and, as superintendent, gradually eliminated it as a mode of treatment for his patients. In this he was adopting current practice. In 1877 the Legislative Assembly of Ontario made it known that it did not approve of the use of alcohol medicinally for mental patients, and by the mid-1880s it was used very little.[1] In a lecture he gave in May 1888, to the London Young Men's Prohibition Club, Bucke summarized the change in policy over a fifteen-year period.[2]

		1872-76	1877-81;1882-87
Cost of alcohol/per patient	$3.50	3-1/2 cents	0
Number of patients treated in hospital	1,068	1,440	1,635
General death rate in hospital	5.5%	4.5%	4.35%
General recovery rate in hospital	37%	41%	45%

Bucke implied that the decline in death rate and the increase in recovery rate were related to the change in policy. Although theoretically this may have been so, we have already seen in Bucke's belief in the Baconian authorship issue his propensity to find what he was looking for and to fashion his rationale around it. This was most flagrant in his approval on the effect of gynecological operations in helping insane women.

Bucke has been credited with being the first to abolish the use of restraint in the treatment of the mentally disturbed, but this was not so. When he arrived at the asylum he made no objection to its use and, as Mitchinson has pointed out, he ordered six more restraint chairs.[3] Within a few years, however, Bucke, like other superintendents, was criticizing the use of restraint, and eventually abandoned it.

Bucke did initiate an open-door policy, to give patients a sense of freedom. He also introduced the use of female attendants in male wards, and found that "a greater tidiness in person, a greater activity in employment, and a general brightening of the condition of those in the male wards is perceptible."[4]

Bucke also developed occupational therapy by encouraging but not forcing patients to work constructively at the hospital. But the treatment of the insane remained basically custodial, while the cause of insanity was unknown. Bucke attempted to develop a theory and a classification of the causes of insanity, and in this he was much influenced by societal attitudes of the time. He introduced two radical forms of treatment; one, which was short-lived, at the beginning of his career in London; the other, in the last six years of his life, although successful in Bucke's eyes, was criticized at the time and discontinued after his death.

The first was a procedure which involved wiring of the penis to prevent masturbation. Bucke believed, like others of that time, that masturbation was a contributing factor to mental illness. The Victorians were hostile to *excessive* sexual activity, which they defined as any sexual activity outside of marriage including masturbation. Bucke got the idea of partially closing the prepuce with a suture from an article by a Scottish physician, Dr. Yellowlees.[5] The intention was to inhibit erection by the pain of the suture. In his first year as superintendent Bucke wired fifteen male patients.[6] In most of them masturbation continued and the procedure was discontinued; but in every instance in which the habit stopped Bucke claimed that mental improvement occurred. Mitchinson compared the medical records of these cases with Bucke's public report on the subject and discovered several discrepancies:

For example, Bucke claims that patient J.Z. had been prevented from masturbating and had mentally improved whereas the records show that there was an improvement in bodily health but nothing else. In patients J.D. and M.M., Bucke claimed the wiring prevented self-abuse and improved mental health but the records show that no change occurred at all.[7]

In spite of his claims, Bucke abandoned wiring altogether, and between 1877 and 1895 treatment at the London Insane Asylum was largely custodial and devoid of any specific therapeutic attempts. The few drugs which were used included opium, potassium bromide and chloral hydrate for sedation, and magnesium sulphate for seizures. The expenditure on drugs in 1887 was 0.6% of the annual cost of patient maintenance. Although medicine in general had gone through a phase of therapeutic nihilism, both medicine and surgery in the 1880s were beginning to emerge into the modern era. The stimulus in general medicine was the new understanding of bacterial diseases, and in surgery the introduction of antiseptic techniques. No comparable innovations affected psychiatry.

The therapeutic ethos at Bucke's asylum revolved around three types of activity: work, play and religion. The great majority of the patients contributed to the maintenance of the institution: the men worked on the farm, in the laundry or kitchen, and the women were engaged in sewing or helped in the kitchen and dining room.[8] Industrious, productive activity was seen as the cornerstone of treatment and reflected the Victorian concept of work as a virtue. This view was echoed in a lecture given to the graduating class at the University of Toronto by William Osler. Osler, in eloquent prose, enjoined the young graduates to find and cherish "The Master Word in Medicine", which was the simple four letter word — WORK.[9]

But the Victorian ethos also admonished that "all work and no play makes Jack a dull boy." Bucke was fortunate in having as his bursar Charles Sippi, a musician, who directed the asylum orchestra at weekly concerts and helped with productions by the Asylum Dramatic Club, which included citizens of London and the families of the medical officers. Constant encouragement backed up by a system of fines was imposed on those who did not come to the concerts.[10]

The third prong of the therapeutic trident was religion. Though Bucke himself was always anti-clerical and, as an adult, had never embraced orthodox Christianity, he had gone to church sporadically, more as a social custom, while practising in Sarnia. He recognized the need for an orthodox religious focus at the asylum, and Sunday morning services were held by rotation of Protestant clergymen of various denominations. It was such an occasion that Whitman described in his recollection of his 1880 visit to the London Asylum. Thus, in the absence of specific remedies for the insane, the approach was rational and a reflection of the values held by Victorian society. Although the important role of heredity in the genesis of insanity engendered therapeutic pessimism among alienists, a chink of light was visible. Insanity was associated with both poverty and anti-social behaviour, and the Victorians believed that honest, productive work, alloyed with the correct amount of leisure and coated with a respectable adherence to Christianity, was the key to a sane and happy life. The alienist, understandably, hoped that occupational therapy employing these ingredients might restore sanity and allow the patient to re-join society.

Although at the 1881 meeting of American asylum superintendents, which Bucke attended, entreaties were made for a more aggressive and scientific approach to institutional treatment of the insane, no real advances were made throughout the decade. At the 1894 meeting Weir Mitchell, a distinguished American neurologist who was known to have a poor opinion of American alienists, was invited to address the asylum superintendents. He refused at first, but then, reluctantly agreed to take on the task of rebuking them.[11] He criticized his audience for stagnating by remaining aloof from the mass of physicians. As administrators, business managers and custodians, it was small wonder they were mediocre physicians. The consequence, he pointed out, was that the treasure house of pathological material at their disposal was little used.[12]

Bucke was in the audience, and two days later, at the same meeting, he delivered his first lecture on cosmic consciousness. Though not offered as a mode of therapy for the insane, the concept could certainly not be considered either mediocre or stale. What Bucke thought of Weir Mitchell's scathing address is not known, but we do know that four years later to the day he delivered the presidential address, describing a bold and aggressive new mode of therapy. It was on 10 May 1898 that Bucke gave his lecture entitled "Surgery Among the Insane in Canada". Thus, eighteen years after his first and abortive attempt at aggressive treatment by "wiring" the penis, in February 1895 he began his second campaign. It was a concatenation of several factors that stimulated Bucke to consider gynecological procedures as a means of treating insane women.

The physiological theory that underlay Bucke's enthusiasm for gynecological surgery had its origin in the old belief that pathology in a specific organ might manifest itself as a symptom in another part of the body. Today, a century later, we know this to be true of many endocrine disorders as well as in cases of referred pain. In Bucke's time the connection was believed to be due to reflex nervous action, and Bucke himself had nearly twenty years earlier addressed the same association of asylum superintendents on the relationship of the sympathetic nervous system to man's emotions or moral nature. He had pointed out that the rich sympathetic nerve supply to the uterus was responsible for the female's greater intensity of feeling than the male's. It was only a short step to hypothesize that a diseased uterus could be responsible for aberrations of those intense feelings. This relationship also had the sanction of leading gynecologists. Alexander Skene had written in his *Medical Gynecology* (1895):

I take it for granted that all will agree that insanity is often caused by diseases of the procreative organs, and on the other hand, that mental derangement frequently disturbs the functions of other organs of the body, and modifies diseased action in them.

Either may be primary and causative, or secondary and resultant. In the literature of the past, we find the gynecologist pushing his claims so far as to lead a junior in medicine to believe that if the sexual organs of women were preserved in health, insanity would seldom occur among them.[13]

Whether Weir Mitchell's critical address spurred Bucke to more aggressive psychiatric treatment is not known; there is little doubt that the arrival at the London Asylum of Dr. A.T. Hobbs as assistant physician in February 1895, determined the timing of the new approach.

Bucke gave his first report on the results of gynecologic surgery in mental patients at the 1896 meeting of the asylum superintendents. He reported that surgery for diseased ovaries or uterus in thirty-four women had produced physical improvement or recovery in twenty-six, and mental improvement or recovery in twenty-one.[14] Many comments on the paper were favourable, a few critical. Dr. James Russell of Hamilton observed that the patients might have improved without the operation, that the improvement might have been due to extra nursing care, and that the follow-up period was brief and that relapse might be common. Bucke replied with caution that, indeed, the follow-up period was brief, but that the procedures had been carried out to improve or cure the diseased ovaries or uterus, and that the improvement in the patient's mental disease was simply an observation he had made.[15]

By the time of his presidential address in May 1898, the number of operations had increased to 109. Bucke had been well aware of opposition to the surgical approach to treatment of the insane: he announced that a request for funds for an infirmary to improve his treatment facilities had been turned down because "the government was advised by certain doctors that the work was unnecessary and in fact undesirable."[16]

This did not deter him. With political adroitness he had sent out to the 350 practitioners in southwestern Ontario a circular describing his work with Hobbs and a questionnaire asking if they thought the work should go on and whether the government should support the work by providing suitable buildings. He informed his audience that only two respondents actually opposed the work, and went on to say that the favourable responses resulted in a deputation to the government to support his cause. Bucke then proceeded to describe the favourable results in the 109 patients.

There was further opposition the following year when Dr. Clarke, the superintendent of the Kingston Asylum and with whom Bucke had acted as expert witness in the Shortis case, wrote to the inspector of hospitals, Mr. Christie, charging that Bucke and Hobbs had been soliciting support from the National Council of Women.[17] Christie replied sympathetically to Clarke but nothing more was done and the operations continued. Clarke's failure to criticize Bucke may have been a reluctance to condemn someone of Bucke's stature in the medical world, especially in view of the results of Bucke's questionnaire which appeared to give him the overwhelming support of rank and file practitioners.

By 1900, 228 patients had been operated on, some apparently more than once as a total of 409 operations were performed. The gynecologic diagnoses were:

Endometritis	29
Prolapsed uterus	68
Lacerated perineum	33
Lacerated cervix	29
Hypertrophied cervix	6
Retroverted uterus	15
Tumor	31
Unknown	17
TOTAL	228

Bucke reported that 66% of these patients recovered or improved mentally. These good results could be explained through the initial choice of patients with good psychiatric prognoses. For example, among the patients selected were few with delusional symptoms, known to carry a poor prognosis.[18] As the experiment had no controls, the placebo effect may also have been important. Finally, the special care and support surgical patients received might have contributed to the good outcome.

But an examination of the individual case notes reveals a significant discrepancy with the outcome Bucke reported. When the mental status after the post-operative follow-up period is tabulated, only 21% of the patients appear to have recovered or to have improved.[19]

Bucke was not dishonest but he tended to see what he wanted to see. He wanted to see psychiatric treatment vitalized, keeping pace with recent and dramatic advances in surgery and medicine. He gave evidence of this need in the concluding remarks of his presidential address. He felt that removal of diseased ovaries was the gynecologic procedure most likely to confer psychiatric benefit. He speculated on the reason for benefit, saying:

> It seems to me that the recent physiological theory of so-called internal secretion will furnish the clue that we want. According to this theory, there is a "normal and constant contribution of specific material by the reproductive glands to the blood or lymph and thus to the whole body". This contribution may be supplied or produced artificially, as by the daily injection of testicular juice, with very marked effect. But in case of disease of the organ that supplies it, it is not only liable to be changed to a pathological contribution and the internal secretion which was a source of health and energy to the whole economy to become a toxic agent of unknown but probably great virulence. The removal of the diseased ovaries would of course cut short this poisoning process and enable the vis medicatrix to re-establish the health of the individual.[20]

Bucke was framing his hypothesis in terms of the new science of endocrinology, which had already demonstrated the successful treatment of hypothyroidism by the administration of an extract of sheep thyroid glands.

It all ended abruptly when Dr. Hobbs resigned in 1901 to enter private practice. For reasons unknown, Bucke did not have him replaced and with his own death a year later the brief era of psycho-gynecology came to an end.

During this same period, Bucke had conceived a totally different approach to the treatment of mental illness. It was born of his conviction that the province contained many more mentally ill patients than those who found their way to the asylums, and his concern that the total number would increase inexorably as the population continued to swell, and so impose an unbearable burden on existing facilities. Rather than building additional expensive institutions, he formulated an imaginative plan for what could become a self-sufficient, therapeutic community stressing genuine rehabilitation, an idea decades ahead of its time.

In his 1896 Annual Report he included his suggestion for the "Care of a Certain Class of Lunatics".²¹ He proposed that the Provincial Government set aside an area of land approximately five to ten miles square and adjacent to a good-sized river like the Severn, having nearby in its course waterfalls and rapids. A portion of the land should be suitable for cultivation, some of it should have large tracts of pasturage for cattle, sheep and horses, and some should have clay for bricks and stone which could be quarried. The land should be within ten miles of a railway station and reasonably near navigable water.

The superintendent should be carefully selected for qualities of vision, courage, stamina and practicality, and, Bucke felt, should be young, no more than 35 or 40, and preferably non-medical. The next step would be to erect a few temporary buildings with lumber from the land. Upon completion, some 200 working patients, 150 men and 50 women, together with hired labour, would clear the land to make farms, gardens and roads.

For the first few years wood could be used for heating and cooking until waterpower could be harnessed to produce electricity. An electric railway could then be built from the executive building in the centre of the community to the nearest railway station. Within several years the community would become not only self-sufficient but might also produce excess for sale. Bucke estimated that the community should consist of 90% working and 10% non-productive patients. The latter would consist of epileptic and severely retarded individuals and patients who had not been successfully rehabilitated and who had become old and less able to work. He advised that the growth of the community should not be rapid, and concluded that it would probably not reach maturity for forty or fifty years.

Bucke saw it as a community without restraints, in which patients whose lives would otherwise be useless and miserable could become productive and fulfilling. This farsighted project was buried in government archives, and Bucke does not appear to have referred to it again. Perhaps if he had been twenty-five years younger, he might have pursued it with the determination he had brought to the other convictions that shaped his life. Bucke was an innovative nineteenth century alienist and administrator, but his lasting reputation owes nothing to his medical activities. Pelvic disease as a cause of insanity fell into disrepute, and by the time therapeutic communities, genuine psychiatric rehabilitation with half-way houses, and insight therapy catering to a whole new clientele had arrived, Bucke as a prototype nineteenth century psychiatrist was long forgotten. By contrast, his reputation as the original proponent of cosmic consciousness as part of our evolutionary equipment has continued to grow.

The Bucke family, December 1893. Left to right: Pardee (b.1875), Will (b.1873), Ina (b.1877), Jessie Bucke (b.1839), Robert, in front (b.1881), Maurice (b.1868), Harold (b.1879), Clare (b.1870) and R.M. Bucke (b. 1837)

Maurice Andrews Bucke, 1893

R.M. Bucke (1899) and Walt Whitman (1880)
whom Bucke emulated in many ways

R.M. Bucke and Romaine Elliott, 1899

The Bucke summer home on Liberty Island on the Severn River in Muskoka, Ontario, circa 1900

August 25, 1919: Horace Traubel, helped by George W. Morris and Colonel Cosgrove, on their way to the dedication of "Old Walt" at Bon Echo. In the background are Betty Bain and Anne Traubel.

Crossing The Narrows of Lake Mazinaw, August 25, 1919, at Bon Echo for the dedication of "Old Walt". From left to right: George Morris, Bessie Morris, Paul Bain, Anne Traubel, Horace Traubel and Flora MacDonald

—— Chapter 17 ——

Cosmic Consciousness

BUCKE'S convictions realized their final expression in *Cosmic Consciousness* published in 1901, a year before his death. Over the preceding twenty-five years he had been building upon the original optimistic view, expressed in his first book, that man's moral nature was evolving and becoming progressively more elevated, that love and faith were increasing at the expense of hate and fear. Other ingredients in the final view included his belief that individual human beings would continue to make the leap into cosmic consciousness in increasing numbers because acquisition of the ability to do so was part of their continuing evolutionary development as a species. An integral part of experiencing cosmic consciousness was the certainty of personal immortality, and belief that in the fullness of time, when the possession of this higher awareness would become common, mankind would finally be happy. It would be the true liberation of man; the human soul would be revolutionized. Religion would have no need for sacred texts, priests, ecclesiastical institutions, or the saving of man from his sins. Mankind would have no fear of death, knowing itself to be immortal, and would therefore live in harmony with itself. Although there would be daily problems and frustrations, a race truly informed by cosmic consciousness would have the capacity to deal with these maturely and without anxiety. The vision was truly apocalyptic.

The first public expression of the completed theme was Bucke's address to the American Medico-Psychological Association in Philadelphia on 18 May 1894. He was working on the book at the time, and the main difference between the speech and the book is in the amount of detail and in the number of individuals he had discovered who had acquired the new faculty.

The book itself was dedicated to his son Maurice whose unexpected death had nearly killed Bucke with grief. He was sustained in that grief by the knowledge that he had, twenty-eight years earlier, glimpsed the eternal for a few moments and gained his certainty of personal immortality, thereby ensuring that he would be with his son again. It was the same source of strength which enabled him to bear the final parting with Whitman:

> If I have been permitted — no, not to enter, but — through the narrow aperture of a scarcely opened door, to glance one instant into that other divine world, it was surely that I might thereby be enabled to live through the receipt of those lightning-flashed words from Montana which time burns only deeper and deeper into my brain.(CC,Foreword)

Bucke saw cosmic consciousness as the next inevitable evolutionary stage in the growth of man, preceded by past stages he called simple consciousness and self consciousness. He used the analogy of a tree to describe the historical relationship: the roots of the tree of life are sunk deep in the organic world; the trunk at earth level is composed of the lowest forms of life which in turn led up to organisms with simple consciousness many millions of years ago. From its dawn, simple consciousness grew in these gradually emerging species until it reached its highest expression in the dog, the ape, the elephant, etc. The transition from simple to self consciousness occurred some 300,000 years ago; self consciousness is the faculty by which a creature is aware of himself as a distinct being, and knows that he knows this. It is the faculty that separates human beings from other forms of life.

From the tree of life, branches emerge from lower down (simple consciousness) and from higher up (self consciousness): examples of the former would be simple limb movement and the instinct of self-preservation, of the latter the qualities of judgement, reason, imagination, etc.

Bucke believed that the various qualities that constitute self consciousness appeared at different times in man's evolutionary development. Some idea of the chronology of appearance of these human characteristics could be gleaned from the average age at which each appears in the individual as he grows up, from the frequency of its appearance in the population, and from the ease with which it may be lost. For example, the sense of colour, according to Bucke, is a relatively recent acquisition. It is not surprising, therefore, that colourblindness is common, occurring in one out of every forty-seven people. Man's moral nature is also relatively recent. Evidence for this is given by its relative or complete absence in savages and, surprisingly, in children. Bucke believed that the human moral nature was still often absent at puberty, and that the average age of its appearance was about fifteen.

Even more surprising were his reasons for believing that man's musical sense is recently acquired. He stated that it had existed for less than 5,000 years and did not appear in the individual before adolescence. Moreover, he contended that the musical sense did not exist in more than half of the human race. He used his experience as a psychiatrist to state that in insanity the musical sense was invariably lost; over a quarter of a century of observing some 5,000 cases of lunacy, he couldn't recall a single case where the musical sense was retained. For a bibliophile, well read in the classics, it seems strange that Bucke apparently did not believe in the existence of the mad lament, the Ophelian dirge.

Using the concept that the more recently a faculty has been acquired, the more frequently it will either be found wanting or become deranged, Bucke reiterated his theory of mental defectiveness and insanity. Thus, in the Aryan race, the faculties that have evolved most in the last few thousand years are the mental ones: the intellectual, arising from the central nervous system, and the moral, arising from the sympathetic nervous system. Because these have evolved so rapidly it is logical, according to Bucke, that defects and disintegration should be common. Thus a mentally defective person is one in whom the intellectual and moral qualities have been omitted to a greater or lesser extent, marking severe or mild mental retardation, with all gradations in between. Similarly, those who seem to develop normally at first but who suffer derangement of the mind as they reach adolescence have a very poor prognosis. These individuals represent the most malignant end of the spectrum of mental illness. Bucke was probably referring here to schizophrenia. People who develop mental instability only under exceptional duress are at the benign end. Between these extremes lie all the other more or less severe cases of insanity.

Bucke cited the prevalence of insanity in whites and blacks in the United States as supporting his theory. Because the mind of the white population has had a more rapid evolution than that of the black it is not surprising, according to Bucke, that insanity is so much commoner in the former (one in five hundred, as compared with one in eleven hundred).

Bucke saw human biology, both physical and mental, in evolutionary terms, and viewed mental deficiency, moral deficiency and insanity as natural and expected. At a time when Freud was fashioning his revolutionary theory of mental illness, Bucke, along with other North American alienists, was committed to an organic approach: mental disease was simply the price the species paid for continuing evolutionary progress.

When a new faculty such as cosmic consciousness appears for the first time, it does not appear by chance. It appears in a person who is exemplary, in someone who has an exceptional physique, exceptional beauty, exceptional health, exceptional sweetness of temper and abundant charisma. That is, it will appear in an individual who has reached the highest plane of the species' development. Bucke, of course, cited Whitman as the perfect example, a man thought by some to be the greatest spiritual force the race had ever produced.

The sense of cosmic consciousness is often perceived as a separate force which fuses with the individual. Paul called it "Christ", Mohammed called it "Gabriel", Dante called it "Beatrice", and Whitman called it "My Soul" as though it were another person, a beloved:

O soul repressless, I with thee and thou with me ....
We too take ship O soul ....
With laugh and many a kiss ....
O soul thou pleasest me, I thee ....(CC,52)

Bucke believed that the sense of cosmic consciousness appeared not only in the best specimens of the race, but at the time when the individual was at the peak of his powers, nearly always in the fourth decade. He believed that self consciousness had appeared in the same way hundreds of thousands of years ago, that is, in superb specimens of examples of simple consciousness at the height of their powers. As the millennia passed and more individuals developed the faculty, it began to appear earlier in life, and is now evident at the age of three; it is so common that an individual without it (severely mentally retarded) is considered abnormal. Similarly, the time will come when most human beings will have the cosmic sense and those who do not will be considered abnormal.

Bucke felt that as the extent of variation in the plane of self consciousness is much greater than in simple consciousness, so the variation in those with cosmic consciousness will be greater still. After a new faculty appears, in time it becomes present in increasing numbers. Bucke calculated that between Gautama and Dante, a period of eighteen hundred years, five cases of celebrated individuals had arisen. From Dante to 1899, a period of six hundred years there were eight cases. Bucke was, of course, aware of a number of lesser cases, some of whom he knew personally, but he argued logically that they could not be included because earlier anonymous possessors of cosmic consciousness had anticipated them but had left no mark of their existence. His total collection, which included himself, came to forty-three.

Bucke pondered the possibility that the attainment of cosmic consciousness was a delusion, as individuals who suffer from a delusion are certain of its reality. But there are important differences. Individuals who attain cosmic consciousness are moral; their sense of morality is further exalted by the experience, whereas the psychotic view of the deluded is often immoral or amoral. Another difference is the quality of self-restraint characteristic of the possessors of cosmic consciousness. Finally, Bucke argued, that since all great civilizations rest on the teachings of such enlightened men as the Buddha, Jesus, Mohammed and Whitman, it follows that if these leaders were deluded, then all our civilizations would be delusions.

From Bucke's reading and his own experience he concluded that the possession of the cosmic sense among individuals would have certain features in common though, naturally, many differences in detail would also exist. Generally, the experience occurs suddenly and unexpectedly; there is a sensation of being immersed in a bright light or flame, or of the mind being filled with an incredibly clear sensation. There is usually a brief period of alarm at what is happening, but then awareness is suffused by an intense feeling of joy. This joyful, orgasmic sensation contains an intellectual illumination imparting a clear conception of the sense and meaning of the universe which no longer seems inert but alive and eternal. The individual has the sensation of being an integral part of that eternity; he experiences his own sense of immortality. There is certainty about the whole, an absence of a sense of sin, and all fragmentation, differences and uncertainties are abolished during the trance state.

The transcendental experience is difficult to express in words; Bucke quotes Whitman:

When I undertake to tell the best I find I cannot,
My tongue is ineffectual on its pivots,
My breath will not be obedient to its organs,
I become a dumb man.(CC,65)

Bucke compared the state of a person who had acquired cosmic consciousness with that of a child who has just become self conscious: he sees life through a new lens. This is a mirror image of Jesus's injunction that the childlike vision is a pre-condition of entering the Kingdom of Heaven. Bucke was careful to point out that attainment of the cosmic sense in no way prevents lapses to the self conscious level of existence, just as the self conscious man will sink at times below the higher animal to simple consciousness. For, after all, it is a new and fragile acquisition historically and, perforce, susceptible to relapses. This new man, imbued with cosmic consciousness, must not be considered infallible or omniscient. Indeed, if mankind should reach an intellectual and moral plane as far above the best man of today as the latter is above the simplest form of organic life, he would still aspire to reach higher. Thus the evolutionary trend would even then continue upward.

The largest sections of the book consist of a catalogue of individuals who have acquired the cosmic sense through illumination, and of those who came close, such as Emerson, Tennyson and, surprisingly, Wordsworth, whom Bucke felt had not actually pierced the veil. The undisputed cases are presented in roughly chronological order beginning with Gautama, the Buddha, and include Jesus, Paul, Mohammed, Dante, Pascal, Blake, Balzac, Bacon and Whitman, the last two, not unexpectedly, being given the most attention.

In the next section Bucke describes numerous instances of historical figures who came close, but who did not actually break through the cosmic curtain. These include Moses, Socrates and Pushkin, as well as some celebrated contemporaries, such as Thoreau, Wordsworth and Tennyson. Finally, Bucke adds a number of less well-known friends and acquaintances of his own, or whose cases had been reliably reported to him. This last group includes his Lancashire friend, Wallace, who had all the features of illumination except the presence of subjective light, and Horace Traubel whose 1889 and subsequent illuminations are described in detail. Of Whitman's inner circle only Traubel and Bucke qualified with the elect who had tasted of the Brahmic splendour.

Bucke's format was to describe briefly the life of the subject and then to quote from his/her writings the passages showing that cosmic consciousness had been achieved. He took passages that expressed the elevated state in other metaphors and translated them into the language of cosmic consciousness, or pointed out what aspect of the cosmic sense the passage illustrated. Often he used a quotation from Whitman as a reference source for the explication. For example, in his case study of Paul, Bucke quoted the celebrated verses from I Corinthians:*

Behold, I shew you a mystery; We shall not all sleep, but we shall all be changed, In a moment, in the twinkling of an eye, at the last trump: for the trumpet shall sound, and the dead shall be raised incorruptible, and we shall be changed. For this corruptible must put on incorruption, and this mortal must put on immortality. So when this corruptible shall have put on incorruption, and this mortal shall have put on immortality, then shall be brought to pass the saying that is written, Death is swallowed up in victory.(CC,9)

Then, in a rather proprietary fashion, he pointed out that the passage expressed the sense of immortality and thus belongs to cosmic consciousness. He then invited the reader to compare the above with a Whitman passage:

There is that in me — I do not know what it is — but I know that it is in me. Wrenched and sweaty — calm and cool then my body becomes, I sleep, I sleep long. I do not know it — it is without name — it is a word unsaid — it is not in any dictionary, utterance, symbol. Something it swings on more than the

---

* Bucke made several minor errors in the quotation which have been corrected.

earth I swing on, to it the creation is a friend whose embracing awakes me. Perhaps I might tell more. Outlines! I plead for my brothers and sisters. Do you see, O my brothers and sisters? It is not chaos or death, it is form, union, plan — it is eternal life — it is happiness.(CC,99)

Bucke devoted more space to Bacon than to anyone else. This was because he found irresistible the temptation to include his theory that Bacon wrote the Shakespeare sonnets and plays. Bucke used much imagination in incorporating circumstantial evidence from Bacon's life with the hidden authorship of the plays and sonnets; he interprets the sonnets as proof that, save for Whitman, Bacon was the most sublime example of cosmic consciousness. The first problem to face was that there was no positive historical evidence that Bacon, like the others in Bucke's collection, had experienced an illumination. Bucke tackled this obstacle by finding a period in Bacon's early life in which solitude played an important part. Bucke pointed out that following the sudden and unexpected appearance of the transcendental experience, a period of solitude was a prime necessity. With his newly endowed riches the neophyte visionary, having had the gum rubbed from his eyes, was reluctant to return at once to the old world. Instead, for weeks he longed to remain alone, as did Balzac, Paul and, as Bucke surmised, Whitman too.

There is no better example of Bucke's need to fashion facts to suit his purpose than in his attempt to find and date Bacon's supposed acquisition of the cosmic sense. He misquotes Bacon's biographer James Spedding in one instance (CC,130) and misunderstands him in another, in order to strengthen the case for Bacon's supposed post-illumination need for solitude. The incorrect quotation states falsely that in the years 1590 and 1591 not much is known of Bacon's activities, whereas we know that Bacon continued as a lawyer at Gray's Inn, and that he made the important acquaintance of the Earl of Essex.[1]

The misunderstood quotation is:

I do not fear that action shall impair it [my health] because I account my ordinary course of study and meditation to be more painful (more labourious*) than most parts of action are.(CC,130)

---

* Bucke's insertion.

Bucke infers from this extract of a letter written to the Lord Treasurer, Burghley, by Bacon that he had retreated from an outwardly active life for a period of reflection, and that the latter was indirect evidence of his post-illumination period of solitude. The true intention of the letter was to explain and plead his case for wishing to pursue his ambitious philosophical plans — "I have taken all knowledge to be my province." Bacon pointed out that he was getting on (aged 31) and, obliquely, that he was without substantial funds.[2] What he was really trying to do was to ingratiate himself with Burghley, to whose guardianship Essex had been entrusted,[3] and with the help of the dual friendship to increase his access to and support from the Court. Bucke went on to speculate that during this period of seclusion Bacon wrote a number of the Shakespeare sonnets.

As a sort of running commentary upon his mental experiences and his work, he wrote the earlier "Sonnets", the rest being written one or two at a time as occasion called them forth, between this period and the date of their publication — 1609.(CC,131)

Thus did Bucke create Bacon's illumination and his subsequent period of retreat from public life, during which he allegedly wrote many of the sonnets and at least some of the early plays. An even larger obstacle to admission into the cosmic club had yet to be addressed: Bacon's conviction of bribery in 1621.

Bacon's considerable merits had been recognized. He was knighted in 1603, became King's Counsel in 1604, Solicitor-General in 1607, Attorney-General in 1613, a Privy Councillor in 1616 and Lord Chancellor in 1618. In this year he was also elevated to the House of Lords as Baron Verulam. He had a well-deserved reputation as an efficient and fair judge. However, in 1621 he was accused of corruption, found guilty by the House of Lords, dismissed from parliament and all offices, imprisoned for two days in the Tower and fined £40,000. He suffered for having accepted presents from two men whose cases were being tried in his court. His decision was not affected by the gifts as, indeed, it went against both men, but his name was blackened for a long time. Although Bacon was careless and naïve and the act was immoral, it was the custom of the times and thus not particularly heinous. In the course of his very detailed account of the pros and cons of the incident, Bacon's nineteenth century biographer, James Spedding, succinctly summed up the issue wisely and compassionately:

> If I were asked to sum up Bacon's case in the fewest words, I should call it a little fault meeting with a great accident; and whenever that happens you will find that the fault bears all the blame.[4]

How did Bucke approach the bribery conviction as it affected Bacon's eligibility for cosmic sense? Earlier in *Cosmic Consciousness*, he had listed the eleven marks of the cosmic sense, and the second of these was "the moral elevation". In the chapter on Bacon he writes:

> The question which concerns us here is (of course): were his intellect and moral nature (especially the latter) such as belong to persons having Cosmic Consciousness? ... The point cannot be argued here. All that can be said is that the present writer believes that Bacon was as great morally as he was intellectually.(CC,131)

Not surprisingly, Bucke was unwilling to concede a moral lapse in his Hero Number Two, however understandable it was within the historical context; he simply avoided handling the issue directly, referring the reader to Spedding's works. He ended the section with two long quotations from Spedding testifying to Bacon's good character and his astonishing burst of creativity in his few remaining years, free from the demands of public office.

The next section brings out three points which Bucke considered important. The first is a quotation from Bacon's contemporary biographer, William D. Rawley, extolling Bacon's intellect:

> I have been induced to think that if there were a beam of knowledge derived from God upon any man in these modern times, it was upon him.(CC,132)

Bucke interpreted that passage literally, asserting that because Bacon did not openly live for the cosmic sense, he published his inspired writings (i.e., the plays and sonnets) under a concealed authorship.

The second point Bucke made from his interpretation of Bacon's unconcealed writings, related to the essay "Of Truth", in which Bacon wrote:

The first creature of God, in the works of the days, was the light of the sense, the best was the light of reason; and his Sabbath work ever since is the illumination of his spirit.(CC,133)

Bucke read this as a realization by Bacon that in the evolution of the mind there was simple consciousness, followed by self consciousness and finally by cosmic consciousness.

Lastly, Bucke made an interpretation of this fragment from Bacon's great prayer:

I am a debtor to Thee for the gracious talent of Thy gifts and graces, which I have neither put into a napkin, nor put it (as I ought) to exchangers, where it might have made best profit; but misspent it in things for which I was least fit; so as I may truly say, my soul hath been a stranger in the course of my pilgrimage.(CC,133)

He saw this as Bacon's confession that the talent in question, the cosmic sense, while not buried, was not utilized to the fullest extent; that is, Bacon did not live continuously in the cosmic sense, as Jesus and Paul had. It is as though Bacon was apologizing for letting himself and others (e.g., Bucke) down. For Bucke goes on to muse,

The Cosmic Sense produced the plays — if Bacon had openly lived his whole life for the Cosmic Sense what other perhaps greater works might he not have produced?(CC,134)

Throughout the whole Bacon chapter, Bucke vacillates on how much he should include of the Bacon-Shakespeare controversy. Although he has stated his bias unequivocally at the beginning, it is as though he has to keep reminding himself that this is a treatise on the cosmic sense, not a presentation of evidence for Bacon as Shakespeare. But the temptation proved irresistible for two reasons. First, his own passion and excitement concerning his discovery; this led him to summarize in several pages the reasons why he felt convinced that Bacon wrote Shakespeare. The section culminates in Bucke's proud statement that he has discovered the cipher — proof positive of Baconian authorship:

The evidence upon which this statement rests, if not already published by the time this volume is issued, will very soon thereafter be given to the world.(CC,139)

The second reason was Bucke's belief in the importance of the sonnets in illustrating Bacon's cosmic sense. The reader will recall Bucke's excitement when, completely unexpectedly, while riding on a train in November 1899, he worked out the missing clue which unravelled for him the cryptographic meaning of the dedication of the sonnets. He believed the sonnets were written by Bacon in the early 1590s, shortly after his presumed illumination; in the chronology of the sonnets he was in company with traditional Shakespeare scholarship. However, his reading of them was certainly not in the conventional mould. He saw them as written from the perspective of the self conscious man, but addressed to the cosmic sense. This was, in Bucke's view, different from the plays, which flowed directly from Bacon's cosmic sense, that is, they were inspired, and almost wrote themselves.

Bucke was at least in agreement with traditionalists in viewing the overall theme of the first seventeen sonnets as that of regeneration, phrased by Bucke as "urging the Cosmic Sense to produce".(CC,139) The usual view is to see them as exploring the theme that to marry and have children is the best means of defeating Time and Decay, better even than devotion to the distilling power of art. The theme is neatly summed up in the couplet of Sonnet XVII.

But were some child of yours alive that time,
You should live twice, in it and in my rhyme.

Bucke's method in dealing with the Sonnets was to print several in their entirety on the left-hand side of the page, and then to insert his commentary opposite on the right. He quotes six (Sonnets I, II, III, XV, XVI, XVII) from the first group. He sees these as addressed to the cosmic sense and then, as usual, Bucke indulged his habit of finding what he needed to confirm his view. For example, in Sonnet I, the couplet from the third quatrain,

Thou that art now the world's fresh ornament,
Only herald to the gaudy spring,

he interpreted as referring to the time of year in which illumination is most likely to occur. He reminds the reader that in forty-three cases of cosmic consciousness, the time of year of the first illumination was known in twenty, and in fifteen of these it occurred between January and June, a rather liberal view of the span of springtime.

From Sonnet II, Bucke, having concluded that Bacon's illumination occurred in the spring of 1590, calculates that the addressee, the cosmic sense, would be forty years old when Bacon reached seventy. His source for this exercise in mathematics is the first couplet from the initial quatrain,

When forty winters shall besiege thy brow,
And dig deep trenches in thy beauty's field....

However, in the last (Sonnet XVII) of this group, Bucke's analysis is consistent and parallel to the usual interpretation: that succeeding generations would believe the adored subject of the poet's labour was surely exaggerated and great as it might be, it would lack breath. But should a future generation see the flesh and blood offspring of the object of the poet's adoration, that person would live twice, both biologically and believably appreciated in the poem itself. Here is Bucke's interpretation of this poem addressed to the cosmic sense from a person (Bacon) who has achieved it, but who writes from the vantage point of the self conscious man:

Let me say what I may about you, no one could realize from my words what you really are. Let me tell how you appear to me and it will be said I have exaggerated, lied. But produce — leave behind children like yourself — worthy of yourself — as they must be — then you cannot be denied. You will live, unmistakably, twice: (1) in your own offspring, whose divinity none will be able to question, and (2) in my description of you in the "Sonnets", which description will be seen, from a comparison with your own offspring, to be truthful.(CC,141)

As the sonnets progress, Bucke's explications tend, on the whole, to become longer. This is, in part, because he quotes heavily from other individuals who have acquired, in Bucke's terms, the cosmic sense, and who have written about it. In Sonnet XXXIII, for example, the poet praises his friend, using the sun as the image, and the clouds which come along to obscure it as the poet's rejection by the friend. Bucke saw this sonnet as illustrating the intermittent character of illumination in instances where there is more than "one flash of the divine radiance". He went on to quote from Yepes, Behmen and Paul, all included in Bucke's list, relating the usually transient nature of the transcendental experience, and the contrasting relative darkness which surrounds them.

Sonnet XXXIX expresses very clearly to Bucke an important aspect of cosmic consciousness: the duality in the person's life. Once he has acquired his new sense (the old part being the persona of his daily round of business, politics and family life, his life between illuminations), the new part is the experience itself with its halo of the cosmic sense. He concludes his analysis of this sonnet by reminding the reader of Whitman's phrase "the other I am" as an example of this duality.

In the justly famous Sonnet LV, Bucke departs radically from the conventional interpretation. In this magnificent sonnet, the conventional reading is more eschatological than Bucke's.

Not marble, nor the gilded monuments
Of princes, shall outlive this powerful rhyme;
But you shall shine more bright in these contents
Than unswept stone, besmear'd with sluttish time.
When wasteful war shall statues overturn,
And broils root out the work of masonry,
Nor Mars his sword nor war's quick fire shall burn
The living record of your memory.
'Gainst death and all-oblivious enmity
Shall you pace forth; your praise shall still find room,
Even in the eyes of all posterity
That wears this world out to the ending doom.
So, till the judgement that yourself arise,
You live in this, and dwell in lovers' eyes.

In the poem Shakespeare recognizes that the beloved has his own personal immortality, not only in the poem and in personal resurrection at

Judgement Day, but that "You live in this, and dwell in lovers' eyes". The poet's beloved becomes, then, the image of love. Bucke saw this sonnet as an affirmation by Bacon that the cosmic sense would endure not so much in the rhyme of the Sonnets, as in the early plays such as *Romeo and Juliet*. Cosmic consciousness would live on in those plays to delight the eyes and hearts of lovers until such far off time as the elevation of human taste — an integral part of the cosmic sense — would prevail.

Sonnet LXII falls into three parts. The octave expresses the poet's self-love:

Sin of self-love possesseth all mine eye,
And all my soul, and all my every part;

After the self-glorification of the octave comes a sharp descent, as the truth is revealed in the mirror:

But when my glass shows me myself indeed,
Beated and chopp'd with tann'd antiquity.

Then in the final couplet there is a suggested redemption. The poet's beloved is the poet's better self and, in effect, a second looking glass which throws back to the poet an image of himself as he would like to be:

Tis thee, myself, that for myself I praise,
Painting my age with beauty of thy days

Bucke's reading of this sonnet is imaginative. When the individual ruminates on his cosmic conscious self, he is pleased and filled with admiration for himself, but when he reflects on his physical, ordinary self, he tends to despise himself. Bucke wrote in his annotation to this sonnet:

Whitman's admiration for the Cosmic Conscious Whitman and his works (the "Leaves") was just such as pictured in this sonnet, while he was absolutely devoid of egotism in the ordinary way of the self conscious individual.(CC,145)

Bucke was, in a sense, doubly wrong. The closing sestet begins with the distasteful truth of the mirror, reflecting a most unflattering light, as Bucke recognized. But it hardly expresses Bucke's intended analogous view of Whitman as "absolutely devoid of egotism". The second error is understandable: Whitman was the paragon of egotism, but it was a quality that never filtered through Bucke's lens.

Bucke did not comment on the final couplet, though he might have done so to good effect. Given Bucke's reading of the poem, the couplet would do nicely to express a quality which is characteristic of the self conscious and cosmic conscious man: the pleasure such a person experiences in thinking about his cosmic self as Bucke did so frequently and to acknowledge that the cosmic self throws back the image to the self conscious self which the latter always aspires to.

In Sonnet LXXVIII the poet expresses his acknowledgement that the beloved has inspired his poetry and by virtue of the poet's work has in turn inspired others:

Thine eyes, that taught the dumb on high to sing
And heavy ignorance aloft to fly,

Bucke saw this poem as expressing the inspiring effect of illumination. This time his use of Whitman is apt. He remarks on the sudden, unexpected and, indeed, inexplicable surge of Whitman's creative outpouring that produced the 1855 edition of *Leaves of Grass*.

In the last of the Sonnets analyzed in his chapter on Bacon, Bucke looked at Sonnet CXXVI. This poem, the last in time of the entire sequence, is traditionally considered to be addressed to the Friend, the third Earl of Pembroke, William Herbert, who is possibly the Mr. W.H. of the dedication. Bucke felt that this marked the close of the Sonnets addressed to cosmic consciousness. His interpretation is quite opposed in mood to the traditional one, which is rueful: a reluctant farewell to the poet's Friend's youthful charms, over which Time the destroyer ultimately triumphs. The theme is summarized in the final couplet in which the poet concedes that Nature, though perhaps delayed, must eventually force the surrender of the Friend's youth:

Her audit, though delayed, answered must be,
And her quietus is to render thee.

From Bucke's perspective the sonnet's message is not only triumphant, but apocalyptic. He saw the opening lines

O thou my lovely boy, who in thy power
Dost hold Time's fickle glass, his sickle-hour

as addressed to the cosmic sense, which has the power to control Time and Death. The second couplet contrasts the withering of mortal lovers with the growth of Bacon's progeny, his plays:

Who hast by waning grown, and therein show'st
Thy lovers withering, as thy sweet self grow'st;

But more important, the decline and eventual disappearance of Nature, i.e., self consciousness, will mark the evolutionary victory of cosmic consciousness. Bucke thus saw the final line

And her quietus is to render thee

as the ultimate surrender of self consciousness to cosmic consciousness, and the attendant destruction of ''death, the fear of death, sin and practically time and space.''(CC,149)

Bucke concludes the chapter on Bacon with the assertion that he was, as creator of the plays, perhaps the greatest intellect in history, and morally in no way inferior to others who have entered cosmic consciousness, and that the sonnets reveal their author has acquired the cosmic sense and has used these poems as an invocation with truly apocalyptic implications for the future of mankind.

The remaining case illustrations include individuals who sufficiently fulfill Bucke's criteria for definite assignment as possessors of the cosmic sense. As mentioned earlier, they include the sixteenth century mystic Jacob Behmen, William Blake, Balzac, Edward Carpenter, the English writer and acquaintance of Bucke, and, of course, Walt Whitman.

Though not thoroughly conversant with Blake's poetry, and by his own admission incompetent to judge his drawings,(CC,164) Bucke was familiar with the details of Blake's life from Alexander Gilchrist's biography. Gilchrist's widow, one of Whitman's most passionate admirers, came to America to court him. In his account of Blake, Bucke quotes heavily from W.M. Rossetti's Preface to his 1891 edition of *The Poetical Works of William Blake*. Blake qualified for cosmic consciousness on several counts, such as his high moral standards and his sense of immortality. He also exemplified another quality of the creative person who has the cosmic sense: the divine inspiration which is the true source of any work of art, the writer or artist being, in effect, merely the agent or transmitter. The contention, then, is one of divinely inspired automatic writing.

> In the preface to "Jerusalem" Blake speaks of that composition as having been "dictated" to him; and other expressions of his prove that he regarded it rather as a revelation of which he was the scribe than as the product of his own inventing and fashioning brain.(CC,160)

In the chapter on Balzac, Bucke makes several interesting observations pertaining to the cosmic sense. He emphasizes that literary ability, even of the first rank, is unrelated to the presence or absence of cosmic consciousness in the author. Indeed, the possession of the cosmic sense is very unlikely, by mere chance, to endow the owner with significant literary talent. However, such an individual has a compelling need to impart to the world his vision and concept of mankind. Thus the importance of his message causes him to be read, and by the force of his personality everything surrounding him is admired, including his literary style which may be held up as the ultimate model.(CC,174)

Bucke also points out that those who acquire cosmic consciousness, although having a strong religious sense, seldom adhere to any orthodox religion. The great ones, of course, may found a religion, but are themselves for *"religion,* not for *a religion."*(CC,174)

Finally, Bucke introduces a new consideration. In noting the "antagonistic attitude" of many of the most celebrated cases towards marriage (Gautama, Jesus, Paul, Whitman, etc.), he asserts that as the cosmic sense becomes a general possession, marriage as an institution will disappear.

The chapter on Whitman contains much that will already be familiar to the reader. In describing the biographic details of Whitman's life, Bucke simply lifts verbatim much of chapter 10 of his book on Whitman, written more than fifteen years earlier. He began the second section as follows:

Walt Whitman is the best, most perfect, example the world has
so far had of the Cosmic Sense, first because he is the man in
whom the new faculty has been, probably, most perfectly developed, and especially because he is, par excellence, the man who
in modern times has written distinctly and at large from the point
of view of Cosmic Consciousness, and who also has referred to
its facts and phenomena more plainly and fully than any other
writer ancient or modern.(CC,126)

Although Bucke stresses the duality of cosmic consciousness with former
self, a sort of alter ego, he also emphasizes that if the cosmic sense is
complete it will express itself both in daily life and in creative works. It
was in this sense that Bacon, for Bucke, is a lesser god than Whitman,
since his day-to-day life had little of the transcendent splendour which
Bucke, and others, saw in Whitman.

As a corollary of this theory of artistic creation, Bucke attempts to
account for the extraordinary, incandescent and quite unpredicted artistic creation of the 1855 *Leaves of Grass*. He reminds his readers that in
the early writings of such poets as Shelley, one can see the seeds of greatness, followed by their artistic evolution to maturity. In both Balzac and
Whitman, on the other hand, there is no trace of latent genius:

It is upon this instantaneous evolution of the "Titan" from the
"Man", this profound mystery of the attainment of the splendour and power of the Kingdom of heaven, that this present volume seeks to throw light.(CC,187)

Bucke then interprets the famous lines from Section 5 of "Song of
Myself":

I believe in you my soul, . . . the other I am must
    not abase itself to you,
And you must not be abased to the other.
Loafe with me on the grass, . . . loose the stop
    from your throat,
Not words, not music or rhyme I want, . . . not
    custom or lecture, not even the best,
Only the lull I like, the hum of your valved voice.

I mind how we lay in June, such a transparent summer
   morning;
You settled your head athwart my hips and gently
   turned over upon me,
And parted the shirt from my bosom-bone, and
   plunged your tongue to my bare-stript heart.
And reached till you felt my beard, and reached till
   you held my feet.
Swiftly arose and spread around me the peace and
   joy and knowledge that pass all the art and
   argument of the earth;
And I know that the hand of God is the elder hand
   of my own,
And I know that the spirit of God is the eldest
   brother of my own,
And that all the men ever born are also my brothers,
   . . . and the women my sisters and lovers,
And that a kelson of the creation is love.(CC,188)

The poem is a dramatic representation of a mystical experience. It is not generally regarded as a transcript of an actual mystical experience, but rather as a work of art in which such an experience is conceived in the imagination and represented dramatically with the author as protagonist.[5] This section from the early part of the poem describes entry into the mystical state. The soul materializes and is invited to loaf on the grass. The poet then proceeds to describe the union of body and soul resulting in the consummation of the marriage. Most remarkable, in terms of the mystical state, is the celebration of the senses as an equal partner in the union with the soul. The interfusing is beautifully described as the spiritual tongue informs, and the physical heart receives. The passage suggests that it is only through the ultimate fusion of the physical and spiritual, the ennobling of the physical through the spiritual, that transcendence is experienced reality. The immediate outcome is a new awareness, not rational knowledge; it represents the spiritual awakening of the physical self.

Bucke read this passage rather more historically. He took note of the month (June) as part of spring, the time when the experience is most likely to take place. He estimated that the lines were written in 1853 in

Whitman's thirty-fifth year, the usual time in life when the cosmic sense is acquired. He saw the soul as the new cosmic sense, and the body as the old self conscious state; the old self conscious self must not abase itself to the new sense — they must be equal partners. Thus, Bucke did not view the union as essentially sexual, nor interpret the lines as celebrating the physical as a novel ingredient in the expression of a mystical union. We know that Bucke did not reject heterosexual imagery as such, and had praised the "Children of Adam" poems in his biography of Whitman for helping to remove the shame associated with the sexual act.

Whereas Bacon's weakness was in failing to give cosmic consciousness adequate play in his daily life, Gautama and Paul, and even Jesus to a lesser extent, were taken over or mastered by the cosmic sense. Whitman's great glory was in

determining, on the contrary, to subdue it and make it the servant along with simple consciousness, self consciousness, and the rest of the united, individual SELF.(CC,192)

The last to be included in the section of the book entitled "Instances of Cosmic Consciousness", was the English writer, Edward Carpenter. With the exception of Whitman, he was the only one whom Bucke had actually known. There were some similarities between Carpenter and Bucke in their relationship with Whitman. Carpenter had first encountered *Leaves of Grass* in Rossetti's edition in the summer of 1868,[6] as had Bucke, and both men believed their life had been changed by the experience. Each wrote to Whitman subsequently, and each had an overpowering need to meet the poet. Carpenter crossed the Atlantic to do so and knocked on the door on 2 May 1877,[7] just five months before Bucke's first visit. Like Bucke, Carpenter expected an important experience:

Ever since, in my rooms at Cambridge, I had read that little blue book of Whitman, his writings had been my companions, and had been working a revolution within me — at first an intellectual revolution merely — but by degrees the wonderful personality behind them, glowing through here and there, became more and more real and living, and suffusing itself throughout rendered them transparent to my understanding.[8]

There were differences though. Whitman's literary style had no apprecia-
ble effect on Bucke's literary expressions, but Carpenter's best known
book, *Towards Democrary*, owes much to *Leaves of Grass*.

We have already seen that Bucke's relationship to Whitman had a
homoerotic texture but there is no evidence that Bucke was overtly homosexual. Carpenter *was* homosexual and, like his countryman John Addington Symonds, derived comfort from the "Calamus" poems in a way
which was quite different from Bucke's experience with them. As Carpenter confessed,

> What made me cling to the little blue book from the beginning
> was largely the poems which celebrate comradeship. That
> thought, so near and personal to me, I had never seen or heard
> fairly expressed.[9]

Carpenter's illumination occurred in the spring of 1881, that is, four
years after he had met Whitman, whereas Bucke's occurred several years
before the first meeting. The combination of the effect of *Leaves of Grass*
and Whitman the prophet, and the mystical experience of 1872, finally
culminated in Bucke's theory of cosmic consciousness a quarter of a century later. The incubation period was considerably shorter for Carpenter,
whose illumination in 1881 led to an abrupt decision to abandon his position as lecturer in the recently formed Cambridge University extension
lecturing scheme. As soon as the term was over in April he left Cambridge and spent his days on a farm near Sheffield, writing the long poem
Towards Democrary, which he completed by the end of that year. *Towards
Democrary* has similarities with *Cosmic Consciousness* in describing the
immortality of life and of love, and the insignificance of death except as
a partner in that trinity. It is fundamentally different, however, in its style,
and in making no claim that the new life is part of the evolutionary process. Carpenter subsequently read *Cosmic Consciousness* and acknowledged:

> Some evolution into a further order of consciousness is the key
> to the future, and that many aeons to come (of human progress)
> will be ruled by it. Dr. Richard Bucke, by the publication (in 1901)
> of his book Cosmic Consciousness made a great contribution to
> the cause of humanity. The book was a bit casual, hurried, doc-
> trinaire, un-literary, and so forth, but it brought together a mass

of material, and did the inestimable service of being the first to systematically consider and analyse the subject.[10]

Carpenter's own contribution in Bucke's book was significant. His extensive description of the altered state is the most detailed of any in the whole section and the chapter on Bucke consists almost entirely of long direct quotations.

Of his second pilgrimage to America to see Whitman in 1884, Carpenter remarked in disappointing therapeutic terms that

the visit to Whitman did not help me so much as the first time... his self-centeredness had increased and seemed difficult to overcome.[11]

It was following this visit, and at Whitman's suggestion, that he crossed Lake Erie and spent four or five days with Bucke in London, where they talked a good deal about Whitman. Bucke, in his spiritual isolation at the asylum, must have enjoyed having an eager and informed audience to whom he could show his Whitman pictures and books.

In the penultimate section of *Cosmic Consciousness* Bucke describes "Additional — Some of Them Lesser, Imperfect and Doubtful Instances". He begins by speculating that there must be many people who ascend above the self conscious level, but who do not fully enter cosmic consciousness. This is the first mention of a grey zone, which Bucke calls "the twilight".(CC,211) He considers whether the twilight would include cases of religious conversion when the individual has a spiritual ascent without the full-blown incandescence which accompanies the actual bursting of the cosmic veil. The section is composed of the accounts of thirty-one men and three women who for one reason or another do not quite make the first team. It is a hodge-podge of Moses, Socrates, Roger Bacon, Pascal, Spinoza, Wordsworth, Pushkin, Thoreau, Emerson and Tennyson. It also includes many contemporaries of Bucke, some of whom he knew. It is the weakest section of the book, and some of the inclusions seem unwarranted. For example, all Bucke knows about the anonymous E.T. is that he/she was born in 1830 and entered cosmic consciousness at the age of thirty. Some of the contemporaries, even some whom Bucke knew, are identified by initials, while others are named. Thus J.W.W. is Bucke's Bolton friend Wallace, but Horace Traubel is identified by name.

Traubel's assignation to this twilight group is puzzling. Traubel's description of his illuminations would seem to render him eligible for inclusion in the previous section, along with Bucke's much more distant friend, Carpenter.

In the last section, Bucke confesses his original intention of dealing with other departures from normal, self conscious, mental life, such as hypnotism, miracles and spiritualism. He admits that not only time, but also a lack of ability, now made this impossible. He contents himself with describing one case in considerable detail, the levitation experienced on some ten occasions by William Stainton Moses, a clergyman in England and a contemporary of Bucke's, though not known to him personally. Bucke flirted with the possibility of kinship between such phenomena and the cosmic sense. For example, he points out that in the case of William Stainton Moses the phenomena began at age 33. He emphasizes that, in spite of protestations to the contrary, the "medium", in this case the clergyman, was the source of the force responsible for the phenomenon, and that there were no supra-normal or extra-human forces involved. This was very important to Bucke because he viewed cosmic consciousness in exactly the same way. In spite of the assertions by some possessors of cosmic consciousness that they were agents only, and not the authors of their artistic expression, Bucke felt definitely that the source of their power lay within themselves. Bucke saw the cosmic expression, either in their lives or their works, as evidence of a nascent faculty, acquired not by magic or bestowed by some extra-human Providence, but simply as part of the continuing evolution of the species. In this sense, his was a rationalist view.

He finally conjectures that perhaps, buried within himself, the self conscious being has several higher faculties of which the cosmic sense is but one. He uses the analogy of equating the primitive totipotential unicellular organism with self conscious man. Lying within self conscious man may be several possibilities, the germ of not one superior race but many; for example, a cosmic conscious race, a race with clairvoyant powers, a race with miraculous healing powers.

Bucke lamented that not only Christians, but also Buddhists and Mohammedans tended to limit their studies to the exemplars of their own faith and culture. He enjoyed a more catholic view that would give the individual a wider concept of spiritual growth, increasing his chances of advancing to the new vision.

Bucke concludes by summarizing the pre-conditions most favourable to the attainment of cosmic consciousness: 1) full maturity — i.e., between thirty and forty years; 2) a strong, spiritual and highly moral mother; 3) a father of superior physical and spiritual qualities; 4) the most propitious blend genetically from both parents: the possesion of at least three, if not all four of the Galenic humours (choleric, phlegmatic, sanguine, melancholic). This was most likely to occur if each parent possessed an opposite pair, passing on to the offspring a blend of all four; 5) birth at the right time of the year, the first half; 6) the right mental attitude, the ability to listen to one's inner self.

As an afterthought, Bucke mentions the altered state alcohol and certain such drugs as chloroform can produce, ''a kind of artificial and bastard consciousness.''(CC,314) He quotes the account of the Whitman disciple, John Addington Symonds, of the ecstatic, mind-altering effect of chloroform:

a sort of actual Cosmic Consciousness.(CC,315)

Symonds compared his experience with that of Saul of Tarsus, and Bucke simply concludes that Symonds had instinctively picked a genuine (presumably permanent) case of cosmic consciousness to compare with his own *temporary* state, conveniently forgetting that almost all cosmic illuminatory experiences, including his own, last only a few moments.(CC,8)

Bucke ends the book with an admission of the dilemma that confronts all mystics who attempt to explain their experience; the frustration of inadequate linguistic tools. Bucke was not only keenly aware of this, but he also saw an essential unity in the message of Cosmic Man, Jesus, Gautama, Whitman, etc., and the unfortunate and largely artificial schisms which result when men of self conscious stature attempt to interpret their visions.

Carpenter pointed out fifteen years after its publication that *Cosmic Consciousness*

has elicited no serious recognition or response from the accredited authorities, philosophers, psychologists and so forth; and the subject with which it deals is in such circles practically ignored — though in comparatively unknown centers it may be warmly discussed.[12]

However, *Cosmic Consciousness* is still in print nearly one hundred years later, and has been a seminal work for those interested in man's potential mental evolution; Barbara Marx Hubbard's recent book, *The Evolutionary Journey*, for example, draws directly on the well-spring of Bucke's theory.[13]

Cosmic Consciousness gestated for some twenty years after the three events that called it to life: the first exposure to *Leaves of Grass* in 1868, the illumination in 1872 and the first meeting with Whitman in 1877. Bucke's labours spring from many characteristics typical of nineteenth century men; he was self-educated and self-reliant, industrious, highly disciplined and inner-directed, to use David Riesman's term.[14] The sources of his wisdom were his reading and his introspection, not, as in other-directed twentieth century men, his peers and public opinion.

As the nineteenth century drew to a close, the toil of *Cosmic Consciousness* was finished. Bucke was glad to be done with 1899, the year of Maurice's death, while the new century, of which he would see so little, gave promise. The most immediate challenge was to be the completion of his manuscript on the Bacon-Shakespeare mystery.

—— Chapter 18 ——
The Riddle Solved

Bucke ENTERED the new century pragmatically. He wrote Harry Forman on January 1st, to express his disappointment that he had not heard from the British Museum concerning the earlier epitaph on Shakespeare's grave. The original gravestone, partially disintegrating by the early nineteenth century, had been replaced and Bucke was very keen to apply the cipher to the original epitaph. A few days later the sense of disappointment, not to say paranoia, was sharper,[1] and Bucke could not refrain from confessing his fear that someone else would get on the track of his discovery and deprive him of the credit which he very much wanted for himself. On January 17th, Bucke expressed contrition to Forman, and ascribed his behaviour not only to his sense of urgency over the cipher question, but also to his emotional fragility since Maurice's death. By way of atonement, but also because of his irrepressible desire to share his secret with Forman, Bucke went on to delineate in every detail how one could read the cipher in Shakespeare's dedication of the *Sonnets*. Forman himself was sceptical of the whole Bacon-Shakespeare cipher issue and, although he may have simply been too busy to act promptly to Bucke's continuing requests for books, frontpieces, etc., his tardiness may well have been an expression of his lack of conviction. In any case, it was his brother, Alfred, who throughout the next year strove nobly to follow all of Bucke's instructions.

But, during that first month of the century, Bucke did express feelings other than impatience and disappointment. In a note replying to his Bolton friend J.W. Wallace's December 7th letter of condolence, Bucke wrote of his own consolation:

> I am glad to suffer I am content — I find no fault — I have never felt more deeply than now that there is no flaw in the universe — that it is perfect — that it is God.[2]

A similar feeling expressed more as a credo went to Elliot, whose daughter Romaine, adored by Bucke, had recovered from typhoid fever.

> All we have to do is to see (if that is possible) that our own lives are noble and clean, if they are we shall not need to worry about the rest for if we are really right about ourselves we shall not see so-called evil — we shall look abroad and see that all things that God has made are good.[3]

In May, Bucke and his daughter Ina repaid the previous autumn's visit of Elliot and Romaine. Elliot lived in Milford, near Cincinnati. After travelling to Richmond, Virginia and Terre Haute, Indiana, where Bucke lectured, they spent two days with his friend. Perhaps the highlight of the journey for Bucke was re-visiting the farm where he had worked as an adolescent boy forty-seven years earlier, his first job after leaving home in 1853, and the first part of his *Wanderjahre* during which he reached maturity, nearly died, and returned home minus one and a half feet. There were other lectures on Whitman in London and Sarnia, and the annual month of restoration at Liberty Island, where Bucke's son Pardee, now a physician, and his daughter Clare and her infant son, together with the younger children and many friends swelled the total number at times to as high as 25.[4]

In 1901, Bucke's main concerns were the publication of *Cosmic Consciousness* and to find a publisher for his Bacon authorship discoveries, entitled *New Light on the Life of Francis Bacon*.[5] In an attempt to raise money to finance the publication, he sent a circular to some acquaintances and to certain men in Cincinnati whose names Elliot had given him. Not surprisingly, none of the latter replied.[6] By the time *Cosmic Consciousness* was published at the end of June by Innes and Sons in Philadelphia, the cost had risen to $1,300. In September Bucke was still sending letters asking for subscriptions.[7]

It all ended abruptly and unexpectedly. On the evening of 19 February 1902, Bucke and Jessie were visiting friends. He was in great spirits and had been expostulating on his momentous discovery of the Baconian authorship.[8] After returning home, Bucke decided to wander onto the verandah to admire the cold and starry night.

A few minutes later his family heard a heavy thud on the porch. Alarmed, they hurried out to investigate. Bucke was lying on the floor. They carried him inside but there were no signs of life. Bucke's assistant, Dr. Beemer, arrived to find Bucke dead. The only mark of injury was a bruise on the back of his head.

Bucke's death has always been ascribed to a head injury resulting from the fall, but the evidence that he was dead within minutes makes this very unlikely. Bucke must have died from ventricular fibrillation, at his age no doubt a consequence of coronary heart disease; exposure to cold is well known to be capable of triggering such arrhythmias.

He was buried in Woodland cemetery in London, Ontario, beside his first child, Clare Georgina, who had died in infancy, and his beloved son Maurice Andrews. Twenty-five years later, Jessie, aged 87, joined him.

As for Dr. Bucke himself, what remains to be said about this extraordinary man?

He was honest and open, not reticent or misleading in his writing about himself. An exception was his often repeated account of his departure from home at the age of sixteen. Throughout his life Bucke was not only vague about the reason why he left home, but definitely misleading concerning the events surrounding it. Using the third person, he wrote in *Cosmic Consciousness*:

The boy's mother died when he was only a few years old and his father shortly afterwards. The outward circumstances of his life in some respects became more unhappy than can readily be told.(CC,7)

In the article for the *Mail and Empire*, written in 1900, but published as his obituary, he had written:

By the time Maurice was sixteen he had lost his father and mother, and having become dissatisfied with his home he left it....[9]

Bucke's mother had died in 1844, but his father re-married. Bucke never referred to his stepmother, who died in 1847, nor to his father's subsequent unrequited amour for Miss Alison. Equally interesting is the fact that his father did not die before Bucke's departure, but moved from London to Moore township, near Sarnia, with the rest of the family. His father died on 31 March 1856, when Bucke was about to head west on a wagon train from Kansas. There is no record of any correspondence between father and son during the preceeding three years when he was away from home.

We see, then, a boy who never acknowledged his stepmother, nor his father's emotional vicissitudes following her death. The Bucke family knew the Alisons and probably young Bucke had met Lowell Alison.[10] He was aware of his father's amorous but frustrated feelings towards Miss Alison, as he not only had had access to his father's poems (see chapter 1), but had written a poem of his own on the page opposite his father's last tormented verses to L.C.A. He left home in 1853, five months before the L.C.A. poem was written, and thereafter considered his father dead. There are few dates a son is less likely to remember incorrectly than that of his father's death. Bucke's repeated references to his father's death having occurred prior to his departure is, therefore, best understood as being factually erroneous but symbolically true.

During the next four years Bucke, without family support or religious faith, courageously survived severe hardship and the imminence of death from exposure to cold. He emerged with an unsatisfied and unexpressed longing for the missing father, a void which had to be filled. He yearned for a prophet and a creed which would satisfy the true believer's need for certainty. Although the longing was not expressed, perhaps not even perceived by Bucke during his years at medical school and his early years in practice, in the summer of 1868, when he first read *Leaves of Grass*, the moment was propitious for the eager supplicant. As he recalled later:

The fixed feeling of conviction ... that the writings of this man contained a message for me, never left me, but I could neither discover the message nor find any clue to it.[11]

Bucke was emotionally ripe for the plucking. Although in 1868 *Leaves of Grass* was baffling to him and he knew nothing of the author, he had the true believer's conviction that the man and the message were meant for him. This conviction was enriched by his illumination four years later after an "evening reading Wordsworth, Shelley, Keats, Browning, and especially Whitman."(CC,7)

There had thus been added the important ingredient of mystical insight. The third component in the recipe that would fill the void created by the loss of the dissapointing and rejected father was the initial meeting with the Master in 1877. The conversion was complete. He had found an idealized father figure.

This idolatry led Bucke to misread *Leaves of Grass* as a sacred text, as holy writ, an approach fundamentally alien to Whitman's purpose. Yet Bucke understood the essential unity of the poet and his poems in a way that future generations of critics have not. That first generation of Whitman admirers, of varied backgrounds and intelligence, including O'Connor, Colonel Ingersoll, Burroughs, Traubel and perhaps Bucke most of all, saw Whitman as seer first and poet second, but inseparably linked. Sentimental and extravagant though they were, they saw in Whitman the incarnation of modern man, the prophet with a new and purer vision of the world. They sensed that the fiction which he created of himself as a mythmaker embodied a truth available to everyone. Whitman's rejection of religious dogma, of original sin and of guilt itself, all entrenched in Western man's credo, could now be accepted. His celebration of the human body, and at its core its sexuality, was to be proclaimed proudly, not repressed.

Although Bucke's understanding did not extend to the inclusion of homosexuality as a component of comradeship, the empty core was nevertheless filled, giving him a sense of grand purpose. It also gave him a model to represent the most complete expression of cosmic consciousness. Bucke and Whitman became linked by Whitman's inhabiting not only his own works but Bucke's as well. It may seem less absurd in this light to consider Bucke's biography of Whitman a fusion of the two, as textually it actually was.

Although none of Bucke's family, colleagues or local friends, with the possible exception of James Coyne, his first biographer, shared his vision, there is no sense that he felt deserted on that account. He operated at two levels. In his day-to-day relationships he was pragmatic, politically adroit and in no sense the impractical dreamer. At the other, deeper level, he was the illuminated visionary and disciple, unembarrassed by his unconventional beliefs. Not only had he discovered a Messiah but he would, thereby, enjoy a measure of eternal fame himself; strong medicine to ward off the blues which threatened him intermittently throughout part of his adult life.[12] Bucke's affirmation was clear:

> We are coming to the front at last — and should come. I have no fear, no doubt. It is only a question of waiting a few years till men have time to take it in. Another quarter or half a century will see Leaves of Grass acknowledged to be what it really is — The Bible of America.[13]

Among the second generation of Whitman acolytes, none was more enthusiastic than the group organized by Flora MacDonald, who had taught school in the backwoods north of Belleville, Ontario. She had attended a lecture on Whitman given by Colonel Ingersoll in 1892; later when she inherited a house and property at Bon Echo on Lake Mazinaw sixty miles north of Belleville, she declared:

> My life's work from now on will be propagating the ideals of Whitman with Bon Echo as a glorious vantage ground, away up in the Highlands of Ontario.[14]

Flora MacDonald's Whitman club had its inaugural meeting at the King Edward Hotel in Toronto on 7 January 1916. The literary organ of the club published its first issue in March. The large house was called Bon Echo Inn and stood across a narrow strait from the huge rock on Lake Mazinaw.

It seemed to Flora MacDonald and the Whitman club that Bon Echo would be a fitting Canadian monument to dedicate to their patron saint. She had met Horace Traubel at the home of shared friends in Toronto in 1916 and plans began to unfold to hold the dedication ceremony in 1919, the year of Whitman's centennial. The rock was to be known as "Old Walt" and the ailing Traubel agreed to come from Camden to Bon Echo for the commemoration. He and his wife Anne arrived on August 4th. Traubel was very feeble and, like Whitman, prematurely aged, and there was considerable doubt that he would be able to descend the steps and get into the boat to travel the fifteen or twenty feet across the narrows to touch the huge rock on which was to be carved the formal dedication and signed, "Horace Traubel".

On August 25th, sunshine and the merest breath of a breeze conspired to allow the frail Traubel to keep his appointment at the rock. Assisted into the small boat, Traubel, his wife, Flora MacDonald and a few friends, crossed the narrow strait. Traubel and Flora MacDonald placed their hands together on the face of the rock where the inscription was to be carved, and uttered the simple invocation, "Old Walt".

Traubel became more feeble in the following days, suffered a stroke and died at Bon Echo on September 8th. The inscription of Whitman's lines was duly carved and Horace Traubel's connection acknowledged. Twenty-three years later as an adolescent I first responded to those lines. It was some seventy years after they had been inscribed that they were fully illuminated for me.

My foothold is tenon'd and mortis'd in granite
I laugh at what you call dissolution
And I know the amplitude of time.[15]

My journey with Bucke was over.

Notes

Works by Richard M. Bucke, Letters, Diary, Autograph Notebook, Manuscripts and the Seaborn Notebooks, are all held in the Richard Maurice Bucke Collection, The D. B. Weldon Library, The University of Western Ontario, London, Canada. Other works in this collection are identified by the abbreviation, RMB.

Works frequently cited have been identified by the following:

Lozynsky — Artem Lozynsky, ed. *The Letters of Dr. Richard Maurice Bucke to Walt Whitman* (Detroit: Wayne State University Press, 1977).

Miller — Edwin Haviland Miller, ed. *Walt Whitman: The Correspondence*. 6 vols. (New York: New York University Press, 1961-1977).

The following abbreviations are cited in the text:

CC — Richard M. Bucke, *Cosmic Consciousness: A Study in the Evolution of the Human Mind* (Philadelphia: Innes and Sons, 1901).

WWC,2 — Horace Traubel, *With Walt Whitman in Camden*, 2 (reprinted, New York: D. Appleton and Company, 1908).

WWC,3 — Horace Traubel, *With Walt Whitman in Camden*, 3 (New York: Mitchell Kennerly, 1914).

WWC,4 — Horace Traubel, *With Walt Whitman in Camden*, 4 (Philadelphia: University of Pennsylvania Press, 1953).

WWC,5 — Horace Traubel, *With Walt Whitman in Camden*, 5 (Carbondale, Illinois: Southern Illinois University Press, 1964).

With respect to correspondence references, Richard M. Bucke is identified by the surname only, *i.e.*, Bucke.

Chapter 1

1. William Walpole Bucke, interview with author, Oakville, Ontario, 27 July 1987.
2. Francis M. Brookfield, *The Cambridge Apostles* (New York: Charles Scribner's Sons, 1906), 3.
3. Anna Brownell Murphy Jameson, *Winter Studies and Summer Rambles in Canada* (London: Saunders and Otley, 1838), 2:146-147.
4. Seaborn Notebooks, I:39.
5. *Daily Mail and Empire* (Toronto), 20 February 1902, RMB.
6. Richard M. Bucke, "An Episode in the Life of R. M. B.," Seaborn Notebooks, 4:526.
7. Seaborn Notebooks, 8:1072.
8. [Original Manuscript of Poems. Written by members of the Bucke family] 1798-1880, RMB.
9. Ibid.
10. Ibid.
11. Ibid.
12. Ibid.
13. Ibid.
14. Seaborn Notebooks, 8:1072.

Chapter 2

1. *The Bury, Norwich Post and Suffolk Herald*, 13 July 1880, RMB.
2. Garnett Laidlaw Eskew, *The Pageant of the Packets* (New York: Henry Holt and Company, 1929), 277.
3. Richard M. Bucke, "An Episode in the Life of R. M. B." Seaborn Notebooks, 4:537.
4. Richard M. Bucke, "Twenty-Five Years Ago," *The Overland Monthly*, 2nd ser., 1(6): 554(June 1883).
5. Seaborn Notebooks, 5:795.

6. Richard M. Bucke, "Twenty-Five Years Ago," 559.
7. Ibid., 560.
8. James H. Coyne, *Richard Maurice Bucke A Sketch* (Toronto: Henry, S. Saunders, 1923), 29.
9. Rev. A. B. Grosh to Bucke, 5 November 1858.
10. Seaborn Notebooks, 4:569.
11. [Original Manuscript of Poems. Written by members of the Bucke family] 1798-1880.RMB13.

Chapter 3

1. Bucke to Jessie Gurd, 19 November 1859.
2. Ibid., 19 August 1860.
3. Ibid.
4. T. Brookes to Gurd, 29 October 1862, 10 November 1862, 4 December 1862, and 20 December 1862.
5. Gurd to Brookes, 1 December 1862.
6. Bucke, Diary, 30 June 1862.
7. Ibid., [n.d.] 1862.
8. Richard M. Bucke, "The Correlation of the Vital and Physical Forces," *British American Journal* 3(6): [161]-167(May 1862), 3(7): [193]-200(June 1862), and 3(8): [225]-233(July 1862).
9. Ibid., 3(7): 199(June 1862).
10. Ibid., 200.
11. Bucke, Diary, 12 March 1863.
12. Ibid., 3 April 1863.
13. Ibid.
14. Ibid., 5 May 1863.
15. Ibid.
16. August Comte, *A System of Positive Polity*, trans. John Henry Bridges (New York: Burt Franklin, n.d.), 4:45.
17. Bucke, Diary, 26 September 1863.

Chapter 4

1. Bucke, Diary, 5 March 1864.
2. Richard M. Bucke, "The Discoverers of Silver in Nevada," Seaborn Notebooks, 5:795.
3. Seaborn Notebooks, 3:292.
4. Bucke, Diary, 5 March 1864.

5. Ibid., 9 March 1864.
6. Ibid., 14 March 1864.
7. Ibid., 14 September 1864.

Chapter 5

1. Richard M. Bucke, "Memories of Walt Whitman [I]," *Walt Whitman Fellowship Papers* 1(6): 35(September 1894).
2. William Blake, *The Complete Writings*, ed. Geoffrey Keynes (London: Oxford University Press, 1966) *Auguries of Innocence*, 431.
3. Walt Whitman, *Poems*, selected by W. M. Rossetti (London: Chatto and Windus, 1868), 16.
4. Idem., *Leaves of Grass* (Philadelphia: David McKay, 1900), 367.
5. Bucke to Harry Buxton Forman, 13 March 1872.
6. Bucke to Jessie Gurd Bucke, 22 May 1872.
7. Biggs Andrews to Bucke, 4 August 1872.
8. Bucke to H. B. Forman, 10 December 1872.
9. Ibid., 18 June 1873.
10. Ibid., 30 November 1873.
11. Ibid., 28 October 1874.
12. Ibid., 17 February 1875.
13. Alfred William Forman to Bucke, 31 January 1875.
14. Richard M. Bucke, "The Functions of the Great Sympathetic Nervous System," *American Journal of Insanity* 34(2): 115-159(October 1877).

Chapter 6

1. Bucke to H. B. Forman, 20 May 1876.
2. Ibid., 26 November 1876.
3. Ibid.
4. Artem Lozynsky, ed., *The Letters of Dr. Richard Maurice Bucke to Walt Whitman* (Detroit: Wayne State University Press, 1977), 1.
5. Bucke to H. B. Forman, 24 October 1877.
6. H. B. Forman to Bucke, 1 January 1878.
7. Bucke to Jessie Bucke, 26 March 1878.
8. Ibid., 17 May 1878.
9. Ibid., 12 May 1878.
10. Bucke to H. B. Forman, 12 May 1878.
11. Bucke to Jessie Bucke, 19 May 1878.

12. Jessie Bucke to Bucke, 25 May 1878.
13. Bucke to H. B. Forman, 14 July 1878.
14. H. B. Forman to Bucke, 28 July 1878.
15. Ibid.
16. Bucke to H. B. Forman, 27 November 1878.
17. Ibid., 11 September 1871.
18. Ibid., 8 November 1871.
19. Ibid., 23 December 1878.
20. Robert M. Young, *Mind Brain and Adaptation in the Nineteenth Century* (Oxford: Clarendon Press, 1970), 23.
21. Francis Schiller, *Paul Broca* (University of California Press, 1979), 177-78.
22. Richard M. Bucke, *Man's Moral Nature: An Essay* (New York: G. P. Putnam's Sons; Toronto: Willing and Williams, 1879), 113.
23. Ibid., 169.
24. Comte, *System of Positive Polity*, 1:262.
25. Ibid., 265-266.
26. Bucke, *Man's Moral Nature*, 190.
27. Bucke to H. B. Forman, 11 December 1871.

Chapter 7

1. Bucke to Jessie Bucke, 23 May 1880.
2. Ibid., 31 May 1880.
3. *London Advertiser*, 28 February 1880.
4. Ibid.
5. Ibid., March 1880.
6. *London Free Press*, 5 June 1880.
7. Walt Whitman, *Specimen Days in America*, rev. ed. (London: Walter Scott, 1887), 249-251.
8. Bucke to Jessie Bucke, 1 July 1880.
9. Ibid., 30 July 1880.
10. Ibid., 1 August 1880.
11. Ibid., 6 August 1880.
12. Bucke, "Memories of Walt Whitman [I]," 39.
13. Philip Eustace Bucke to James Coyne, 27 December 1908.
14. Bucke to H. B. Forman, 17 September 1880.
15. Bucke to Jessie Bucke, 16 June 1881.
16. Ibid., 19 June 1881.

17. Ibid., 23 June 1881.
18. Ibid., 26 June 1881.
19. Ibid., 27 July 1881.
20. Ibid., 23 August 1881.
21. Ibid., 25 August 1881.
22. Bucke to H. B. Forman, 26 August 1881.

Chapter 8

1. Bucke to H. B. Forman, 22 May 1881.
2. "Notes for Introductory Lecture to Second Session of Medical School of Western University [and] Annual Report, 1884" [London, Ontario: 1882-1884], Autograph Notebook.
3. Sir Samuel Baker, *The Albert N'Yanza, Great Basin of the Nile, and Explorations of the Nile Sources* (Philadelphia: J. B. Lippincott and Company, 1868), 231-232.
4. Richard M. Bucke, "Notes on Education", (n.p., after 1882), Autograph Notebook.
5. Ibid.
6. Ibid.
7. Bucke to H. B. Forman, 12 May 1878.
8. H. B. Forman to Bucke, 28 July 1878.
9. Richard M. Bucke, *Walt Whitman* (Philadelphia: David McKay, 1883), 86.
10. Bucke to Walt Whitman, 18 March 1883, Lozynsky, 18.
11. *Walt Whitman: Walt Whitman's Autograph Revision of the Analysis of "Leaves of Grass"* (New York: New York University Press, 1974), 112.
12. Bucke, *Walt Whitman*, 163.
13. Whitman, *Leaves of Grass*, 101.
14. Ibid., 126.
15. Bucke, *Walt Whitman*, 166.
16. Ibid.
17. Ibid., 195, and *Brooklyn Daily Times*, 29 September 1855.
18. Bucke, *Walt Whitman*, 204.
19. Review of *Walt Whitman*, by Richard M. Bucke, *Nation*, 943:84(26 July 1883).
20. A. W. Forman to Bucke, 24 October 1873.
21. Bucke to H. B. Forman, 30 November 1873.
22. Seaborn Notebooks, 8:1185.

Chapter 9

1. Harvey Williams Cushing, *Life of Sir William Osler*, 2 vols. (Oxford: Clarendon Press, 1925), 1:264-266.
2. Roger Asselineau, *The Evolution of Walt Whitman* (Boston: Harvard University Press, Belknap Press, 1960), 253.
3. Ibid., 254.
4. Ibid., 255.
5. Bucke to H. B. Forman, 13 July 1885.
6. *London Free Press*, 17 November 1885.
7. Joseph Edmund Collins, *The Story of Louis Riel, the Rebel Chief* (Whitby, Ontario: J. S. Robertson and Brothers, 1885), 185.
8. *London Free Press*, 11 August 1885.
9. Thomas Flanagan, *Riel and Rebellion: 1885 Reconsidered* (Saskatoon: Western Producer Prairie Books, 1983), 139.
10. Bucke to H. B. Forman, 13 July 1885.
11. *London Free Press*, 17 November 1885.
12. Ibid.
13. Bucke to H. B. Forman, 11 October 1885.
14. Ibid., 4 January 1886.
15. Ibid.
16. Bucke to Whitman, 13 May 1886, Lozynsky, 28.
17. Ibid.
18. Bucke to H. B. Forman, 23 July 1886.
19. Ibid., 5 September 1886.
20. Ibid., 24 September 1887.
21. Bucke to Horace Traubel, 13 July 1888.
22. Asselineau, *Evolution of Walt Whitman*, 210.
23. Bucke to Traubel, 13 July 1888.
24. Ibid.
25. Ibid., 24 September 1888.
26. Ibid., 22 September 1888.
27. Ibid.
28. Ibid., 28 September 1888.
29. Ibid., 13 December 1888.
30. Bucke to Whitman, 24 August 1888, Lozynsky, 30.
31. Artem Lozynsky, ''Whitman's Complete Poems and Prose: 'Bible' or 'Volume'?,'' *Walt Whitman Review* 19(1): 29(March 1973).
32. Ibid.

33. Ibid.

Chapter 10

1. Bucke to Traubel, 6 November 1888.
2. Ibid.
3. Horace L. Traubel, ed., *Camden's Compliment to Walt Whitman, May 31, 1889* (Philadelphia: David McKay, 1889), 57.
4. Traubel, *Camden's Compliment*, 57.
5. Ibid.
6. Bucke to Traubel, 31 December 1889.

Chapter 11

1. Bucke to Whitman, 24 April 1889, Lozynsky, 123.
2. Whitman to Bucke, 6 May 1889, Miller, 4:332.
3. Bucke to Traubel, 29 January 1890.
4. Ibid.
5. Richard M. Bucke, "'Leaves of Grass' and Modern Science," *Conservator* 1(3): 19(May 1890).
6. Horace L. Traubel, Richard M. Bucke, and Thomas M. Harned, eds., *In Re Walt Whitman* (Philadelphia: David McKay, 1893), 250.
7. Bliss Perry, *Walt Whitman: His Life and Work* (Boston and New York: Houghton Mifflin Company, 1906), 255.
8. Bucke, *Man's Moral Nature*, 192-195.
9. Richard M. Bucke, "Sanity," *American Journal of Insanity* 47(1): 17-26(July 1890).
10. Edwin Haviland Miller, ed., *Walt Whitman: The Correspondence* (New York: New York University Press, 1961-1977), 5:38.
11. Traubel, Bucke and Harned, *In Re Whitman*, 253.
12. Whitman to Bucke, 29 October 1890, Miller, 5:107-108.
13. Bucke to Traubel, 13 October 1890.
14. Ibid., 26 September 1890.
15. Richard M. Bucke, "The Case of Walt Whitman and Colonel Ingersoll," *Conservator* 1(8): 59(October 1890).
16. Ibid.
17. Traubel, Bucke, and Harned, *In Re Walt Whitman*, 252.
18. Bucke to Traubel, 9 November 1890.
19. Traubel, Bucke, and Harned, *In Re Walt Whitman*, 282.
20. Bucke to Traubel, 23 November 1890.

21. Ibid., 19 December 1890.
22. Ibid., 26 November 1890.
23. Ibid., 31 December 1890.
24. Ibid., 3 April 1891.
25. Traubel, Bucke, and Harned, *In Re Walt Whitman*, 314-315.
26. Ibid., 311-312.
27. Ibid., 323.
28. Miller, *Walt Whitman: The Correspondence*, 5:72.
29. Ibid.
30. Traubel, Bucke, and Harned, *In Re Walt Whitman*, 302-303.
31. Whitman to Bucke, 23 May 1891, Miller, 5:202-203.
32. Bucke to James William Wallace, 3 January 1891.
33. Ibid., 23 November 1891.
34. Miller, *Walt Whitman*, 5:221.
35. *Camden Post*, 1 August 1891.
36. Ibid.
37. Traubel, Bucke, and Harned, *In Re Walt Whitman*, 231-248.
38. Whitman to Bucke, 26 June 1891, Miller, 5:219.
39. Artem Lozynsky and John R. Reed, eds., *A Whitman Disciple Visits Tennyson; an Interview Describing Dr. Richard Maurice Bucke's Visit of 9 August 1891 at Aldworth* (Lincoln, [England]: The Tennyson Society, 1977), 27.
40. Ibid., 30.
41. Ibid.
42. Ibid., 14.
43. Ibid., 32.
44. Ibid., 33.
45. Ibid.
46. Ibid.
47. *Camden Post*, 5 September 1891.
48. Ibid.
49. Bucke to Traubel, 18 July 1891.
50. John Johnston and James W. Wallace, *Visits to Walt Whitman in 1890-1891* (London: Allen and Unwin Ltd., [1918]), 98.
51. Ibid., 99.
52. Ibid., 92.
53. Ibid., 105.
54. Whitman, *Leaves of Grass*, 33.

55. Richard M. Bucke, *The Value of the Study of Medicine*, (London, Ontario: Advertiser Printing Company, [1891]), 33.
56. Ibid.

Chapter 12
1. Bucke to Traubel, 2 December 1891.
2. Whitman to Bucke, 12 November 1891, Miller, 5:265.
3. Ibid., 10 July 1891, Miller, 5:225.
4. Bucke to Traubel, 7 November 1891.
5. Bucke to Whitman, 14 November 1891, Lozynsky, 261.
6. Ibid., 17 October 1891, Lozynsky, 255.
7. Whitman to Bucke, 18 November 1891, Miller, 5:266.
8. Bucke to Whitman, 21 November 1891, Lozynsky.
9. Bucke to Traubel, 10 February 1892.
10. Ibid., 19 January 1892.
11. Ibid., 4 February 1892.
12. Ibid., 20 March 1892.
13. Traubel, Bucke, and Harned, *In Re Walt Whitman*, 434.
14. Ibid., 434.
15. Ibid., 406-410.
16. Richard M. Bucke, "At the Graveside of Walt Whitman: Harleigh, Camden, New Jersey, March 30th," *Conservator*, Supplemental 3(2): iii(April 1892).
17. Ibid.
18. Bucke, "Memories of Walt Whitman [I]," 35.
19. Ibid., 38.
20. Ibid.
21. Bucke to Jessie Bucke, 19 June 1881.
22. Seaborn Notebooks, 1:31.
23. Plato, *The Dialogues of Plato*, trans. Benjamin Jowett (Oxford: Clarendon Press, 1953), 1:547-554.
24. "London Asylum: Report of Medical Superintendent and Statistical Information 1876-7," in *Tenth Annual Report of the Inspector of Asylums, Prisons, etc., for the Province of Ontario*, Ontario Legislative Assembly Sessional Papers, 1878, 4:280.
25. Havelock Ellis and John Addington Symonds, *Sexual Inversion* (New York: Arno Press, 1975), 14.
26. Bucke, "Memories of Walt Whitman [I]," 37.

Chapter 13

1. Maurice Andrews Bucke to Bucke, 30 March 1892.
2. Bucke to M. A. Bucke, 28 August 1892, Seaborn Notebooks, 10:1569.
3. Ibid., 8 March 1893, Seaborn Notebooks, 10:1570.
4. Ibid.
5. Ibid., 16 June 1893, Seaborn Notebooks, 10:1572.
6. M. A. Bucke to Bucke, 13 August 1893.
7. Ibid., 6 November 1893.
8. Ibid., 26 January 1893.
9. Ibid., 1 October 1893.
10. Ibid., 29 August 1894.
11. Jessie Bucke to Edward Pardee Bucke, 14 December 1893.
12. M. A. Bucke to Bucke, 15 May 1894.
13. *Globe* (Toronto), 30 June 1894.
14. Bucke, "Memories of Walt Whitman [I]," 35-45.
15. Richard M. Bucke, "Was Walt Whitman Mad?," *Conservator* 6(4): 55-58(June 1895).
16. Idem., "Was Walt Whitman Mad?," *Journal of Hygiene and Herald of Health*, 45(9): [225]-232(September 1895).
17. Idem., "Was Walt Whitman Mad?," *Walt Whitman Fellowship Papers* 2(9): 23-30(November 1895).
18. Edgar Fawcett, "Two Letters Indicating the Con of Whitman," *Conservator* 6(7): 103-104(September 1895).
19. Richard M. Bucke, "The Pro of Whitman," *Conservator* 6(8): 119-120(October 1895).
20. Whitman, *Leaves of Grass*, 21.
21. Richard M. Bucke, "Mr. Fawcett's Objections to Whitman Reviewed," *Conservator* 6(11): 170(January 1896).
22. Bucke to Wallace, 25 March 1894.
23. *Saturday Night*, 5 June 1897.
24. Bucke to Coyne, 14 July 1894.
25. *Globe*, 14 September 1895.
26. M. A. Bucke to Bucke, 7 April 1895.
27. Ibid., 9 September 1894.
28. Ibid., 18 September 1894.

Chapter 14

1. Martin L. Friedland, *The Case of Valentine Shortis* (Toronto: University of Toronto Press, 1986), 33-34.
2. Ibid., 61.
3. Ibid., 71.
4. Ibid., 72.
5. Ibid., 37.
6. Ibid., 85.
7. Ibid., 105.
8. Ibid., 117.
9. Ibid., 159.
10. *Saturday Night*, 29 May 1897.

Chapter 15

1. Bucke to H. B. Forman, 9 March 1896.
2. Richard M. Bucke, "The Shakespearean Authorship: Questions to William Sloane Kennedy," *Conservator* 7(9): 133-134 (November 1896).
3. William Frederick Friedman and Elizabeth Smith Freedman, *The Shakespeare Ciphers Examined* (Cambridge: Cambridge University Press, 1957),2.
4. Ibid., 3.
5. Ibid., 28.
6. Bucke to H.B. Forman, 15 October 1900.
7. M. A. Bucke to Bucke, 13 January 1896.
8. Ibid., 15 May 1896.
9. Ibid., 17 June 1896.
10. Ibid., 10 November 1896.
11. Ibid., 15 February 1897.
12. Richard M. Bucke, "What Ben Jonson Thought about Shakespeare," *Conservator* 7(11): 165-167(January 1897).
13. Idem., "Lawyer or Actor?," *Conservator* 8(2): 20-23(April 1897).
14. Richard M. Bucke, "Shakespeare or Bacon?," *Canadian Magazine* 9(5): 363-378(September 1897).
15. Idem., "Ben Jonson and Shakespeare," *Conservator* 8(8): 119-121(October 1897).
16. Idem., "Bacon-Shakespeare," *Canadian Magazine* 9(1): 85-86(November 1897).
17. *Globe*, 25 December 1897.

18. Richard M. Bucke, ed., *Calamus* (Boston: Laurens Maynard, 1897).
19. Ibid., 18-19.
20. Ibid., 23.
21. Ibid., 55.
22. Seaborn Notebooks, 6:869.
23. Ibid., 867.
24. Ibid., 861.
25. Ibid., 855.
26. M. A. Bucke to Bucke, 20 February 1897.
27. Ibid., 16 April 1897.
28. Bucke to H. B. Forman, 7 August 1900.
29. Richard M. Bucke, "Mental Evolution in Man," *British Medical Journal* 2: 643-645(11 September 1897).
30. Idem., "Mental Evolution in Man," *Journal of the American Medical Association* 29(17): 821-824(23 October 1897).
31. *Montreal Star*, 6 October 1897.
32. Bucke to H. B. Forman, 21 October 1897.
33. Ibid., 3 January 1898.
34. M. A. Bucke to Bucke, 1 February 1895.
35. Ibid., 12 January 1898.
36. Ibid., 11 June 1898.
37. Richard M. Bucke, "An Open Letter to Edgar Fawcett," *Conservator* 9(4): 56-58(June 1898).
38. Ibid.
39. Ibid.
40. M. A. Bucke to Bucke, 11 September 1898.
41. Ibid., 3 December 1898.
42. Ibid., 2 May 1899.
43. Ibid., 3 October 1898.
44. Ibid., 9 February 1899.
45. Bucke to M. A. Bucke, 3 October 1899.
46. Bucke to Charles Nathan Elliott, 2 May 1899.
47. M. A. Bucke to Bucke, 3 December 1899.
48. Bucke to H. B. Forman, 11 December 1899.
49. Bucke to Elliott, 16 December 1899.
50. Sir William Osler, *Science and Immortality* (Boston and New York: Houghton Mifflin Company, 1905), 43.
51. Bucke to Elliott, 8 November 1899.

Chapter 16

1. Wendy Mitchinson, "R. M. Bucke: A Victorian Asylum Superintendent," *Ontario History* 73(3): 242(September 1981).
2. *London Advertiser*, 5 May 1888.
3. "Annual Report of the Medical Superintendent of the Asylum for the Insane, London, Ontario," in *Twentieth Annual Report of the Inspector of Prisons and Public Charities for the Province of Ontario*, Ontario Legislative Assembly Sessional Papers, 1888, 13:36.
4. "Annual Report of the Medical Superintendent of the Asylum for the Insane, London, Ontario," in *Sixteenth Annual Report of the Inspector of Prisons and Public Charities for the Province of Ontario*, Ontario Legislative Assembly Sessional Papers, 1884, 8:52.
5. D. Yellowlees, "Notes and News," *Journal of Mental Science* 22:336-337(July 1876).
6. "London Asylum: Report of Medical Superintendent and Statistical Information 1876-7," in *Tenth Annual Report of the Inspector of Asylums, Prisons, etc. for the Province of Ontario*, Ontario Legislative Assembly Sessional Papers, 1878, 4:280.
7. Mitchinson, "R. M. Bucke: A Victorian Asylum Superintendent," 247.
8. Samuel Edward Dole Shortt, *Victorian Lunacy: Richard M. Bucke and the Practice of Late Nineteenth-Century Psychiatry* (Cambridge: Cambridge University Press, 1986), 132.
9. Sir William Osler, "The Master Word in Medicine," *Aequanimitas* (Philadelphia: P. Blakiston's Son and Company, 1905), 365-388.
10. Shortt, *Victorian Lunacy: Richard M. Bucke and the Practice of Late Nineteenth-Century Psychiatry* (Cambridge: Cambridge University Press, 1986), 133.
11. Ibid., 140.
12. Ibid.
13. Alexander Skene, *Medical Gynecology* (New York: 1895), 930-931.
14. Richard M. Bucke, "Gynecology Notes," *American Medico-Psychological Association Proceedings* 3:[139]-146(1896).
15. Ibid.
16. Richard M. Bucke, "Surgery Among the Insane in Canada," *American Medico-Psychological Proceedings* 5:75(1898).
17. Charles Kirk Clarke to R. Christie, 1 February 1899, Correspondence of the Inspector of Asylums, Archives of Ontario.

18. Shortt, *Victorian Lunacy*, 148.

19. Ibid., 149.

20. Bucke, "Surgery Among the Insane in Canada," 87.

21. "Annual Report of the Medical Superintendent of the Asylum for the Insane, London, Ontario," in *Twenty-eighth Annual Report of the Inspector of Prisons and Public Charities of the Province of Ontario*, Ontario Legislative Assembly Sessional Papers, 1896, 11:39-46.

Chapter 17

1. James Spedding, *An Account of the Life and Times of Francis Bacon* (Boston: Houghton, Osgood and Company, 1878), 1:49.

2. Ibid., 57.

3. Ibid., 50.

4. James Spedding, *Evenings With a Reviewer* (London: Paul Trench and Company, 1881), 2:328.

5. James E. Miller, *A Critical Guide to Leaves of Grass* (Chicago: University of Chicago Press, 1957), 6-35.

6. Edward Carpenter, *My Days and Dreams* (London: Allen and Unwin Ltd., 1916), 64.

7. Edward Carpenter, *Days with Walt Whitman* (London: Allen and Unwin Ltd., 1916), 3.

8. Edward Carpenter, *My Days and Dreams* (London: Allen and Unwin Ltd., 1916), 85-86.

9. Ibid., 65.

10. Ibid., 206.

11. Ibid., 117.

12. Carpenter, *My Days and Dreams* (London: Allen and Unwin Ltd., 1916), 206-207.

13. Barbara Marx Hubbard, *The Evolutionary Journey: A Personal Guide to a Positive Future* (Berkeley, California: Mindbody Press, 1982), 125.

14. David Riesman, *The Lonely Crowd* (New Haven: Yale University Press, 1950), 89-96.

Chapter 18

1. Bucke to H. B. Forman, 8 January 1900.

2. Bucke to Wallace, [January 1900].

3. Bucke to Elliott, 10 January 1900.

4. Ibid., 18 August 1900.

5. Richard M. Bucke, "New Light on the Life of Francis Bacon, AMs, RMB.
6. Bucke to Elliott, 14 March 1901.
7. Bucke to Coyne, 21 September 1901.
8. *London Advertiser*, 22 February 1902.
9. *Daily Mail and Empire*, 20 February 1902.
10. Mollie R. Hill to Ina Bucke Seaborn, 28 November 1944, Seaborn Notebooks, 8:1054.
11. Richard M. Bucke, "Memories of Walt Whitman," Walt Whitman Fellowship Papers 1(6): 36(September 1894).
12. Shortt, *Victorian Lunacy*, 21-23.
13. Richard M. Bucke, *The Sunset of Bon Echo* 1(5): 24(Centennial Edition, 1919).
14. Flora MacDonald, "Flora MacDonald," *The Sunset of Bon Echo* 1(1): 8(March 1916).
15. Whitman, *Leaves of Grass*, 51.

Index

R.M. Bucke : journey to
cosmic consciousness /
Peter A. Rechnitzer.
Book Stacks
RC 438.6 .B8 R4 1994